RĒWENA AND RABBIT STEW

THE RURAL KITCHEN IN AOTEAROA, 1800–1940

KATIE COOPER

AUCKLAND UNIVERSITY PRESS

First published 2024
Auckland University Press
Waipapa Taumata Rau
University of Auckland
Private Bag 92019
Auckland 1142
New Zealand
www.aucklanduniversitypress.co.nz

© Katie Cooper, 2024

ISBN 978 1 77671 111 6

Published with the assistance of
Creative New Zealand

A catalogue record for this book is available from the National Library of New Zealand

This book is copyright. Apart from fair dealing for the purpose of private study, research, criticism or review, as permitted under the Copyright Act, no part may be reproduced by any process without prior permission of the publisher. The moral rights of the author have been asserted.

Every effort has been made to trace copyright holders and obtain permission to reproduce copyright material. The publisher apologises for any errors or omissions in this book and would be grateful if notified of any corrections that should be incorporated in future reprints or editions.

Design by Kalee Jackson

Cover image: *Wining's Wairau NZ April 1851*. Charles Emilius Gold, Alexander Turnbull Library, A-447-002.

Frontispiece: A threshing team taking a meal break in front of a mobile cookshop, Canterbury region, date unknown. Cooper photograph, Canterbury Museum, 19XX.2.778.

This book was printed on FSC® certified paper
Printed in China by 1010 Printing International Ltd

For my dad
Murray Leicester Cooper
(1958–2018)

Contents

	Introduction	9
1	**What makes the ideal kitchen?** Houses and homes in rural New Zealand	23
2	**Hāngī stones and hot stoves:** Changes in cooking technologies	75
3	**Rēwena and rabbit stew:** Provisioning the rural kitchen	123
4	**Women's work?** Gender roles in rural Aotearoa	177
5	**Hākari, feasts and picnics:** Manaakitanga and rural hospitality	225
	Conclusion	269
	Notes	277
	Bibliography	292
	Glossary of Māori words	330
	Imperial to metric conversion	333
	Acknowledgements	334
	Index	337

∧
A reconstruction of a pioneer hearth with colonial oven, as exhibited in the Women's Court of the New Zealand Centennial Exhibition (1939–1940). John Dobree Pascoe photograph, Making New Zealand: Negatives and Prints from the Making New Zealand Centennial Collection, Alexander Turnbull Library, MNZ-1867-1/2-F.

Introduction

Introduction

As I look at this image of Maud Adkin, sitting alone at her kitchen table, I can almost hear the gentle scrape of the peeler as she prepares potatoes for her next meal. I imagine she is daydreaming, enjoying a moment of quiet contemplation as she carries out a routine task. In the photograph of the outdoor kitchen in Kaikohe, the faint whisper of smoke coming from the chimney brings to mind the distinctive smell of a burning fire, the cluster of people to the right suggesting a scene animated by chatter and laughter, jackets flung off as the fire heats up and work gets underway. These images, so different in composition, setting, subject and style, represent the kitchen as I hope to depict it in this book. They show cooking spaces both indoors and out, the presence of men, women and children, moments of leisure and of work, an intimate family scene and a communal gathering. They invite us to imagine what those spaces might smell, feel and sound like. These are spaces with real people in them, and they set the scene for this history of rural New Zealanders as revealed through their kitchens.

In many ways the kitchen is the perfect vantage point from which to examine aspects of everyday life, for social practices relating to food are fundamental in every household and in every society. We need food to survive, and the work undertaken in order to secure and prepare food must be ranked among the most vital of all human endeavours.[1] More than that, as human beings we make meaning out of producing and cooking food, ritualising its consumption in a 'seemingly needless overcomplication' that is uniquely our own.[2] We transform basic biological nourishment into a form of communication, using food to mark social boundaries and to cement family and community relationships.[3] To borrow a phrase from anthropologists Carole Counihan and Penny Van Esterik, 'Food is life, and life can be studied and understood through food.'[4] The lives examined here are those of rural New Zealanders in the

◁
Preparing dinner.
Maud Adkin preparing vegetables, Hastings, 28 December 1913. Leslie Adkin photograph, Gift of G. L. Adkin family estate, 1964, Museum of New Zealand Te Papa Tongarewa, A.008597.

◁
An outdoor kitchen at Kaikohe, April 1911. Unknown photographer, Auckland Libraries Heritage Collections, 236-7504.

nineteenth and early twentieth centuries, and I use the kitchen space as a framing device to capture some of the key processes by which rural people produced, cooked and shared food. These processes are shaped by a wide range of economic, environmental, social and cultural factors, which operate at scales from the global to the local.

The word 'rural' requires some explanation at the outset, for the ubiquity of the term obscures its complexity. My own personal image of rural life took shape on a small sheep farm just outside of Gore, Southland, in the 1990s. My family, and all of my neighbours, were Pākehā farmers who drew on the principles of scientific farming to grow acres of introduced grasses, fatten lambs for overseas markets, control weeds and boost soil fertility. I loved that world, I cherish my memories of it, and it has inevitably impacted on how I think about rural New Zealand. It gave me just one very narrow understanding of rural, though – specific to that time, place and community. This book, I hope, provides a much more expansive view, encompassing different peoples and different forms of land use, environments, perspectives and ways of living.

In New Zealand's history and historiography, the term 'rural lives' has often been taken to mean rural Pākehā lives, despite the fact that until the mid-twentieth century the vast majority of the Māori population (almost 90 percent in 1936) lived in rural areas. As sociologist Hugh Campbell explains, rural Pākehā created bounded farming worlds based on their own ideologies and beliefs with no reference to Māori values, and social histories of rural New Zealand have tended to reinforce those boundaries.[5] There are some good reasons for this, as rural history and Māori history do not necessarily sit comfortably together. Rural and urban are colonial constructs introduced to New Zealand by settlers. Māori ways of being traverse these locales.[6] Certainly in the sources I have studied, Māori tend to describe their lives in terms of a Māori world rather than a rural one. Pākehā farmers wielded such ideological and economic power in New Zealand that it is vital we understand the dynamics of the worlds they created. The danger of studying rural Pākehā society in isolation of other rural population groups, however, is that it obscures Māori and Pākehā interactions in rural spaces, does not give due prominence to Māori farmers and farming practices, and allows us to pretend that Pākehā farming worlds were built in a void. This book is a study of the rural population in its broadest sense, incorporating Māori and Pākehā farmers, station owners and swaggers, those who held tight to an idealised view of the rural world and those who could not identify with it.

Taking my cue from Richard Waterhouse's *The Vision Splendid: A Social and Cultural History of Rural Australia*, I adopted a 'catholic and elastic attitude towards the term "rural"'.[7] Combining demographic, structural and sociocultural approaches to rural studies, I defined rural New Zealanders as those living in counties and town districts that fit at least one of the following criteria: a population of under 1000; economic dependence on primary production; and physical isolation from major and secondary urban areas to the extent that it affects the social and economic characteristics of the locality.[8] This wide-ranging definition gave me the freedom to investigate a rich body of primary material, and it provided the scope necessary to examine the full spectrum of rural society – Māori and Pākehā, land-owning families and seasonal workers, stock agents and store owners.

The study begins in the early nineteenth century, when colonisation commenced and tangata whenua, the indigenous people of New Zealand, were introduced to a range of new tools, foods and culinary traditions. This was the point when the rural landscapes and industries we are now familiar with – and the communities they were built on – were brought into being through a series of dramatic and traumatic transformations. The Eastern Polynesian ancestors of Māori who arrived in 1250–1300 CE precipitated ecological transformations with their use of fire, hunting and horticulture, but the impact of European settlement was of an entirely different scale.[9] As one geographer put it in 1940, one century of European settlement in New Zealand brought environmental change the equivalent of twenty centuries of settlement in Europe.[10] Across five thematic chapters I explore aspects of this profound change through histories of rural housing, cooking technologies, food production, gender dynamics and mealtime rituals.

The study ends at the outbreak of the Second World War in late 1939 – a time of major social, economic and technological upheaval. In the postwar period rural kitchens were transformed once again. The demand for electricity increased as wartime restrictions ended, and power boards renewed their efforts to extend powerlines to backcountry areas.[11]

˅
A group outside a kāuta at Parihaka, c. 1900. One woman
is holding buckets; others are holding poi. A woman in
the foreground is scraping potatoes with a shell.
William Andrews Collis photograph, Negatives of Taranaki,
Alexander Turnbull Library, 1/1-012053-G.

Appliances such as refrigerators were within the means of most families by the 1950s, and more money was spent on New Zealand kitchens in that decade than in any previous decade of the twentieth century.[12] Urban drift was evident across the population in general but was particularly rapid in Māori communities, which changed from 83 percent rural to 83 percent urban between 1936 and 1986.[13] Women – both urban and rural – increasingly took up paid employment, meaning they had less time and flexibility to participate in community groups and social gatherings, while improved roading meant rural people could travel more easily to larger centres for recreation and entertainment.[14] These changes – just a few examples among many – all have their own fascinating histories, but it was beyond the scope of one book to consider them all.

Rural is a slippery and imprecise concept, and the notion of the kitchen no less so. Merriam-Webster defines kitchen as 'a place (such as a room) with cooking facilities', but of course this can encompass an infinite number of different places and a vast range of cooking facilities. In some chapters I consider the kitchen as a relatively bounded space closely linked to the cooking fire or stove, although not necessarily contained within four walls. In many cases this is primarily a place of work, and mainly (although not exclusively) a space associated with women, although it can also be a site of leisure activities and socialising. In other chapters, I imagine the kitchen not as a fixed place but as the centre of a range of processes and networks: the point of convergence for a whole host of people and goods. This approach owes much to the thinking of geographer Doreen Massey, who understood place as 'particular moments in . . . intersecting social relations, nets of which have over time been constructed, laid down, interacted with one another, decayed and renewed'.[15] The kitchen is given life by social relations stretching across neighbourhoods and regions, and can only function because of connections to disparate other places, including paddocks, oceans, factories and forests. In this sense, the kitchen is a rural space not necessarily because of how it looks, but because of the distinctly rural networks laid down in it.

To provide as many vantage points on the kitchen as possible I have drawn evidence from a wide range of primary sources, including diaries and journals, autobiographies, photographs, guidebooks, oral testimonies (either published, as in Waitangi Tribunal reports, or recorded and stored in heritage institutions), magazines and official publications. None of these sources offer more than a glimpse of historical kitchens, so I do not follow particular case studies through the book. When taken together, however, they provide a broad picture of economic, technological, environmental and social change in rural New Zealand, and demonstrate the diversity of rural lives and experiences.

Personal manuscripts by rural Pākehā – many of which were written in the later twentieth century, and which reflect on the 'golden age' of farming in the 1920s – need to be read with care, for they tend to repeat and reinforce accepted themes such as the challenging but rewarding nature of farming, the necessity of 'improving' land by making it more productive, and the deep social bonds that family farms were built on.[16] As Hugh Campbell points out, such personal accounts are also extremely selective: they have little to say about the destabilised ecosystems within which family farms exist; and they all but ignore past and present Māori lives.[17] Still, if we are to take historian Paul Star's advice and consider the making of rural New Zealand as thousands of individual pictures, these personal narratives cannot be overlooked.[18]

I found that because key sources such as magazines and government publications were national rather than local, I was not able to limit my study to a particular place or region. This approach has allowed me to draw on a rich variety of sources but it does have limitations, as it obscures important environmental, cultural and economic differences across New Zealand's varied rural landscapes. Wherever possible I have tried to show how the history and landscape of a place shape the routines and relationships of the people who live there, but there is much more that could be written on this topic.[19] This broad scope also precludes detailed analysis of the unique culinary practices of different iwi and hapū, and although I have indicated some distinctive traditions, I have had to make comments about a more generalised 'Māori' history which does not do full justice to those distinctions. Māori scholars have carried out fine-grained analyses of foodways in particular places, and where possible I have drawn on their valuable work.[20]

Given New Zealand's investment in individual home ownership it is perhaps not surprising that there has been sustained interest in

A boy in a tin bath in front of the kitchen range, probably at the Burrell family farm, Waimauku, 1930s. Alfred Burrell photograph (assumed), Auckland Libraries Heritage Collections, 7004-30-07.

different housing forms, and a number of architectural histories have traced the country's built heritage and the development of distinct architectural styles such as the villa and bungalow.[21] In recent years this scholarship has come to include social, political and cultural analysis, recognising the importance of the dwelling as a site of cultural maintenance and contestation.[22] Anthropologist Helen Leach has been at the forefront of research into culinary traditions and cooking spaces. Her most recent book on twentieth-century New Zealand kitchens uses advertisements, cookbooks and consumer manuals to analyse changes in the layout and material culture of cooking spaces, focusing on the issues affecting consumer choices as revealed in marketing materials.[23]

I build on Leach's analysis by integrating a broad survey from architectural and social histories with archival material and images, demonstrating the uneven development of domestic interiors 'on the ground'. Johanna Rolshoven suggests in *The Kitchen: Life World, Usage, Perspectives* that '[e]veryday kitchen culture has developed largely independently of architectural plans or of the attractive, glossy images provided by kitchen manufacturers. The architect's model has, it would seem, played a very small role in how dwelling has evolved.'[24] My approach gives a sense of this everyday kitchen culture, demonstrating the diversity of kitchen forms and the ways in which rural people adapted their domestic interiors to suit particular functions.

Chapter 1 'What makes the ideal kitchen?' draws on architectural histories and studies of material culture to analyse the variety of built forms that constituted the kitchen, and demonstrates how those forms varied in different geographic and cultural landscapes. Utilising personal manuscripts allows me to integrate material, emotional and symbolic constructions of domestic space within the same framework. In doing so, I explore an approach developed by geographers Alison Blunt and Robyn Dowling, who suggest that the home might be viewed both as a place we live in and an idea imbued with feelings and cultural meanings.[25] European settlers came to New Zealand with preconceived ideas about how the ideal house should look and function; and with the assumption that nuclear Christian families were the ideal social unit and that they should be sheltered in private, detached dwellings. To be 'at home' – in the sense of being in the place where you felt you belonged – meant, for Pākehā, being in your own house, and the kitchen was imbued with those feelings.

Chapter 2 'Hāngī stones and hot stoves' outlines the development of cooking technology from open fire to electric oven, and highlights important economic, cultural, infrastructural and personal reasons why this progression was not consistent or universal. While the basic sequence of open fire to camp oven, colonial oven, coal range and electric stove is roughly chronological, in practice the progression of cooking technologies was never unilinear. Often kitchen appliances were kept in use for decades, either because the household could not afford to replace them or because they were found to be fit for purpose – or both.

Popular discourse has tended to represent rural people as somewhat backward; rural sociologist H. C. D. Somerset, for example, suggested in *Littledene*, his 1938 study of small-town New Zealand, that 'the voice of the majority is resistant to change'.[26] I argue, however, that rural people did not eschew the trappings of modernity simply for the sake of tradition, and that pragmatism rather than conservatism was their overriding concern. Rural New Zealanders adopted new domestic technologies as convenient and necessary (although farm technologies were given priority when money was scarce), but there were also good, practical reasons to keep existing appliances.

Chapter 3 'Rēwena and rabbit stew' considers the various ways in which food was produced, acquired, preserved and distributed. The kitchen is still the vantage point, although this chapter also considers a range of other places associated with food gathering and preparation. Over the course of the nineteenth century a system of land ownership prioritising individual smallholdings was set in place in rural New Zealand, and this allowed Pākehā families to develop largely self-sufficient lifestyles that were more comfortable than those of their counterparts in rural Britain.[27] The strategies they implemented in order to achieve those lifestyles are certainly to be admired, and their innovation is acknowledged here. The security they enjoyed, however, relied on the dispossession of Māori from their lands and the displacement of previous forms of land use. Denied access to traditional food resources and with insufficient land or government support to participate profitably in the export economy, many Māori communities fell into a cycle of poverty that could only be broken by leaving their ancestral lands and moving to urban areas in search of employment.[28] In recent decades these injustices have been recorded as part of the Waitangi Tribunal's proceedings, and these reports, supplemented by personal manuscripts and photographs, provide powerful first-hand accounts that are used throughout the chapter.

Chapter 4 'Women's work?' explores aspects of class, rank and gender in rural Māori and Pākehā communities, in reference to cooking and food preparation. It interrogates the popular understanding of the kitchen as a private women's sphere, and considers whether this holds true in rural settings. Using personal manuscripts, photographs and extracts from the rural press, I demonstrate that rural kitchens could serve both public and private functions, that they were not used exclusively by women, and that women's work extended beyond the kitchen to other areas of rural life. That said, it is true that women did spend a lot of time and energy on domestic work in and around the kitchen, so I devote the final part of the chapter to an analysis of how they navigated and wrote about those roles and responsibilities. Rural women attached a range of meanings to their kitchens and to the work performed there, and their writing reflects this multiplicity of perspectives.

Chapter 5 'Hākari, feasts and picnics' focuses on meals. Here I argue that the sharing of food has been an important mechanism for the formation and maintenance of community relationships in rural New Zealand. In te ao Māori, food was traditionally a key measure of wealth and a symbol of prestige. Communities and whānau kept their storehouses full so they could always offer manaakitanga to guests, while iwi and hapū staged elaborate feasts that were planned and prepared for many months in advance. The sharing of food at hākari demonstrated the hosts' capacity for hospitality, provided an opportunity for social and political connections to be made or strengthened, and allowed for the repayment of obligations.[29] Everyday expressions of manaakitanga, meanwhile, demonstrated care for others and a recognition of interconnectedness.

The extent of cohesion in the Pākehā community in the nineteenth century has been the subject of debate. Miles Fairburn argued in his controversial classic *The Ideal Society and Its Enemies* that until the end of the nineteenth century settler communities had only minimal social organisation and social isolation was acute, leading to loneliness, alcoholism and interpersonal conflict.[30] I suggest that the social isolation and transience of the early settlers in fact contributed to a tradition of open hospitality that came to define rural Pākehā communities in the twentieth century. Geographic isolation meant that resources and practical assistance usually had to come from within the community, and local people were reliant on one another.[31] It did not pay to distance yourself from your neighbours, and under these circumstances an atmosphere of relative social equality and magnanimity developed. Sharing meals was one way of encoding those community relations, and Maori and Pākehā alike used food to make social statements.

∨
A domestic scene, Oct 16 1918, Levin. Leslie Adkin photograph, Gift of G. L. Adkin family estate, 1964, Museum of New Zealand Te Papa Tongarewa, A.006402.

In *Respectable Lives*, anthropologist Elvin Hatch explores questions of class and status in rural Canterbury by examining the eating arrangements on farms and stations, which he divides into one-table and two-table households. One-table households had all members, as well as workers and other guests, eating together: this had the effect of dignifying labour, and it demonstrated the importance of work as a measure of personal worth. Two-table households, however, had different eating arrangements for those perceived to be in different social strata – thus reinforcing social distance.[32] Following Hatch's methodology, I suggest that by the early twentieth century the majority of households had a 'one-table' eating arrangement, and those who laboured on the land had their work dignified by sharing meals with their employers. This echoes Tom Brooking's suggestion that the relatively egalitarian order that prevailed in most communities had to be actively consolidated.[33] While some of this consolidation would undoubtedly have occurred in the field or shed, I argue that community was also made through the sharing of meals.[34]

There are many kitchens described in this book, all of which look and function slightly differently. What unites them is, of course, the presence of food, but more than that they all share a connection to the land around them; they demonstrate the importance of food and cooking as forms of social connection and communication; and they show the power of mealtimes to draw people together or to divide them. The kitchen was at the centre of a web of social relations that stretched across and connected distant places, but it could also be an intimate familial space where personal relationships were built and nurtured. As such, the kitchen provides the perfect frame for capturing both the overarching structures of rural life and the diversity of individual experiences. By gazing into the kitchens of rural New Zealand in the nineteenth and early twentieth centuries, we gain insights into how sweeping structural changes impacted on the routines and rituals of daily life, and how the making of rural New Zealand was enacted and experienced by individuals, families and communities.

1
What makes the ideal kitchen?

Houses and homes in rural New Zealand

'The house is the thing; the home is the thing enlivened.'[1] In the introduction to their history of buildings in the British Atlantic, Daniel Maudlin and Bernard Herman offer a new response to an old question: what makes a house a home? A house, they suggest, is an artefact, a dwelling of wood, stone, brick or turf built by human hands. A house becomes a home when enlivened by human experience, by people eating, sleeping, talking and dreaming, using domestic spaces in ways that suit their own social, spiritual and practical needs. It is a simple enough distinction on paper and a useful place to start, but as we shall see these concise definitions open up complex and contested histories. The ways that houses are built and used are specific to the time, place and culture in which they are constructed, and ideas about what an ideal house or home should look like are both personal and political. With particular reference to kitchens – broadly defined as places with cooking facilities – this chapter considers both the built form of houses in New Zealand, and the ideas and activities that contributed to perceptions of 'homely' houses for different people at different times.

In a series of essays published in 2020, the authors of *Imagining Decolonisation* explore an analogy put forward by lawyer and Māori rights advocate Moana Jackson (Ngāti Kahungunu, Ngāti Porou, Rongomaiwāhine) that colonisation is the process of replacing one house with another.[2] While they imagine the house very broadly as the systems and resources that shelter a society, the metaphor can usefully be applied to physical structures as well as social ones.[3] Pākehā New Zealanders came here with very particular ideas about how domestic spaces should be built and used, shaped by culturally specific notions of home and family. These were in contrast to, and sometimes in conflict with, tikanga Māori. Māori and Pākehā buildings had very different symbolic and spatial boundaries; their houses spoke a language that those on the outside could not always understand.[4] The contact and clash between cultures in the nineteenth century resulted in a huge variety of housing types, as some Māori communities adopted and adapted tools and technologies introduced by Pākehā, and some settlers lived in houses built by Māori (albeit usually only temporarily). While this organic development continued throughout the nineteenth century and into the twentieth, missionaries, politicians and health officials attempted to regulate housing in New Zealand and introduce the types of dwellings they considered most conducive to the building of 'homely homes'.[5] By the 1930s, these efforts had resulted in an almost universal transition from whare raupō and other traditional housing types, to weatherboard, brick, stone or cob cottages.

Changes to the form and construction of houses did not necessarily alter underlying understandings of domestic spaces, however. This is perhaps best demonstrated by the continued separation of kitchens or cooking areas from other buildings in some Māori communities until well into the twentieth century. Furthermore, if for most Pākehā New Zealanders being 'at home' – in the sense of being in a place where you could find meaning and feel you belonged – meant being in your house, this was not necessarily the case in te ao Māori.[6] Communities invested in marae, meeting houses and wharekai as places for their people to come home to; homes enlivened by waiata, kōrero and tikanga Māori.

The first section of this chapter provides an overview of the construction of houses and kitchens in Aotearoa New Zealand from the early nineteenth century to the mid-twentieth. I consider the role of sojourners, settlers, missionaries, state officials and entrepreneurs in the development of housing; and I use photographs to illustrate key changes. The second section of the chapter explores the ideals supposedly encapsulated within the preferred colonial form of housing – the specific notions of family, piety, privacy and economic security that underpinned the Pākehā idea of home and gave the kitchen many of its emotional associations. These ideals had limited relevance in the Māori world, and where possible Māori families and communities used their homes in ways that reflected their own ideals, not the colonial ideals built into the structure and layout of Pākehā-style houses. Nevertheless, as Jackson put it, the colonisation of Aotearoa was the process of replacing one house with another – and an aspect of that process is explored here.[7]

Building houses

In most contemporary contexts, the word 'kitchen' is taken to mean a room or part of a room dedicated to food preparation in a private dwelling or a commercial enterprise.[8] The broadest definition of the kitchen, though, is simply a place with cooking facilities, and that is the definition I adopt here.[9] Places devoted to cooking can be very grand, housing an imposing arsenal of tools and appliances wielded by an expert staff, or they can be quite rudimentary, comprising nothing more than an open fire and a few utensils. Both types of kitchens, and countless other forms that fall somewhere in between, have been used in rural New Zealand.

The elements that make a kitchen (or a house) distinctly rural are often the ways in which it is used rather than how it is designed or constructed. In the nineteenth century, box cottages were built to standard patterns in rural and urban areas alike, and architectural styles such as the villa and bungalow were common all over the country. In the twentieth century, however, as house planning and construction were increasingly regulated by the state, greater attention was given to the specific housing needs of rural people, and planned for accordingly.

The history of the kitchen is distinct from, but related to, the history of the house. Both were influenced by the availability of materials, changing architectural styles, and government regulations. That said, changes in the form and function of houses were not always reflected in the kitchen; for example, in some early twentieth-century Māori communities weatherboard houses replaced whare raupō, but the kāuta or cookhouse remained relatively unchanged. In this section I look at the evolution of houses and kitchens in tandem.

Kitchens in the eighteenth and nineteenth centuries

I wandered at whim through his village, followed by the children and a few young slaves. At the doors of the huts women were pounding *phormium* fibre to make it ready for weaving those beautiful, fine mats which are so supple and strong. The huts looked like Lilliputian dwellings, they were so low; at the most scarcely three or four feet high and about as wide, they were about six or seven feet long. They are rectangular in shape, having side walls supported by supple peeled branches, and a roof made of a layer of close-packed rushes. At the front there is a kind of alcove where they come to sniff the air when it rains. The partition which separates this part from the other, in which two people sleep on the straw which serves as a bed, can be passed only by crawling, and is closed by a little door. It is easy to keep these burrow-like dwellings warm, and the rigours of the winter are not felt.... The service buildings are some distance from each family's hut. A straw roof supported by four sticks protects the open ovens from the rain; these ovens, near the kitchens or kaouta [kāuta], are large, wide-mouthed holes, lined with stones which they heat in the Oceanian manner. I have eaten sweet potatoes cooked in this way, and they tasted delicious.[10]

In 1824 René Primavère Lesson, of the French naval vessel *La Coquille*, was given leave to 'wander at whim' through Kahuwera pā in the Bay of Islands, where he observed ways of living that were wholly unfamiliar to him. Many other European visitors to Aotearoa in the eighteenth and nineteenth centuries recorded written descriptions of Māori housing. Although these narratives do not provide a balanced account of tangata whenua (not least because a good proportion of them relate primarily to the Bay of Islands), if assessed alongside archaeological evidence and traditional narratives they can provide some insight into the construction and use of dwellings and the dynamics of community life at that time.[11]

When James Cook arrived in 1769 he observed large Māori communities in fortified pā with dozens or even hundreds of dwellings, although smaller hapū- or whānau-based kāinga were more common.[12]

In permanent settlements the most common dwelling type was the rectangular wharepuni, which has a long history in all parts of New Zealand with only minor variations in style.[13] What Cook and his contemporaries did not observe and could not have understood were the beliefs and principles underpinning the use of domestic spaces in Māori communities, although they recognised that the people they were encountering had a very different way of living than their own.[14]

The use of domestic spaces in te ao Māori was governed by the principles of tapu and noa. According to scholar Māori Marsden, tapu is 'the sacred state or condition in which a person, place or thing is set aside by dedication to the gods and therefore removed from profane use'.[15] Noa, on the other hand, is defined as a neutral state, 'or that which is mundane, everyday and having a lesser degree of restriction'.[16] Cooked food is noa – free from the restrictions of tapu – and can infringe on the sacredness of people or places. For this reason, Māori never cooked food in wharepuni, and spaces and structures associated with cooking and eating were distanced from other buildings. Anglican missionary James West Stack observed in *Early Maoriland Adventures* that his house at Mangapouri had a detached kitchen 'because Maoris thought it as shocking to cook food in a dwelling-house as we should to do so in a church'.[17] When weather permitted, cooking was carried out in the open, but in most kāinga there were also dedicated cooking structures associated with each dwelling.[18] These structures had a number of names, including kāuta, whareumu, hereumu and kāmuri.

Those of chiefly rank were vulnerable to having their tapu contaminated or diminished by contact with prepared food, so cooking was the work of those of lower rank – often slaves or captives.[19] Because of their role, servants and captives came to be associated with the black soot and charcoal created by cooking in close spaces.[20] In one story Whakatau, son of Tuwhakararo and Apakura, rubs his face all over with charcoal to hide his chiefly status, allowing him to move unobtrusively among the workers in his enemy's village.[21] French voyager Jules Dumont d'Urville reported during his visit to the Bay of Islands in 1824 that while 'the real word for a slave or prisoner was *tao reka-reka* [taurekareka] and for a servant *wari* [n]owadays they are more frequently known by the name of *kouki* [kuki], which is a corruption of the English word *cook*'.[22]

> *Titari's house and cooking place at Taiamai. August 20 1841.* This sketch shows the chiefly dwelling at Taiāmai (Ōhaeawai, Far North), with the cooking shed to the right, separated by a fence. Richard Taylor, Sketchbook 1835–1860, Alexander Turnbull Library, E-296-q-025-3, reproduced with permission of Richard Woodman, chairperson of Ngāwhā marae and descendant of Titari.

> *A feast at Mata-ta, on the east coast; Mt Edgecumbe in the distance.* This plate is based on a sketch made by Joseph Merrett between 1841 and 1843. The image shows a large whata at Matatā stacked with baskets of food, and with drying fish hanging beneath it. Detail of Plate 36, from George French Angas, *The New Zealanders*, Thomas McLean, London, 1847, Gift of Charles Rooking Carter, Museum of New Zealand Te Papa Tongarewa, RB001054/084a, acknowledging Ngāti Rangitihi.

Kāuta were exclusively functional buildings and were not associated with those of the chiefly classes, and therefore did not need to be adorned with symbols of rank. Instead, as archaeologist Nigel Prickett has suggested, they were built from a variety of materials and did not conform to a prescribed or uniform design.[23] In *Māori Life & Custom*, first published by ethnologist W. J. Phillipps in 1966 and revised by John Huria in 2008, the authors suggest that open-air structures or lean-tos were most common.[24] In a lean-to, the earth oven was protected from the elements by a thatched covering, usually held up by four posts and often with a rough wall at the lower end.[25] John Savage, a surgeon who travelled to New Zealand in 1805 and spent two months in the Bay of Islands, wrote that Māori cooking operations were 'carried on in a shed at a little distance from the hut, formed by fixing four posts in the ground, about five feet high, on which [was] laid a flat covering of rushes'.[26] An 1841 sketch by Richard Taylor of the pā at Taiamai (Ōhaeawai) shows this type of structure (see opposite). The cooking shed sits to the right of the chiefly dwelling and is separated by a fence.

A number of other types of outbuildings were used for cooking. These varied by locality.[27] In the South Island, for example, cookhouses were often made of ponga logs, and elsewhere the walls were made of wooden slabs or short logs held in place by uprights.[28] During his travels as a naturalist with the New Zealand Company between 1839 and 1841, Ernst Dieffenbach observed Māori cooking both outdoors and in cookhouses. He wrote in *Travels in New Zealand* that '[t]he native oven, *hangi* or *kohua*, made in the well-known manner with heated stones, is situated either in the open air or in a house (te-kauta) constructed of logs at a small distance from each other, so that the smoke may escape'.[29]

Firewood, baskets, mats and other implements were stored in the cooking shed, but separate structures were constructed to store food.[30] The most common of these was the whata, a platform atop a high pole, which in its simplest form was a type of rack used to dry fish and shellfish.[31] Artist Joseph Merrett observed preparations being made for a hui at Matatā between 1841 and 1843, and sketched an image of a large whata laden with drying fish and baskets of food (see opposite). Māori also constructed whata close to cultivations in order to store crops until they could be carried back to the kāinga.[32] Underground pits or excavated,

Augt 20 1841. Tiarii's House and Cooking place at Taiamai.

In this photograph women use a kettle, billy and camp oven to cook over an open fire. The kāuta is to the left of the image, separated by a fence from the other buildings. Frank Denton photograph, Auckland Libraries Heritage Collections, AWNS-19041124-4-1.

roofed storehouses were built to store kūmara and other root crops, and preserved foods were kept in pātaka set on raised platforms.[33]

In some places dwelling, cooking and storage structures remained relatively unchanged for much of the nineteenth century, and twentieth-century ethnographers describe them in detail. Mākereti (Maggie) Papakura (Te Arawa, Tūhourangi) wrote in *The Old-Time Maori* (1938) that in her community of Whakarewarewa, wharau or kāuta were shaped like whare with uprights and rafters of wood.[34] They had sides of split ponga logs fixed slightly apart to allow smoke to escape, and the roof was made of split ponga logs or thatched with nīkau palm fronds.[35] Elsdon Best noted that cooking sheds with 'walls composed of stacks of fuel, and a few posts to support the roof' were common, but he also recorded cooking sheds with walls constructed from the thin trunks of whekī.[36]

The arrival of new tools and technologies in the nineteenth century brought major changes to dwellings and kitchens in some communities. When Anglican missionaries arrived in the Bay of Islands in 1814, they soon recognised the importance of domestic arrangements to their evangelising project.[37] They were the first Europeans to come with the intention of settling permanently, and also the first to deliberately attempt to impose changes on Māori housing and ways of living. The mission at Hohi (Oihi) was founded on the belief that if Māori were to be converted to Christianity, they needed to be convinced of the superior comforts of 'civilised' society.[38] Initially the missionaries' isolation and dependence on Māori meant their homes differed little from whare Māori, but as soon as practicable they set about building houses that 'modelled and inculcated a new social order', based on the ideal of a single family inhabiting a single dwelling.[39] The preference was for internal spaces to be differentiated by function, and for an internal kitchen which 'gave the house a more strongly "European" feel'.[40] Although later missionaries emphasised evangelism over civilisation, they continued to promote domestic arrangements that fitted with their own values and way of life.[41]

Some Māori Christian communities saw possibilities in European housing types and, with missionary encouragement, built neatly laid-out villages of multipurpose wooden houses and manicured gardens.[42] At Ōtaki, where missionary Octavius Hadfield was based, the *New Zealand Spectator and Cook's Strait Guardian* reported that by 1847 the community had 'resolved to abandon their pa, and to build on a more eligible site, about a mile and a quarter from their present locality, and nearer to their cultivations, a village laid out after a regular plan'.[43] The rangatira Tāmihana Te Rauparaha (Ngāti Toa) lived in a weatherboard house with 'wooden floors, doors, and glazed windows . . . furnished with chairs and tables, and a bed'. Food was eaten within the dwelling, and the reporter noted that Tāmihana and his wife Ruta Te Kapu, daughter of Tāwhiri of Ngāti Raukawa, sat down to eat 'in the European manner on chairs'.[44] In other communities, rangatira adopted European-style housing, but the form and function of ordinary whare remained largely unchanged.[45]

Sealers and whalers from all over the world took up temporary residence in New Zealand from the 1790s, and in the 1820s established more permanent shore stations. Often they lived in one-room houses built by Māori, adapted to suit a European way of life – in particular with indoor cooking facilities, as described by Edward Jerningham Wakefield in 1845:

> A whaler's house is generally built by the natives. It is either entirely composed of reeds and rushes woven over a wooden frame, – or else the walls consist of a wattled hurdle made of supple-jack (*kareau* [sic]) covered inside and out with clay, and the roof is thatched. A large chimney nearly fills one end of the house; – and generally swarms with natives, iron pots and kettles, favourite dogs, and joints of the whale's backbone, which serve as stools. . . . Bunks with neat curtains line the greater part of the sides of the house. A large deal table and two long benches stand in the middle of the hard earthen floor.[46]

Some historians have argued that the transience and ruggedness of many sealer and whaler lifestyles meant they did not play a significant role in the introduction of colonial culture. More recent scholarship has challenged this argument.[47] Wakefield, who promoted a view of colonisation as the extension of 'civilised' society, maintained that whalers and sealers, rather than missionaries, had been the first 'civilisers' in New Zealand, introducing Māori communities to the comforts of good housing, food and clothes.[48] Certainly, in districts with large concentrations of Pākehā sealers and whalers in the early nineteenth century, such as Foveaux Strait and the Bay of Islands, changes in the style and use of housing were relatively rapid.[49]

After the signing of te Tiriti o Waitangi / the Treaty of Waitangi in 1840, the settler population of New Zealand increased exponentially: from just 2000 people in 1839, the number of settlers had risen to approximately 30,000 by 1852, when New Zealand ceased to be a crown colony. That was nothing compared to the increase in the decades that followed; by 1870 the population of non-Māori had surpassed 250,000 people, and by the end of the century it had risen to more than 700,000.[50] The majority of those who immigrated to New Zealand in the nineteenth century came from Britain, and like the missionaries, whalers and traders before them, they brought housing designs and domestic goods already heavy with cultural baggage.[51]

Animals in the kitchen

Tucked up under the Curtis's kitchen table is their pet cat, sleeping soundly on a footstool. As Nancy Swarbrick argues in *Creature Comforts*, in the colonial context pet animals were not only companions but were also reminders of home, helping settlers to reconcile themselves to their new lives far distant from friends and family.[52] The presence of familiar animals both inside and outside of the house was an important aspect of home-making, as was the establishment of daily routines and rituals, such as eating. Pets were usually given scraps from the dinner table, so animal and human mealtimes were closely associated, and it is not unusual in sketches of settlers' houses to see pets waiting for their share

∧
Interior of the Curtis family's one-room raupō house, sketched by Joseph Merrett in 1851–52. The all-purpose table in the centre dominates the space, leaving little room for the couch, which has been tucked away behind a screen. A kettle or pot is hanging above the fire at the far end of the room. George and Eliza Curtis arrived in New Zealand in 1849 and settled in Ōmata, Taranaki. Untitled (Interior of George Curtis's House, Omata), 1851–1852, Joseph Jenner Merrett, Collection of Puke Ariki, New Plymouth, A92.158.

of the meal. Thus, as Swarbrick suggests, '[t]he sight of a waiting dog or cat by the dinner table became a powerful and enduring sign of security and contentment'.[53]

Having animals in the kitchen could also cause all manner of problems. Sarah Courage had to have the sod cookhouse on their Canterbury station pulled down because 'it was a dreadful place for flies and fleas (being so warm and dry). Oh, those fleas! I shall never forget them – those wretched atoms knew no repose, their nimbleness surpassed mine, and the floor of that whare was literally alive with them, while their appetite and audacity were unparalleled. I dreaded going into the place to see about meals, and every morning gathered up my skirts and as soon as possible beat a precipitate retreat, Mrs Bacchus [the cook] assuring me that wherever dogs assembled there must be fleas.'[54]

Winifred Carson (née Williscroft) wrote in her autobiography about a severe plague of mice and rats overrunning their Maruia home in the 1920s. She remembered seeing mice 'running around the kitchen floor, for after a period of time [they] became dopey and weren't frightened any more. . . . After the mice came the rats . . . Dad had rigged up a miniature block and tackle clothes line to dry and air our clothes in the kitchen. This line was let down while the clothes were arranged on it, then pulled up again near to the ceiling. One time a woollen garment was left up a little longer and Dad noticed that it was gradually disappearing.'[55] While the kitchen could be a cosy place to curl up with a newspaper or talk after dinner, it was first and foremost a place to store and cook food, and was not always conducive to other functions.

⟨

This 1891 sketch from the *New Zealand Graphic* shows a goldminer and his cat resting in front of the fire, waiting for the billy to boil. *New Zealand Graphic,* 10 October 1891, p. 456, Auckland Libraries Heritage Collections, NZG-18911010-456-8.

The wealthiest settlers brought prefabricated houses with them, and in just a few hours – according to the manufacturer – they were able to erect English-style cottages little different to those they'd left behind.[56] Most settlers, however, relied on Māori to build their first dwelling – often a thatched house of raupō, nīkau, toetoe, wīwī or kākaho.[57] These dwellings looked very different to British cottages but with familiar construction and configuration features, such as higher walls than whare Māori, partitioned internal spaces, windows, and a hipped or gabled roof.[58] Often they included a fireplace for heating and cooking, despite the risk in houses built of highly flammable materials. Fears about fire safety meant that raupō houses were quickly taxed out of existence in urban areas. In 1842 the Legislative Council passed an ordinance allowing for an annual levy of £20 on urban houses made of raupō, straw or thatch, and in just over a decade Auckland, Dunedin, Port Chalmers, Wellington, Lyttelton and Christchurch were all brought under the legislation.[59] As a result raupō houses were replaced by wood, brick and earth within town boundaries, but they remained a popular choice for temporary accommodation in the bush.[60]

˄
Two raupō buildings, one used for domestic purposes and the other as a shed or stables, c. 1863. A note at the bottom of the photograph states that the building was occupied by Chapman and Synnot, runholders at Te Aute in Hawke's Bay; however, it has also been suggested that the buildings were part of Woburn Station near Waipukurau. Possibly James White photograph, Gifted by Mrs G. Wood, Collection of Hawke's Bay Museums Trust, Ruawharo Tā-ū-rangi, 562.

∧
A woman stands with two sheep in front of a shingle-roofed wooden cottage, possibly built in the 1850s–1860s, location unknown. The cottage appears to be a standard two-roomed colonial cottage with hearth and kitchen at one end and bedroom at the other. Unknown photographer, Alexander Turnbull Library, 1/2-050842-F.

Those who couldn't rely on or learn from Māori builders had to fend for themselves when it came to shelter, and find temporary accommodation in tents, lean-to shelters or rough huts.⁶¹ The quality and size of these structures varied greatly, depending on the skill of the builder and the resources and time available: some were sound cottages that included a cooking fire and chimney; others were crude sleeping shelters, with the kitchen outside or in a separate cookhouse. As in other settler colonies, settlers in New Zealand invested in land and economic enterprise before material comfort, but as soon as possible they moved to more permanent dwellings or built on to their existing houses.⁶²

The basic model for a colonial cottage was freestanding, one-storey, with a door in the middle and a window either side, and a medium-pitched gable or hip roof.⁶³ Most two-roomed cottages had one 'day' room with cooking and living facilities – a kitchen of sorts – and one bedroom. This archetypal form could be modified to suit the needs of the

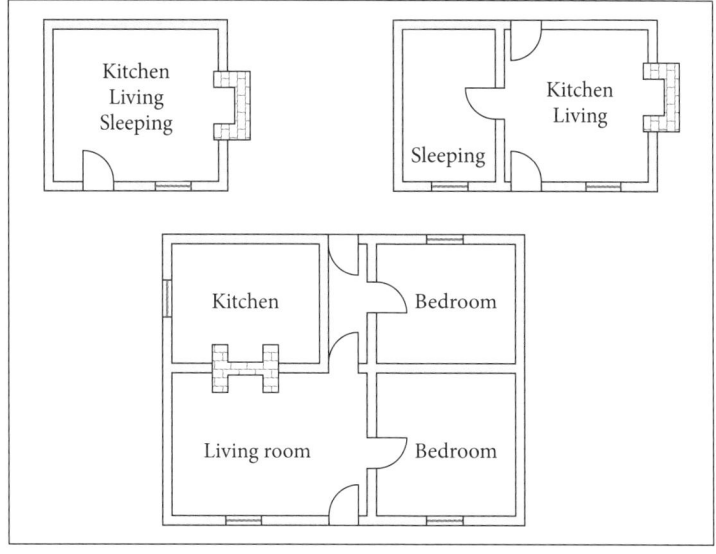

Typical plans for one-, two- and four-room cottages. From Jeremy Salmond, *Old New Zealand Houses 1800–1940*, Reed Publishing, Auckland, 1986, p. 75.

occupants, for example by building an extension of a similar structure, or by adding a verandah or a second storey.[64] In larger cottages the function of each room could be more clearly defined, and a family home might have a parlour or dining room in addition to a kitchen and bedrooms.[65]

Architecturally, the hearth was more of an awkward appendage than the heart of the colonial cottage.[66] As heritage architect Jeremy Salmond points out, the need to contain the cooking fire and reduce the fire risk dictated the layout of the cottage kitchen. A chimney was usually tacked on to one end of the house and, whenever possible, was made of bricks or cobs (lumps of straw and clay) to mitigate the fire risk. Where those materials were not available the hearth could be surrounded by a large enclosure with its own walls and roof, keeping the fire as far as possible from flammable materials.[67] Lydia Mitchell (née Myers) lived with her parents and sister in a small two-roomed tin house at Whangamōmona (near Stratford) in the late nineteenth century. Their kitchen-cum-parlour 'had a tin chimney at one end leaving a space inside for the fire about 8ft long six foot in depth on which big logs of wood could be burnt. . . . The iron kettle was always hung on over the top of the fire & water always kept hot. [A]n iron rod was placed across the chimney from side to side on this lengths of chain hung down & the iron pots and camp oven & kettles were hung on this chain by hooks.'[68] Their kitchen and living space was furnished with a colonial couch (a long settee with arms at either end and a wooden backrest, popular in Australia and New Zealand), a wooden table, chair and stool, and a homemade cupboard with shelves. An enamel basin served as sink and washbasin, and once a week a tin bath would be dragged in front of the fire for more thorough ablutions.

Risk of fire

Nineteenth-century kitchens were designed to limit the risk of fire spreading throughout the house. Still, fires were frequent – and frightening. The McKenzie family lived in a wooden cottage in Martins Bay, Otago. The cottage had an iron chimney with its own roof and walls, to reduce the risk of fire, but on 29 January 1891, Alice McKenzie noted in her diary that 'the kitchen door blew open, and a dress that was on a chair in front of the fireplace caught fire… It was making a great flare, so I got up and threw 2 or 3 buckets of water on it, and then it all went out. There are two of the boards of the floor burned through, and several of the other boards are all charred.'[69]

Johanna Wolff, who lived with her parents in Styx, Canterbury, recorded in her diary how two

A wooden cottage with verandah, attic room and lean-to, c. 1880–1900. The fireplace has its own walls and roof constructed of wooden slabs, which are probably lined with stones or mud. The roof of the chimney structure slopes away from the house to protect the fire from weather and help it to draw well. Most chimneys tacked onto houses were constructed in this way, giving them a characteristic shape (Salmond, *Old New Zealand Houses*, 68). Unknown photographer, Manawatū Heritage image, 2010N_Bur114_3192.

homes were destroyed in separate fires in the neighbourhood in one month in 1888. The first fire, at a neighbour's house, was caused by a poorly installed range that was too close to an adjacent wooden wall; and the second fire, at her aunt and uncle's house, occurred because the chimney was defective.[70]

For some settlers the risk of fire was simply too great, and until a proper brick chimney or iron range could be installed the kitchen was built entirely separate from the house.

∧
William Strutt depicts a settler on the roof of his wooden hut, trying to put out a chimney fire. In places where bricks were not available, and before the widespread adoption of cast-iron ranges, cooking fires posed a major risk to colonial homes. To alleviate the risk, the fire was often positioned in a separate structure tacked onto the end of the house, or in a separate kitchen. William Strutt, 'A collection of drawings in water colour ink and pencil illustrative of the scenery and early life of settlers and Maoris of New Zealand', 1855–1863, 2nd series, Alexander Turnbull Library, E-453-f-003.

Colonial cottages were small by modern standards, and the families they housed were often large. Some commentators have romanticised them as cosy and suggested that '[w]ith hearth and kitchen at one end, and dominated by a large, all-purpose table at the centre of family activities', they epitomised the ideal home life.[71] But what seems cosy in retrospect may in reality have been uncomfortably snug. The Orbell family of Waikouaiti, for instance, had to take their meals in relays because the kitchen–dining area of their two-room cottage was too small to accommodate all twelve of them; and while the parents and five of the children slept inside, the others had to bunk in a nearby granary.[72]

The ease with which the box cottage could be added to or altered, however, meant that by 1860 it was the dwelling of choice for New Zealand's settler population, and it remained a popular style in rural areas into the twentieth century.[73] The basic housing pattern of the mid-nineteenth century endured, too. As the agricultural landscape extended into previously inaccessible areas, a period of 'pioneering' ensued during which settlers had to 'rough it' in temporary dwellings until they could afford more substantial housing. This was often a protracted process, and as Mabel Whitaker (née Wilson) noted in 'Pioneer Tales', 'it took a big slice out of a lifetime to achieve the bright, roomy, comfortable home at which the settlers all aimed'.[74]

The big house

While the box cottage was the home of choice for most country people, some rural settlers had grander aspirations and deeper pockets, and by the 1860s wealthy station holders had begun building large homesteads in the tradition of the English country house.[75] These homes were about ten times the size of an average house, at 10,000 square feet or more, and were often extravagant in their appearance, size and setting.[76] The 'big house' fulfilled various functions, including family home, station administration centre, accommodation for domestic servants, and social centre. Often it was surrounded by a number of other service buildings which meant the station – usually a long way from the nearest town or city – was largely self-sufficient.

The layout varied, but in general the rooms at the front of the house were 'reception rooms', while those at the back served utilitarian functions. In two-storey homes the downstairs spaces were for living, and upstairs for sleeping.[77] The kitchen, usually presided over by a cook and run by domestic staff, was a hub of activity from before breakfast to after supper. At Broomielaw in North Canterbury, Mary Anne Barker employed a cook and housemaid to run the kitchen wing, and she conceded that they both worked 'desperately hard'. They had to do all the washing, which was 'two days severe work', and once that was finished 'there came the yeast making and the baking, followed by the brewing of sugar beer, preserves had to be made, bacon cured, all sorts of things to be done, besides the daily duties of scrubbing and cleaning, and cooking at all hours for stray visitors or "swaggers"'.[78] Because of the range of tasks required to keep a big house running there were often a number of rooms off the kitchen that served a specific purpose. The homestead at Orongorongo Station in South Wairarapa, for example, had a maid's dining room, jam store, dairy, meat safe, numerous pantries, a laundry, ironing room, linen cupboards, boxrooms and covered porches.[79]

The social and economic setting in which homesteads flourished lasted for only a few decades. The number of domestic servants in New Zealand, always inadequate to meet demand, declined rapidly from the 1880s, and palatial homes were impossible to run without staff. Furthermore, many large stations were subdivided in order to distribute family wealth, and the children of the big house often built their own, more manageable homes. Few big houses stayed in the family for more than one generation, and while some were repurposed as schools or health facilities, others were destroyed.[80] In those that survived, the large domestic rooms were more of a burden than a blessing. Rural sociologist Norma Metson observed in 1945 that '[u]nder modern conditions it is the homemaker herself who spends most of her time in the kitchen ... [and] the very large kitchen and adjoining service rooms, which provided necessary space for several workers, mean merely extra and unnecessary steps for someone working alone'.[81] The relegation of the working spaces to the back of the house, almost always on the cold south side, made the house impractical, as it meant that the kitchen was dark and cold.

What makes the ideal kitchen?

^
Longbeach Station homestead, Canterbury, during the Duke of Gloucester's tour of New Zealand in 1934–1935. This house was completely destroyed by fire in 1937. Unknown photographer, Alexander Turnbull Library, 1/4-019093-G.

Alice Carruthers lived at Longbeach Station, South Canterbury, from about 1900, as her father ran the saddlers' shop. In *'There Goes the Bell!!!'* she paints a vivid picture of life on the 13,000-hectare estate. The farm employed about 150 people and was a self-supporting community with a store, butcher, carpenter, saddler, painter, blacksmith, covermaker and wheelwright. As well as the big house – a massive English-style homestead with Queen Anne detailing – there was a cookhouse and dining room with adjoining bakery and sleeping quarters above, two implement sheds, oat lofts, a dairy, milking shed, and a swagger's hut. Of the victuals, Alice writes:

Rēwena and Rabbit Stew

the men's cookhouse as we called it [had a] dining room attached and the wee room alongside was where the bread was baked. At one time there was a large number of loaves baked every night, but later the Baker used to only bake from twenty to thirty a night and in the harvest nearly fifty. Such times as harvest, or shearing time, he also baked a currant loaf we called a 'Brownie'. To us this was a luxury as it always contained a lot of fruit in it....

On the same block was the Butcher's shop where we could buy anything in the mutton line. At one time the Butcher killed from fifteen to twenty sheep a day and during the harvest as many as thirty.... At Christmas time or whenever any visitors were staying at the Homestead (or 'Big House' as it was always called), there would be a big bullock killed; then we could have a lovely joint of beef. Once a year pigs were killed, then we could have pork or any bones from the pig.[82]

The homestead had a large orchard and vegetable garden attached to the flower garden, and workers and their families were invited to gather vegetables and fruit for preserving.

∧
A view of the cookhouse and bakehouse at Longbeach Station (on right), and other farm buildings including a post office and grain store. Hicks photograph, *Otago Witness*, 8 April 1903, p. 45. Hocken Collections Uare Taoka o Hākena, University of Otago.

The effect of encroaching European settlement on Māori housing varied greatly between regions and communities. Places with a higher concentration of European settlers and sojourners in the early 1800s experienced change more quickly, as did communities with Māori converts to Christianity, who saw value in the housing forms constructed on mission stations. Māori labourers who were engaged in farming, cultivation or bush clearing later in the century may also have ushered in broader changes in Māori housing forms and functions. Archaeologist Mary Newman found that houses in the Lake Rotoaira area (between Lake Taupō and Mt Tongariro), which were occupied seasonally by Māori in the late nineteenth and early twentieth century, were functionally and structurally distinct from permanent wharepuni: often they had the fireplace at one end of the house rather than in the centre, and the door was on a side wall.[83] Anthropologist David Robert Martin speculates that changes to the function of Māori dwellings, such as having spaces for cooking and sleeping under one roof, 'may more easily have occurred in temporary seasonal situations'.[84]

Certain changes to the structural fabric of freestanding whare in permanent settlements became more common from the 1880s, such as higher walls and doors, and porches that ran along a side wall rather than the front. Chimneys were incorporated into some whare and eventually this allowed for indoor cooking, although, at the turn of the century, it was still relatively uncommon.[85] Outdoor food preparation and kitchens set apart from the dwelling continued to be built in Māori communities until at least the 1870s and probably well beyond.[86]

Kitchens in the twentieth century: The state steps in

The half-century from 1840 to 1890 has been described as a laissez-faire period in New Zealand housing.[87] The government had very little input into the housing market or housing construction, so dwellings developed according to the preferences and resources of individuals or communities.[88] Settlers could and did take an active role in building their own houses to suit their immediate needs. From the late nineteenth century, however, public health measures were introduced which

established minimum housing standards.[89] The Liberal government, elected in 1890, introduced a 'flurry of legislation' to support individual home ownership, motivated by public health concerns and by an assumption that home ownership promoted social order.[90] The government became involved in providing housing in urban areas, such as building workers' dwellings, but the assistance it offered in rural areas was more indirect, for example in the form of government loans to land-owning settlers.[91] These advances were theoretically available to Māori, but 'so great was the prejudice against the Native title [Māori freehold land] very few were able to secure assistance from that source'.[92]

Instead, it was through the workings of local Māori councils – which were given authority for enforcing sanitary regulations under the Maori Councils Act of 1900 – that the state first became involved in Māori housing, with health reformers such as sanitary inspectors, district nurses and native inspectors aiming to improve Māori health outcomes by eradicating what they considered to be undesirable or insanitary housing practices. Overcrowding and poor ventilation were two areas of particular concern.[93] Māui Pōmare (Ngāti Mutunga, Ngāti Toa) headed the Māori section of the Department of Public Health, set up in 1901 to carry out inspections, improve sanitary conditions and provide education on preventative health measures.[94] Pōmare's work has often been overlooked, but it had a direct impact on Māori architecture by shaping perceptions of what housing forms were considered acceptable.[95]

Pōmare advocated for and encouraged the adoption of European-style housing and kitchens; in 1902 he predicted that 'within the near future we shall see the entire Maori population living in properly constructed, ventilated, and hygienic dwellings, and the old raupo whare become but a dream of the night of his insanitariness'.[96] He condemned kāuta wholesale, calling them 'veritable death traps', and gave a damning description in his first report to the chief health officer.

> Not only our noses, but our eyes, in more ways than one, testify to the fact that surely this is not a place for human beings to live in. There the poor housewife plies her wearied lungs in trying to fan into flame the carbonaceous gases which are making our eyes weep tears – yes, tears, dear housewife, for thee and thine, for death

The Kaiki at The Neck of Stewarts Isle. A Māori family in front of their European-style home at 'The Neck', Rakiura Stewart Island, 1860s. The Neck was home to a mixed Māori and Pākehā community in the nineteenth century. The house has a large chimney at one end, so the interior was perhaps quite similar to the one- or two-room huts described on pages 39–40. Unknown photographer, Richard Taylor, Sketchbook 1835–1860, Alexander Turnbull Library, E-296-q-158-1.

A Māori woman in front of a raupō dwelling at Wairau pā, c. 1880s. The design of the whare incorporates a chimney, high walls and a wooden door. Isabel Clervaux Chaytor photograph, Chaytor family photographs, Alexander Turnbull Library, 1/2-049922-F.

lurks within the very walls of thy realm – in fact, within the very atmosphere you are daily, hourly, breathing in. . . . Our kitchen has no floor. Mother Earth does homage by caressing the bootless foot of the housewife as she plies to and fro getting the *manuhiri* (strangers) their evening meal. . . . What is that chilly sensation stealing up and down our spines? Ah, we find our kitchen at least is well ventilated, for there are many cracks and crannies in its walls, especially between the posts through which the air may find ingress. Though good to have ventilation, yet it can stand the application of the universal law of temperance.[97]

Without the Māori councils, the transition to wooden housing probably would not have proceeded as quickly as it did.[98] The councils had mana and were crucial intermediaries between iwi and the state.[99] Between 1904 and 1909, 1256 'insanitary' houses were destroyed and 2104 new houses built, as well as 301 whare.[100]

The move to weatherboard housing was not universally welcomed; in 1906, for instance, sanitary inspector Elsdon Best wrote that he had been unable to move some of the communities in the Mataatua district from their 'state of apathy' towards the 'improvement' of housing.[101] As Raeburn Lange points out, 'the mere fact that a house was wooden did not mean that it was perfectly satisfactory from a health point of view', and there were complaints that the new buildings were cold and draughty.[102] Te Rangi Hīroa (Peter Buck) of Ngāti Mutunga suggested in *The Coming of the Maori* that '[d]uring the day, the board house impressed the law but at night, the old people stretched out snug on the earthen floor of the beloved *whare puni* at the back'.[103] Nevertheless, when Pōmare left the Department of Public Health in 1909 he claimed that the results of the sanitary reforms had been 'astonishingly satisfactory' and that 'Maori whare of the old stamp' had gone in the 'general awakening' that had taken place.[104]

Māori housing came under the scrutiny of health officials once again in the wake of the influenza epidemic of 1918–19, in which the Māori death rate was seven times that of the Pākehā population.[105] Officials and observers wrote about what they considered to be 'shocking' living conditions in Māori settlements; they frequently described houses as hovels and communities as slums.[106] The Health Act 1920 established a Division of Maori Hygiene within the Department of Health, and Buck was appointed as director.[107] The Māori councils, which had been defunct under native minister W. H. Herries, were revived, and were charged with carrying out sanitary works. The budget for doing this work was tiny and many councils struggled for funding, but in 1925 Buck reported a 'steady improvement in Maori village and home life', which he equated with the disintegration of the communal way of living, the removal of 'crowded clusters of huts', and the relegation of the thatched house to the position of 'ethnological curiosity'.[108] Architecture, particularly at the level of the individual dwelling, had become a focus of the state's Māori health reforms, and as a result, the transition from whare raupō to other housing forms was 'virtually complete' by 1930.[109]

    Although architecturally this transition was dramatic, it did not necessarily denote cultural assimilation.[110] Pōmare had noted in 1902 that many Māori who lived in 'elegant pakeha homes' had kāuta at the back, adopting what he described as 'half-European and half-Maori ways of living'.[111] Despite marked changes in house construction, the use of separate cooking spaces continued until at least the 1930s. Maudie Ruaka Reweti-Logan (née Tamehana; Ngāti Ruaka, Pūtiki, Te Āti Haunui a Pāpārangi) recalled that in the 1920s her family at Pūtiki (near Whanganui) 'slept in a big wooden house at the marae, but didn't eat in there', as they had a whareumu where food was cooked over an open fire.[112] Similarly, all eight women featured in *Ngā Mōrehu*, a collection of life stories from the Bay of Plenty, Urewera and Poverty Bay regions, grew up 'in the kāuta', using an external earth-floor shelter for cooking and eating food.[113]

    Māori found European housing inflexible when it came to accommodating larger groups of people. Although their adoption of the private single-family home seemed to suggest a change from extended to nuclear family living, in fact families still maintained strong connections to their wider whānau, and to other whānau within the hapū and iwi.[114] To be able to offer manaakitanga to members of these networks enhanced the mana of the host, and as Tom Smiler Junior (Te Aitanga-a-Māhaki, Rongowhakaata) recalled of his childhood at Waituhi in the 1920s, '[i]t was not unusual for families to feed up to twenty people at dinner,

including those who were passing by or staying temporarily.'¹¹⁵ Pamera Te Ruihi Warner (née Timoti; Ngāti Whātua) recounted that throughout her childhood in the 1930s her paternal grandmother lived close by in her own little whare, which had a mud-floor cooking area that could seat twenty people.¹¹⁶

State officials were quick to blame Māori for their 'defective use' of housing; they failed to take account of extended family structures in their comments about overcrowding and insanitation.¹¹⁷ Furthermore, there was little in the way of financial assistance available to Māori for housing, and because European-style dwellings required a considerable investment of capital and labour, spacious houses were beyond the means of many families. Government policy in the early twentieth century aimed to give skilled and semi-skilled workers access to housing through state lending, but no direct relief was available to those living in poor conditions.¹¹⁸ From 1894 settlers who lived rurally could apply for state credit through the Advances to Settlers Office (later the State Advances Office), but this scheme was not open to people living on communally owned land.

It was 1929 before public credit was finally made available specifically for Māori land development, through a scheme designed and implemented by the minister of native affairs, Apirana Ngata (Ngāti Porou).¹¹⁹ As well as providing funds for top-dressing, fencing, ploughing, resowing, herd testing and stock, the programme also enabled the construction of farm buildings and houses.¹²⁰ More than 500 homes were built between 1929 and 1936 under the development schemes, and as there was no standard plan for these homes, there was room to experiment with a variety of housing forms.¹²¹ Te Puea Hērangi (Waikato-Tainui) oversaw the land development schemes in the Waikato region, and devised a 'hybrid' house design combining aspects of both Māori and Pākehā architecture. The kitchen was incorporated into the same structure as the living and sleeping spaces. Usually this building had an iron roof and a timber floor, but both thatch and weatherboard were used for the walls: this lowered the construction cost to about one-quarter of the price of a weatherboard home and allowed Māori builders to work with a more familiar weatherproofing system.¹²²

From 1935 loans were made available specifically for Māori housing through the Native Housing Act.¹²³ The Public Works Department

Rawinia Rikihana and Avarua Love, Waikanae, 1924. The wooden house in the background is the wharekai. Unknown photographer, Kāpiti Coast District Libraries, Love Collection, HP1555, reproduced with permission of the Love whānau.

oversaw the construction of houses under the Act, initially offering three standard house plans suited to two, four or six people.[124] The department was asked to make the houses as uniform as possible, but some applicants rejected this standardised approach. At Whakarewarewa and Ōhinemutu, for instance, applicants pushed for houses 'of a Maori character which would conform to the surroundings', while in the Tairāwhiti district the local office produced an additional plan in accordance with residents' wishes, sacrificing the scullery, washhouse, sink and walk-in wardrobes to make room for extra bedrooms.[125] The main barrier to the success of this scheme was that those who could have benefited most from it could not afford the initial deposit. Michael Joseph Savage, minister of native affairs, wrote in 1938 that '[t]he investigations [of Māori villages] undertaken . . . disclose many problems which render a housing scheme for Natives more complex than is the case with Europeans. Indigency, defective land titles, multiplicity of land ownership, insufficient security, Native custom, and even religious beliefs are factors which have retarded the Government's housing policy for Maoris.'[126] That same year an amendment to the Native Housing Act established a special fund for 'indigent' cases, and £50,000 was set aside for those who had no land as security and no way of repaying a loan.[127] Although Savage acknowledged that custom and religious beliefs impacted on Māori housing needs, most of the houses built under this scheme were constructed to standard Public Works Department designs. Many had two bedrooms, and all included a kitchen with a stove.[128] From 1944 the Department of Maori Affairs also offered standard housing plans to potential homeowners, and all had a kitchen just the right size 'for the mother of a biggish family to work in'.[129]

Through these various innovations and interventions, Māori families and communities gradually became more accustomed to 'the Pākehā notion of the "house" as an interior space or spaces where people would gather to be in each other's company, prepare and share food, and sleep'.[130] A transition from wharepuni to European-style housing, from external kāuta to internal kitchen, had taken place in many parts of New Zealand, but this transition was never a wholesale transformation. In 1927 Māui Pōmare and Apirana Ngata spoke to a group of Māori representatives at Pūtiki and summarised the changes they had seen

Te Puea Hērangi (centre) and two others in front of a land development scheme house. The 'hybrid' house was built using both traditional and modern construction techniques. Unknown location, 1930s. Unknown photographer, Alexander Turnbull Library, 1/2-059950-F.

(and overseen) in the preceding decades. They asserted that '[t]he communal Maori has become an individualist in proprietorship and in his home life. . . . [and] the culture complex that centres round the term "home" (in its English significance) has with native modification been adopted'.[131] As Lachy Paterson has argued, the way Māori leaders such as Ngata, Buck, Pōmare and their contemporary Rēweti Tūhorouta Kōhere (Ngāti Porou) responded to assimilatory forces can best be described as 'adaptive acculturation'; 'they made conscious decisions about which Pākehā and Māori tikanga (codes) they thought Māori should practise, rather than promote across-the-board assimilation'.[132] Certainly Māori families sought the security of adequate shelter, and individual home ownership was the only model supported by government policy. However, Māori modified Pākehā notions of the ideal house to incorporate the restrictions of tapu and to accommodate extended whānau.[133]

Houses built under the Native Housing Amendment Act 1938, such as these houses erected near Paeroa, were generally constructed by the Public Works Department to a standard plan. 'Native Land Development and the Provision of Houses for Maoris, including Employment Promotion, Report on – By Board of Native Affairs', *AJHR*, I, 1939, G-10, p. 79.

State intervention into rural settler housing in the early decades of the twentieth century was largely achieved through the provision of loans for erecting buildings or carrying out improvements on freehold land. This indirect assistance promoted closer land settlement and owner-occupied housing, and was rooted in the belief that the 'soil-based family' was the ideal foundation of social order.[134] Around the turn of the century family farming units became commercially viable, and although subsistence farmers still struggled to make a living on marginal properties, established small farmers reaped the rewards of generous state support in the attainment of greater material comfort.

Many rural Pākehā people opted for larger houses in contemporary styles such as the villa and bungalow.[135] The villa reached the peak of its popularity and complexity in the 1890s. Although in its simplest form it was similar to a four-roomed cottage, the villa tended to be bigger and the rooms were more deliberately organised around the idea of a public 'front' (usually the parlour and best bedroom), and a private 'back' (the kitchen, any other bedrooms, washhouse and outbuildings).[136] The central hallway was the main axis of the house, and often featured an ornamental arch at the midpoint that delineated public and private spaces. The 'front rooms' were lavishly decorated and furnished to reflect the wealth and refinement of the family, while the kitchen and other rooms at the back of the house tended to be more sparse and utilitarian.[137] Unlike earlier houses, where one room could serve a number of different functions, each space in a villa was designed for a particular purpose and set of activities.[138]

By the 1910s the bungalow had eclipsed the villa as the house of choice, characterised by simpler design and more open spaces.[139] It suggested a more relaxed lifestyle, and appealed to those who had been 'force-fed on the formality and ornamentation of late Victorian houses'.[140] No longer was it strictly necessary to present a formal face to the world, so rooms took on new names that reflected their function and position

Typical plan for a single bay villa. From Jeremy Salmond, *Old New Zealand Houses 1800–1940*, Reed Publishing, Auckland, 1986, p. 155.

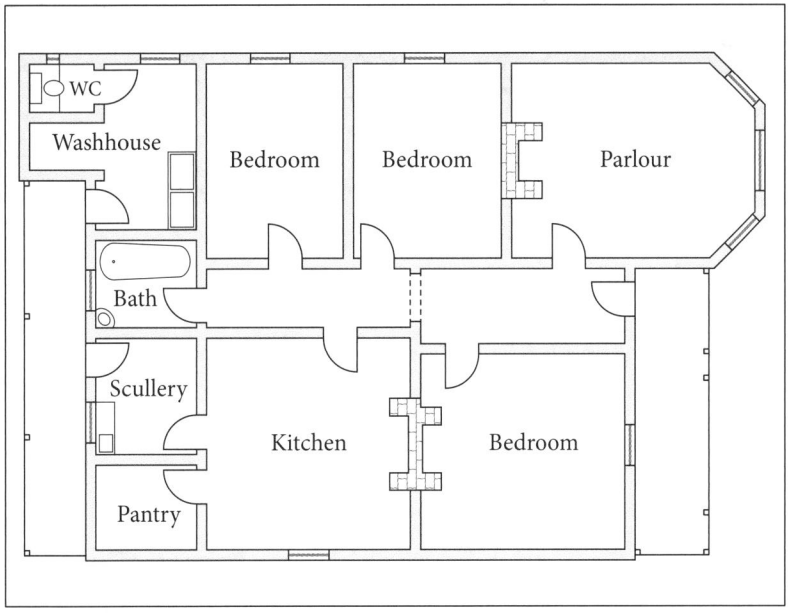

^
A man and woman on the front porch of their villa,
unknown rural location, c. 1900–20. Unknown
photographer, Auckland Libraries Heritage Collections,
900-9621.

within the house. The parlour was replaced by the living room – a less formal space, with simpler furnishings; and the dining room, previously one of the 'best' rooms, became the family breakfast room. Sliding doors were introduced between living and dining spaces to allow for more open-plan living.[141] The bungalow was also designed for those with an interest in home science, and was carefully planned and decorated to achieve maximum efficiency and cleanliness. The family kitchen was replaced by the kitchenette – a small space designed to reduce the number of steps taken, make cleaning easier, and to save labour.[142]

The use of space in rural homes was never so well defined as architectural plans and household guides might suggest. In rural Pākehā houses the kitchen was typically a space for cooking, eating, socialising and relaxing, and this blurred the distinction between public and private.

Typical floor plan for a Californian bungalow in the 1920s or 1930s. From Ben Schrader, 'Housing – Interior Planning and Living', Te Ara – the Encyclopedia of New Zealand, http://www.TeAra.govt.nz/en/interactive/38650/housing-floor-plans

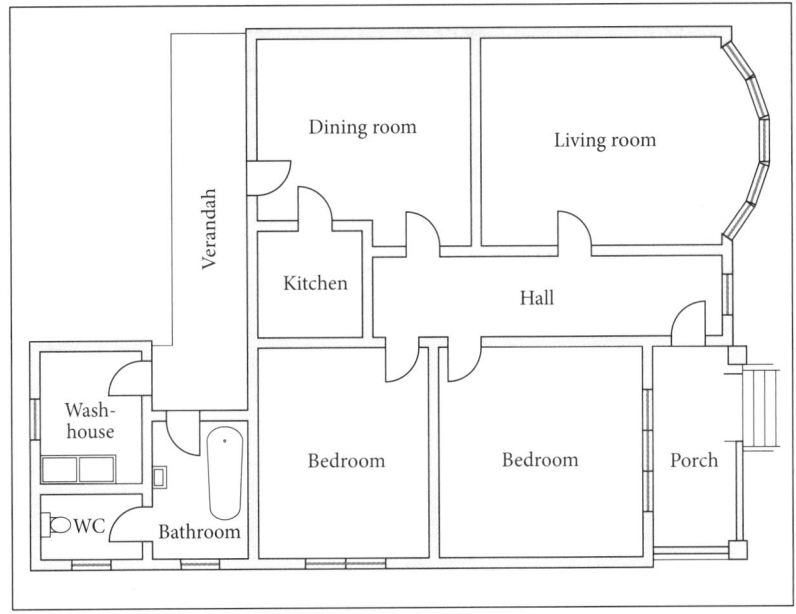

Urban architectural styles proved to be 'quite unsuitable for country conditions', and when the government introduced the Rural Housing Act in 1939 the State Advances Corporation deemed it necessary to create housing plans with rural homeowners specifically in mind.[143] The corporation asked for input from regional branches and farm appraisers throughout the country, and their reports reveal interesting distinctions between rural and urban domestic spaces.

According to the reports, a large kitchen was essential in a rural home. The Nelson advisor gave a list of reasons why the average farmer might want to eat and 'live' in his kitchen: 'He, his wife and children would not always be dressed in a manner becoming to parlour. Coming to meals from cowshed, ploughing etc., he could not be expected to temporarily change and clean up for the "best" room.'[144] The kitchen also needed to be large enough to allow for a range of productive activities, with plenty of storage for staples and preserves. Rural people were still growing or gathering a lot of their own food well into the twentieth century, and they preserved large quantities of fruit and vegetables for use throughout the year. Staples such as flour and sugar had to be stored in bulk, partly for reasons of economy but also because the distance to and from the local store could make it difficult to get provisions regularly. When Myrtle Richards (née Cooksey) moved to a farm on the northern side of the Paturau River in the Tasman region in about 1927, she had to buy stores enough for three months at a time. Her order included a sack of flour, a bag of sugar, a box of sultanas and plenty of treacle, and she had storage bins to keep everything in.[145] The Mitchell family at Umere on the Karamea River could get groceries once a week, but as there were eleven in the family they still needed to be able to store 100 pounds (45kg) of flour and 70 pounds (32kg) of sugar.[146] Because of the need to keep provisions, rural housing advisors noted that built-in kitchen cupboards – a distinctive feature of the modern kitchenette – would not provide sufficient storage for rural households; a separate pantry was preferable.[147]

The Rural Housing Act demonstrated the state's broader aspirations for the rural Pākehā population. Although the provisions of the Act did not explicitly exclude Māori, in practice Māori requests for housing assistance in the 1930s and 1940s were generally dealt with by the underfunded Department of Maori Affairs rather than the State

The kitchen and sitting room in a Pukekohe bungalow, 1924. The bungalow was the house of choice for many New Zealanders in the early twentieth century. Rooms were small and carefully planned according to function, but because rural people used their kitchens as living and social spaces, this architectural philosophy did not suit everyone. Arnold C. Bettany photographs, Auckland Libraries Heritage Collections, Footprints 03222, Footprints 03220.

Advances Corporation.[148] The Act empowered county councils to advance building loans to farmers and to levy rates to pay for the houses.[149] Government largesse had led many farmers into crushing debt, and one of the key goals of the government's intervention in rural housing was to keep families and workers on farms. This reflected not only a fear that a reduction in the labour force would mean a reduction in agricultural productivity, but also a belief, as the MP for Wallace put it, that country people were sturdier than town people and made better citizens.[150] The 1911 census showed for the first time that more Pākehā lived in urban areas than rural, and by 1936 the total urban population (Māori and Pākehā) was 67.9 percent.[151] Although the number of farmers and small farms increased in the late nineteenth and early twentieth centuries, the proportion of the workforce engaged in the primary sector (agriculture, forestry and mining) decreased steadily from a peak of 56 percent in 1871 to 25.2 percent in 1941.[152] Meanwhile the percentage of the workforce employed in the tertiary sector (services such as transport, communication, retail, education and health) increased from 31 percent to 44.9 percent over the same period, and more and more New Zealanders worked for a wage or salary in private enterprise or government.[153]

Nevertheless, politicians continued to idealise family farms – privately and individually owned – as 'the fundamental foundation of the social order'.[154] Successive governments introduced legislation to promote closer settlement despite evidence that many farms were uneconomic and provided an inadequate standard of living. This, Miles Fairburn argues, indicates that the small family farm 'was intended less to serve an economic function than to fulfil a social ideal'.[155] Accordingly, from the late 1930s the state also paid greater attention to agricultural economics and rural living conditions and, in 1944, established a research division within the Department of Agriculture to examine, among other things, farm management and rural sociology.[156] These measures, as with other housing regulations implemented earlier in the century, were underpinned by certain assumptions about what sort of housing forms were most desirable, and what sort of settlement provided the ideal foundation for social order.

Building homes

In an essay on decolonisation and the enduring resonance of stories in the land, Moana Jackson meditates on the 'inexpressible joy of belonging' that characterises the feeling of being at home.[157] This feeling is so personal, so intrinsic, that it seems to defy scholarly analysis, yet notions of home do have histories and those histories are as much political as personal, shaped by particular cultural, religious and familial mores. Māori perceptions of home have multiple facets that are both spatial and metaphysical, centred on whenua and whakapapa.[158] Western notions of the home, meanwhile, tend to centre on the house as a shelter that facilitates domestic life and supports economic aspirations. Given my focus on kitchens and domestic practices I will primarily be exploring notions of the home centred on the house, but I draw on the work of kaupapa Māori researchers and other scholars to demonstrate that this association between house and home is not inevitable or universal.

Houses, homes and home spaces

Papakāinga means, among other things, original home or home base, and this highlights the fundamental connection between the land and Māori concepts of home.[159] Māori identity is rooted in the land, the home space, personified as Papatūānuku (earth mother).[160] Connections to ancestral home places are established through recitations of whakapapa, which express tūrangawaewae – a sense of belonging or attachment. The land binds together all those who have called it home, and collective ownership of land gives a sense of shared identity and purpose.[161]

Traditionally demarcations of space and territory were dictated by iwi and hapū relationships to particular rohe, which became 'home', and the marae was the focal point for those attachments.[162] As the nature of whare Māori changed, there was greater emphasis on the marae as a site of cultural preservation, and a range of new houses, such as wharenui and wharekai (dining halls), were built to meet new needs (see chapter 5). Within these houses, cultural practices that provided a focus for family and community life, individual identity, nourishment, caring and a sense of belonging could continue in some form.[163]

Land alienation as a result of colonisation has had ongoing impacts on Māori conceptions of home, resulting in many Māori being disconnected from their tūrangawaewae and losing the knowledge of whakapapa that allowed a continued metaphysical connection to home places.[164] Discussions of Māori housing often focus on deficits – things that have been lost – and the literature on homelessness and dislocation far outweighs research into Māori understandings of home and belonging.[165] Dominant meanings of home in Aotearoa New Zealand have been shaped by colonial discourse, but Māori have fought to maintain their own sense of home in houses and other places imbued with tikanga and culture.

Family and whānau

Both Māori and European conceptions of the home are inextricably linked with family and whānau, although the composition of families and therefore the structure of domestic spaces is quite different. For Māori, the traditional whānau usually consisted of three or four generations of extended family, who organised and maintained themselves among other whānau of the hapū.[166] Within this whānau environment, members gained a sense of collective affiliation and learnt their obligatory roles and responsibilities to others in the collective. Home was a place where people could live together and maintain the wellbeing of the family through manaakitanga and whanaungatanga.[167]

Anthropologist Mākereti Papakura explains in *The Old-Time Maori* that the internal order of kāinga was designed to support and maintain relationships within and between whānau. She describes her village at Whakarewarewa in depth:

> A kainga would be occupied by a hapu made up of several family groups. No outsider would come and settle in a kainga; he would only come as a guest. Each family group had its own piece of ground which would be fenced off, and within this they would have their houses, two, three, or more. These houses would be used for sleeping, and would be anywhere from 12 feet long by 6 or 8 feet wide to 20 or 25 feet long by 10 or 12 feet wide, the head of the family

using the largest one. There would be space for more houses if necessary. The houses would all face the rising sun, and also face the marae (plaza) of the village. A family group would have a wharau or kauta built close by, to use for cooking in the bad weather. Many things would be stored in the wharau, such as dry wood stacked in a corner, and various necessary things such as baskets for carrying potatoes and floormats would hang up on the wall. In fine weather, all the cooking was done outside, and all meals eaten in the open.[168]

Many whānau converted to Christianity in the nineteenth century, although historian Violeta Gilabert suggests that 'in rural contexts, adherence to Christian beliefs, rituals and moral frameworks seldom extended to the need for a breadwinner, an established domicile, and a nuclear family'.[169] As such, social life still retained its tribal structure, centred on marae and whānau, and household membership remained quite fluid.

In contrast, settler notions of home and family were far more rigid, and closely associated with the growth of the English middle class. Although it encompassed groups with vastly different religious beliefs, political views and occupations, the middle class was united by a distinct moral code and a shared understanding of the domestic setting in which that code was best practised. Middle-class morality stressed the importance of the family as a social unit, faith as a mark of respectability and status, the desirability of separating public and private worlds, and the importance of rationality and order.[170] The nuclear family, shaped by Judaic-Christian tradition and law, was the central institution of this world order. It rested on the separation of generations, whereby a married couple would move into a new residence and live separately from their extended kin.[171]

Within the nuclear family structure men and women had very specific roles, based on women's supposedly innate aptitude for faith and men's natural competence in the world of business. Evangelical belief framed business and professional activities as honest toil, and men could be distinguished by their conduct in these fields. As men's work was increasingly removed from the home, however, the emphasis on professional activities seemed at odds with the focus on family and domesticity. That made the role of women in the home especially important: removed from the temptations of the world, they were to be the guardians of the family's morality and use their 'natural' gentleness and passivity to exercise religious influence. Men could operate in the amoral world of the market 'only if they could be rescued by women's moral vigilance at home'.[172] From these evangelical underpinnings the notion of separate spheres for men and women had become common sense for the middle classes by the mid-nineteenth century, part of a secular language that shaped cultural practices.

A middle-class, Christian concept of family, founded on marriage and with separate spheres for men and women, was introduced to New Zealand by the first missionaries and their families. Within the Church Missionary Society (CMS), men were expected to marry before embarking on a mission, and upon arrival in New Zealand missionary couples set up houses that they hoped would model respectable domestic standards.[173] In the way that they configured their homes missionaries made 'architectural statements' professing their devotion to the conjugal family and Western notions of public and private.[174] Marianne and Henry Williams, CMS missionaries in the Bay of Islands, built their permanent dwelling in 1824 with separate rooms for adults and children, Māori and missionaries, men and women. Marianne and other women of the CMS primarily used the kitchen and parlour, while Henry and the other men used the study and large parlour.[175] Henry noted in his journal that the move to a new home caused a 'very great' change in the household. 'Mrs W.' experienced 'an important change in her domestic duties', while the children and the 'native girls and boys' were 'more orderly and correct in their behaviour. . . . We trust we shall experience much savings of time in every branch of duty besides the comfort of having our household ordered according to the good English fashion.'[176] Williams' confidence that a change of domestic arrangements would provide greater comfort, encourage efficiency and promote 'correct behaviour' indicates just how important the 'good English' house was thought to be as an agent of conversion and colonisation.

The impact of colonial ideas about ideal homes and family structures grew increasingly evident in Māori communities in the early twentieth century, as more and more Māori students were exposed to

Pākehā norms through the education system and increasing numbers of Māori migrated to cities.[177] Amiria Manutahi Stirling (née O'Hara; Ngāti Porou) was born in Tūpāroa in around 1900 and lived with her aunt Mereana Mokikiwa at Taumata o Mihi. She was educated at Hiruhārama and at the Ladies' College in Wellington, and then worked as a housemaid for the Williams family at Kaharau. Since she was a child Amiria had been betrothed to Eruera Kawhia Whakatane Stirling (Te Whānau-ā-Apanui, Ngāti Porou, Ngāi Tahu) and the couple married in 1918. Arrangements for their married life had been made by whānau; they were to live with Eruera's parents and organise their work collectively. Amiria had different plans, however, as she recalled in later life: 'I felt that married life is a house where you can care for your own children, not staying with the old people and looking after all the tribe.'[178] The couple eventually settled on a mixed farm in Otaimina, where they built a two-bedroom house with kitchen and living room. Similarly, when Anglican clergyman Rēweti Kōhere moved with his family to East Cape in 1908 they lived in a small cottage with three other families, and although 'it was not really poky and was well ventilated', Rēweti 'was not altogether happy about living with others in the same house'.[179] He built his family a weatherboard house with an internal bathroom, scullery and kitchen, and his wife Keita Kaikiri Paratene (Rongowhakaata, Ngāti Kahungunu, Te Aitanga-a-Māhaki) was so happy with their home she would go out at night and gaze at it glistening in the moonlight.[180]

    Gradually the proportion of Māori living in individual family dwellings increased, and a 1969 survey of 100 Māori households found that 90 percent of participants lived in single-family units. The researcher suggested that the nature of contemporary housing not only reflected this trend but also exacerbated it, as '[s]mall houses and confined space made it difficult to continue the extended family. . . . [T]he norm was a single family unit to a single dwelling, with each family responsible for its own economic wellbeing.'[181] As we have seen, some modifications were possible to make European-style houses more conducive to Māori ways of living, and at the same time greater emphasis was placed on wharenui as spaces in which communal styles of living could be maintained and key cultural values reasserted. Ernest and Pearl Beaglehole wrote in 1946 that although many Māori at 'Kowhai' (the fictitious name they gave to the community they studied, actually at Ōtaki) worked in Pākehā occupations, lived in Pākehā-style housing, ate Pākehā food, used the Pākehā calendar and observed the rites of the church, there was 'a hard core of persistently surviving Maori beliefs and feelings' that centred on the tangihanga, the marae and the meeting house.[182] Later in the century, Māori architects and other groups pushed for Māori-driven design that reincorporated these beliefs and feelings into the layout and construction of domestic housing. They advocated for larger houses that could accommodate kaumātua, sizeable kitchens big enough for two or more people, and outdoor spaces suitable for food preparation and larger whānau gatherings.[183]

For Pākehā farming families, the cultural and economic assumptions that middle-class ideals of the home were based on were not always applicable to their daily lives (see chapter 4). Still, Christian ideas of home and family were adopted by rural women's groups such as the Women's Institute (WI) and the Women's Division of the Farmers Union (WDFU) in the early twentieth century, and they incorporated these messages into their rhetoric.[184] Explaining the significance of their motto, 'For Home and Country', the editor of the official publication of the WI wrote:

> Home – what a precious word and what a wealth of precious meaning! It is just the dearest place on earth, made so by its associations with your family – their joys and their sorrows – their hopes and their aspirations. It is a refuge from the trials and struggles of the outer world. The peace of home and the healing hands of home, its sweetness, and its power – its love everlasting demanding love in return are all centred there. There is no doubt whatever that our homes are to-day, what they have ever been, the backbone of our country.'[185]

These associations between home and family impacted on how the kitchen was imagined because in many rural homes it was the focal point for family life. Judith Campbell (née Grant), for instance, describes the kitchen in her family home near Takapuna as the hub of their little universe:

> Our kitchen table was the size of a tennis table and was made from two large slabs of kauri on solid, turned legs. None of Mother's table cloths would fit it, so the end was always covered with all the farming magazines and letters that accumulate in any household. . . .
>
> Family life centred on our kitchen. The old kauri sofa beside the fire, with all the newspapers stuffed under its squab, and the comfortable chairs around the fire were the focus of our many games of cards, chess, jigsaw puzzles and draughts. The fireplace was the centrepiece of our Christmas with the pillowcases all hanging expectantly along its mantelpiece. The kitchen walls, with the home-made paper chains draped drunkenly around and up and over the clock and cupboards, epitomised the celebration. . . .
>
> We were *never* bored and lived life to the full, with always the security of Mother, in the kitchen, the centre of our lives.[186]

H. C. D. Somerset noted in his pioneering publication *Littledene* – a detailed sociological study of Oxford in North Canterbury, and for decades the authoritative text on community in rural New Zealand – that the rural family 'lives' in the kitchen and that, of an evening, the kitchen table would need to accommodate the children doing their homework, the father reading the paper, the mother sewing, and the older children talking of their church clubs.[187] This, according to Somerset, was 'the farmer's retreat from the battle with forces over which he has no control', the family's little haven of security.[188]

While most personal manuscripts evoke this sense of sanctity and present rosy pictures of life on the land, there are occasional glimpses of violence in these accounts. Sarah Courage, on a Canterbury sheep run in the 1860s, wrote of her new cook, Mrs Todd: 'The woman was quiet and clean but very forgetful, never troubling to look at a clock. Her desire to be punctual was shown by her absurd precipitancy in doing everything to a cinder an hour before dinnertime. She came to me one day and said, "Please, ma'm, don't you think you could eat your dinner now, for its all ready?" That was just an hour before dinnertime. Yet . . . when her husband's meals were not ready, he would pummel her, as she expressed it.'[189] Although the ideal home was envisaged as a place of peace and refuge, for some rural people there was no safety or comfort there.

Privacy

Another key attribute of the ideal home, as the British middle classes conceived and promoted it, was an emphasis on privacy – the state of being free from observation and disruption. This desire for domestic privacy predated the rise of the middle class but, according to Davidoff and Hall, '[i]t was the middle ranks who erected the strictest boundaries between private and public space'.[190] From the fourteenth century noble families in Europe began retreating from the public, communal life embodied by the medieval hall and instead withdrew to private chambers reserved for them and their staff.[191] In the centuries that followed the idea of domestic privacy slowly unfurled, and individuals came to value not only family privacy but also personal or bodily privacy.[192] Put another way, the architecture of the ideal home increasingly had to provide both privacy of the family from the community, and privacy of family members from each other.[193] From the seventeenth century rooms began to take on specialist functions that enabled physical separation: historian Judith Flanders describes this as the major conceptual leap in the making of the modern house.[194]

The emphasis on personal privacy had both religious and individualist undertones. Eighteenth-century evangelicals 'demanded private space for individual introspection', emphasising the importance of prayer in the quest for self-improvement.[195] Richard Davis, a CMS missionary in the Bay of Islands, wrote to fellow missionary Joseph Matthews in 1861 that '[p]rivate prayer is as essential to the sustentation of our souls, as food is to the nutrition of our bodies, and to make us efficient Christians must be regularly resorted to'.[196] Similarly when Rēweti Kōhere, an evangelical Anglican minister, laid out his design for a model village in 1902, he specified that while communal prayers had their place, 'the best prayers . . . were those with one's own family in one's own home. Some people were good at reciting from a prayer book, but needed to learn how to pray in their own words in their own rooms.'[197] The history of the private home is also bound up with the history of individuality. The growth of individualism – the sense of the self as unique and independent from the social group – has been a defining characteristic of Western modernity, and while some historians see the roots of this conviction in capitalism or political liberalism, others suggest that the home has also been a site for this sharpening sense of self.[198]

Māori developed and maintained a sense of self through tribal structures, deriving identity from membership of whānau, hapū, iwi and waka (the canoe on which their founding ancestors arrived in Aotearoa).[199] Individuals did not conceive of themselves as separate from the social group, and consequently, domestic spaces were not strictly demarcated. Mākereti Papakura writes in *The Old-Time Maori* that traditionally '[t]here was no privacy in a Maori home, such as is known in an English home'. It was usual for all of the family to sleep together in one whare, and children were included in the routines and conversations of daily life to a greater degree than in Pākehā homes.[200]

This lack of personal privacy was of great concern to housing inspectors at the turn of the century. One described the pre-European way of living in these terms: 'Huddled together in *wharepunis* as they used to be, shutters closed, breathing filthy air, thereby ignorantly encouraging all manner of diseases; filthy jesting and very little, if anything, at all edifying; privacy, unknown; and we have the whole of the Maori ways described in that one word, "immorality".'[201] Mākereti counters criticisms like this by explaining that communal living 'did not result, as strangers often suppose, in any lowering of the moral tone. The reason for this is that children were not curious about things which were treated in a matter-of-fact way. Every phase of life was freely discussed by the parents in the presence of the children, even things which western people deem most intimate.'[202] She raises the point that notions of privacy and intimacy are culturally specific – a fact lost on government officials who deprived whānau Māori of privacy as they surveyed and reformed their homes.

In fact, it is likely that only the wealthiest of New Zealand's nineteenth-century settlers could achieve personal privacy in its modern form. When Charles and Johanne Alexander moved to Mangapiko (Manawatū) in 1872, for instance, they lived in a tiny two-roomed cottage with their four children. The bedroom had three beds – one for Johanne and Charles, the others for the children – and the sofa in the kitchen also substituted for a bed at night. Later, when their daughter Bernice married Lindsay Johnstone in 1893, she shared her new home with the ploughman and two of her brothers-in-law. As Bernice's daughter later wrote in a family history, this left 'little time for billing and cooing', and, presumably, little space.[203]

Families who prospered on the land could extend or rebuild their houses, and as Rhoda McWhannell (née McCurdie) recalled of her childhood home in East Taieri, Otago, this did provide some degree of privacy. She wrote that '[t]he old farm kitchen was always an inviting place, with its warm stove, and usually something exciting going on. There was a big table where I could find a corner for myself, if that was where I wanted to be. The maid would be cosy and comfortable in her own easy chair near the fire in the evenings', while Rhoda's parents felt most comfortable in the drawing room.[204] Each member of the household had a space to call their own, but the house was not a private haven for the exclusive use of the family; and indeed, very few rural houses functioned in that way. Rhoda's family had a live-in maid who entertained visitors in the kitchen, and their groceries were delivered each week by a 'wirey little fellow' named Ernie Pleugh.[205] As Judith Flanders puts it in her expansive history of the home, 'the "separate sphere" of the home was routinely breached by others', be they tradespeople, labourers, salespeople, clergy or neighbours, and spaces therefore had to be coded so that only certain rooms were open to public invasion.[206] These codes were built into the fabric of houses using stairs, corridors, archways and separate entrances, signalling to visitors the spaces in which they would be welcome, and those reserved for the inhabitants of the house.

In middle- and upper-class British homes the work of preparing and cooking food had by the late eighteenth century been relegated to backstage, private spaces, and some rural people brought this attitude with them.[207] Those wanting to maintain a careful separation of public and private spaces within their homes saw the construction of a parlour – used for entertaining company and for no other purpose – as a vital step towards domestic order.[208] Newlywed Pauline Perry (née Dickinson) of Te Kawa, Ōtorohanga, reported to her parents in 1927 that she had 'to spring clean the sitting room every few days because of someone coming', presumably because she did not feel it was appropriate to receive guests in the kitchen.[209] Visits weren't always as formal as this implies, however, for in 1928 Pauline wrote that 'Mr C [Cummings, their neighbour] and I had a cup of tea here before milking. He took his gumboots off because they were so hot and came in in bare feet, and I remarked "How clean your feet are! New gumboots I suppose." He'd got a pair a day or two ago, and agreed quite naturally, and then it suddenly occurred to me that this was hardly a topic for afternoon tea!' This may not have been quite the situation Pauline envisaged when she furnished her new home and prepared the sitting room for company, but as she wrote to her parents, 'that is life out here!'[210]

The designation of public and private spaces did not necessarily spell the end of the multifunctional kitchen either as in many homes it was still used for more casual entertaining. A contributor to the *New Zealand Farmer* wrote in 1892 that she had recently paid a visit to a friend and sat in the kitchen with her while she finished the dishes. This would not have been appropriate for new acquaintances, but the writer felt comfortable accepting the invitation because they were well acquainted.[211] Margaret Trotter (née Cowie), meanwhile, described the kitchen in her childhood home at Ōtāpiri, Southland, as the 'living room, playroom, study and dining room', where '[t]he table seemed to be filled often, with room for many who came to the door'.[212] The house had a small sitting room for curling up on cold winter evenings and a front sitting room for best occasions, but Margaret remembers that it was in the kitchen that everything seemed to happen. While there were codes and conventions built into the layout of rural houses, within these private spaces rural people developed their own ways of living; their own ways to feel at home.

When Moana Jackson described colonisation as one house replacing another, he was pointing to the fact that a house is more than bricks and mortar; it is a physical edifice reinforcing a cultural one. A broad range of factors have shaped the form and function of houses in rural New Zealand since the early nineteenth century, resulting in a vast array of cooking spaces. Structural factors such as the availability of materials, risk of fire, and architectural developments played a part, but so too did ideological considerations such as the desire for privacy and the prioritisation of the nuclear family unit. The colonisation of Aotearoa saw those in power attempting to define, both for themselves and for others, what it meant to be 'at home' in this country, and built into their vision of the ideal house were assumptions about the best way for people to live.

This chapter has sketched the outlines of rural houses and cooking spaces in a variety of contexts, but as suggested in the introduction it is people and activities, hustle and bustle, that transform a house into a home. When asked to describe her home for a competition run by the Associated Country Women of the World, Mrs H. Wright of Makarewa, Southland, wrote:

> This is my pen picture of my rural home. Just an ordinary, comfortable home to a stranger, but to me it is part of my life. The memories of forty years' work, the anxieties, sorrows, hardships and the happiness of accomplishment are all built into these walls, and still in fancy I hear the voices of the children, long since grown to maturity and now with homes and children of their own.[213]

In the chapters that follow I will consider the tools, ingredients, people and processes that animated rural kitchens and transformed them from empty spaces to hubs of rural life.

ns and hot stoves:

Changes in cooking technologies

In June 1938, 'A Farmer's Wife' wrote an article for the *Auckland Star* describing the various homes she had lived in since her marriage some thirty years earlier. Moving from place to place in search of opportunities, the author and her husband spent years developing a bush section in the backblocks before 'the hungry King Country' swallowed all their capital and they were forced to leave the land and take up paid employment on someone else's farm. The house they moved to, she wrote, was not uncomfortable, but the most common conveniences still eluded her. 'I am beginning to think that in some former life I must have lived in a luxurious mansion and not appreciated it. If so, I have learnt my lesson and am sure I have earned a home in the next life.'[1] For this woman, living and working in the country meant adjusting to inconveniences: cooking over a tiny stove with a smoky tin chimney; boiling clothes in kerosene tins every wash day; and living in a draughty lean-to house that was 'the last word in ugliness'.[2] The sleek washers, water heaters and gas cookers advertised in the same newspaper had no place in this home, for these were twentieth-century 'pioneers' still searching for their little piece of paradise. The history of the kitchen space in rural New Zealand has been one of adaptability and improvisation, and the history of rural cooking technologies has been no less varied. This chapter explores that diversity of cooking techniques, and considers why and how those technologies were used in rural Māori and Pākehā homes.

The first section of this chapter is arranged in a roughly chronological sequence from the oldest cooking technologies – open-fire and earth oven cookery – to the newest – electric stoves and refrigerators – but that does not mean that rural households adopted technologies in this sequence.[3]

Rural people, by choice or circumstance, used a range of techniques to cook, and the introduction of more modern methods never entirely supplanted others. Cooks made decisions about their domestic appliances for a whole host of personal, practical, cultural and economic reasons, and by examining those decisions we gain glimpses of rural life both inside and outside of the kitchen. This chapter uses personal manuscripts, photographs and material from newspapers and magazines to examine cooking technologies not in gleaming showrooms or stores, but in people's homes: smoky, dirty, cranking out heat, producing delicious (and not-so-delicious) meals.

Cooking techniques ancient and modern

Since the very first days of settlement, cooking in Aotearoa New Zealand has combined ancient strategies with innovative tools and techniques. Earth oven cookery was a well established cooking method in Polynesia, brought to Aotearoa by the first settlers and adapted in this new environment to cook larger forms of protein such as moa. When European settlers arrived in New Zealand, they brought tools and utensils produced by the great modern factories of industrial Britain, but when it came time to use them they had to rely on centuries-old cooking techniques such as roasting over an open fire. This section explores the range of cooking tools used in rural New Zealand in the nineteenth and early twentieth centuries, and looks at how and why technologies were adopted and adapted.

Earth oven and open-fire cookery

At its most basic, a home is a place where technology is used and created.[4] While modern homes can include a vast array of technologies, basic survival depends on a precious few, perhaps the most vital of which is fire. Fire requires for its creation and preservation 'an understanding of how materials of the natural world can be modified for human use', and as a cooking technology it can transform indigestible raw ingredients into life-sustaining meals.[5]

Māori cooking techniques harness the power of fire in a number of ways. Before the mid-nineteenth century, when metal pots were increasingly used, earth oven cookery in a hāngī or umu was the most common.[6] The basic system for cooking in a hāngī is to make a pile of wood and stones, burn the wood, and then transfer the hot stones into a pit. The stones – called taikōwhatu – can reach temperatures of 1100 °C, and are carefully selected so they do not crack when exposed to high heat. Volcanic andesite boulders are best.[7] Food is placed on top of the rocks with layers of green leaves above and below, then the whole oven is covered with earth and the food left to steam; the cooking time depending on the types of food in the hāngī.[8] Kūmara, fish, leafy vegetables and the sugary roots and stem of tī (cabbage tree) were and are all cooked by this method.[9]

Another technique for earth oven cookery is to place the food on embers, rather than stones, and partially cover it with earth until cooked. Some sources distinguish this as an umu rather than a hāngī, while others use umu to describe a style of cooking more common in Polynesia, where food is placed on hot stones in shallow pits and is covered with matting or leaves but not earth.[10] Some scholars use the terms interchangeably.[11] Evidence from Wairau Bar, one of the earliest sites of Polynesian settlement, indicates that different types of earth ovens were used – smaller, shallower pits for everyday cooking, and larger, deeper pits for large protein sources. Earth oven cookery was a well established tradition in Polynesia when the ancestors of Māori sailed to Aotearoa, so they came with a range of techniques for small- and large-scale cooking.[12]

According to nineteenth-century surgeon-turned-historian Arthur Thomson, roasting over an open fire was 'despised' by Māori as a method of cooking; it provided suitable dinner only 'for slaves or men in a hurry'.[13] Sophia Beaton (Ngāi Tahu) suggests that because it was a more convenient way of cooking, roasting was probably common during periods of warfare or long expeditions, but because of those associations was not favoured for everyday cooking.[14] Mākereti Papakura, though, reports in *The Old-Time Maori* that birds were commonly roasted by skewering six or eight on a length of wood and sticking it into the ground near the fire.[15] Shellfish such as pāua were also roasted, as was aruhe, a staple of the pre-European Māori diet.

In the absence of earthenware or metal pots, boiling does not seem to have been a common cooking method, and early European commentators, who saw no evidence of food being boiled, concluded that Māori were 'entirely ignorant of the art'.[16] However, Māori were familiar with the Polynesian technique of boiling food by adding hot stones to liquid in a kōhua (bowl), and this method was recorded in the 1850s as a way of cooking shellfish and making a type of gruel from hīnau meal.[17] Drawing on this tradition, Māori applied the word kōhua to the iron pots Europeans brought ashore to cook their food, and gradually adopted them as a vessel for cooking both Māori and European foods.[18]

Māori adopted the iron 'go-ashore' pots relatively quickly because they 'allowed both the adoption of European cooking technology and a slower and more comfortable adjustment of the tapu system to new living conditions'.[19] Unlike flat-bottomed pots and pans designed to sit on a range or hang above a fire, go-ashores had three short legs which meant they could stand in the fire, and were well suited to cooking in the open air or in a cooking shed.[20] Over the course of the nineteenth century iron pots gradually took over the functions previously performed by the small earth oven, although 'with a capacity of, at most, five gallons in its domestic form, it could not supplant the *hangi* in catering for large groups'.[21]

Many nineteenth-century Pākehā settlers also relied on the iron go-ashores for cooking. For those who had only temporary accommodation or crude sleeping shelters on arrival, cooking over an open fire was expedient and necessary. Eileen Soper describes the arrival of the early settlers in Otago in 1848:

> cooking had to be done outside over an open fire. Circumstances more unusual would have been difficult to imagine but 'everybody was active, happy and exhilarated under the new conditions and the serene skies'....
>
> ... [However] with the cessation of fine weather early in May, just after the arrival of the *Philip Laing* at Port Chalmers, the illusion of an earthly Paradise came to an end. Cooking out-of-doors was no longer the novelty it had hitherto been, for coaxing wet wood into a flame and keeping it alight long enough to produce a hot meal was a grim and disheartening task, which some wives could accomplish only under umbrellas held aloft by their husbands.[22]

Over these sodden fires the cook might place a pot or a camp oven – a heavy cast-iron pan approximately 38cm across 13cm deep.[23] Billycans were a more convenient alternative for those on the move, such as the Otago surveyors depicted in Edward Abbot's 1847 painting (see page 83).

In the more permanent homes the settlers built, the hearth was often positioned in a large alcove at one end of the dwelling, which was sometimes wide enough to accommodate seats and a place to sit by

Te Punaomaru. This 1848 sketch by Walter Mantell shows the interior of Punaomaru pā on the Waitaki River. A go-ashore pot is bubbling over a fire on the left, and a kettle and billy are also visible. Behind the fence is a whata. Walter Baldock Durrant Mantell, Scrapbook, 1840–1872, Alexander Turnbull Library, C-103-078.

∧
A cast-iron camp oven with a lid, three small legs and a wire handle. Cast-iron cooking utensils were extremely heavy and cumbersome: this one from Te Ūaka The Lyttelton Museum probably weighs over 10kg, is 250mm high, 420mm long and 370mm wide. Photograph taken 1 December 2014 (cropped), Te Ūaka The Lyttelton Museum, 703.1.

>
A tin billy with a wire handle that can be retracted for packing. Date unknown, 153mm high, 105mm diameter. Unknown maker, Collection of the Cromwell Museum, CR1977.166.

Hāngī stones and hot stoves

A high country surveyors' camp in bleak conditions. Two men cooking in a billy over an open fire, Otago, c. 1847. Edward Immyns Abbot, Alexander Turnbull Library, B-155-010.

the fire. In his *Rambles with a Philosopher* (1867), surveyor John Turnbull Thomson described such a space in the home of a Bluff fisherman and his wife: 'Our hostess received us with that unsophisticated good humour, which convinced us that our intrusion was by no means disconcerting. She immediately asked us to sit *within* the fire-place, as it was capacious enough for that purpose, it being a huge recess from the room with the fire of wood burning on the hearth in the centre.'[24]

To enable a variety of cooking practices to be carried out simultaneously, indoor fireplaces often had bars or brackets above the hearth. This arrangement, common in eighteenth-century British kitchens, allowed the cook to have a pot or a camp oven sitting in the fire, pots and kettles hanging from the bar above, and perhaps even joints of meat roasting on a spit.[25] Both Pākehā and Māori used this set-up in indoor kitchens or kāuta, particularly from the late nineteenth century.

83

In an extremely rare photograph of the interior of a nineteenth-century Māori home, taken in about 1893, Mrs Karetai of Ōtākou is seen sitting in front of an open fire with pots hanging from a bar above, and a camp oven and kettle sitting in the embers. Reremoana Reweti Koopu (Te Whānau-ā-Apanui) of Ōtūwhare recalls a similar space in the kāuta her family cooked in in the early twentieth century: '[w]e had a kāuta then. It is a big one, though, with a big chimney we cooked in. You have your fire and you would cook all your kai there, with the pieces of iron to hold your pots. We had our kitchen things buried in the chimney – oh, it was nice.'[26] This method of cooking continued well into the twentieth century: when David Maxwell of Waipōua was introduced to what he thought of as a 'truly Maori home' in the early 1920s he noted that it 'had a big open wood burning fireplace with camp ovens and black billies of many sizes standing around the fireplace'. Instead of an iron bar, though, there were two mānuka poles 'horizontally placed about three feet up and from which were suspended wire hooks of various lengths. On these, pots and billies could be hung for cooking as required.'[27]

One benefit of open-fire cooking was that large logs could be put on the fire, meaning less chopping of firewood was needed.[28] An iron bracket or swey could be obtained from the local forge and easily installed.[29] However, as Alice Mackenzie (née McKenzie) wrote in her account of growing up in Martins Bay in the 1870s, cooking over an open fire 'was no easy way for women to cook . . . with gusts of wood-smoke blowing into their faces, making their eyes sore and filling the room, cooking was often a torment.'[30] Winifred Carson, reminiscing about her childhood in Nelson in the 1920s, wrote that '[c]ooking in a camp oven over an open fire isn't the simplest way by any means, it is hot and trying especially in the summer'.[31] To bake bread, for instance, the cook was required:

> to get a really good fire going until the coals were glowing red, as some of these had to be shovelled on to the top of the camp oven lid to help cook the bread. It was inviting trouble trying to remove the lid during the cooking without great care being taken not to sprinkle the ashes and coals on to the contents inside. Lifting the camp oven off the fire was no easy matter either, so it seemed best to manipulate the heat if necessary.[32]

Mrs Karetai, 1893. This rare photograph, taken by John Halliday Scott, shows the interior of the Karetai home at Ōtākou. Mrs Karetai sits in front of the open fire, with a camp oven and kettle in the embers and pots hanging from a bar above the fire. John Halliday Scott photograph, Hocken Collections, Uare Taoka o Hākena, University of Otago, P2008-066-019d.

A woman placing a lid on a camp oven, Te Kaha, c. 1917. In the hearth, a pot and a kettle sit on a stand above the fire; the bar above the hearth has an S-shaped hook to hang a pot from. Mary Frances Mackay photograph, Auckland War Memorial Museum Tāmaki Paenga Hira, PHNEG- C60581-45.

In 1890 a writer for the *New Zealand Farmer* offered a stern rebuke to farmers who refused to purchase a stove for the kitchen because it would require them to chop firewood.

> [I]t never occurs to you that by having a great open fire you are giving your poor wife and daughters a good roasting every day of their lives, and making the cooking twenty times harder than it needs to be. If instead of working out of doors you had to pass the day stooping over a hot fire, hanging a kettle to a hook, or raking hot ashes over a camp oven, or such like antediluvian contrivances, you would very soon have quite enough of it, and ten to one you would burn your fingers, or scald your legs, as well as scorch your face and make yourself tired and hot, as they do every day of their lives.[33]

Cooking over an open fire was dangerous, tiring and uncomfortable work. For these reasons, the colonial oven, first introduced in the 1850s, 'was hailed with joy by those unfortunates who had to admit that they could never manage a camp oven'.[34]

‹
Cast-iron cooking pot with lid and long handle, Kenrick & Sons, England. The pot is 150mm high with a diameter of 200mm, the lid is 60mm high, and the handle is 250mm long – well suited to cooking on a fire or hotplate. Kenrick & Sons exported kitchen equipment to New Zealand for over a century from the 1850s. Collection of the Cromwell Museum, CR1977.220.

‹
Cast-iron kettle, 1890–1900. Unknown maker, Wyndham and Districts Museum, WY.0000.696.

The colonial oven

The colonial oven was a cast-iron box about 100cm long that could be set into the lower part of a brick or stone fireplace.[35] Apparently designed by a Mr Strachan of Whanganui, these devices could be produced in colonial foundries and, in comparison to camp ovens, were said to be a joy to cook with.[36] Agnes Bryant (née Greig), born in 1896, recalled that the installation of a colonial oven in her family home at Reikorangi was 'a big event – a step forward, indeed!'

> The oven was wide enough to span the fire, and was supported on either side by a hob. The fire was built under the oven and embers were spread over the top in much the same way as on the lid of the camp oven. But it was a fixture, and had a door, and trays for baking cakes, etc. A day's baking by this method was still a hot and tiring task, but the women of the day felt themselves to be fortunate to be promoted to a 'colonial oven kitchen'.[37]

Cooking by any of these methods was back-breaking work, but still, each appliance represented a small advance. By the 1870s, however, a new device had become 'associated with the efforts of the colonists to build a better life': the coal range.[38]

The coal range

Cast-iron ranges – generally known as coal ranges although they also burn wood – were imported in relatively large numbers from the 1850s.[39] A range is defined as a kitchen appliance incorporating a hotplate and oven (an enclosed space for baking), with a closed fire designed to burn solid fuel. The first ranges were developed in Europe in the early 1800s: they offered greater fuel efficiency, more usable heat and a wider range of temperatures and cooking options than an open fire.[40] The freestanding American range was initially the most popular model in New Zealand, though bricked-in British kitset models were also available. However, users found that they were not well suited to New Zealand conditions as both were designed to burn bituminous coal, whereas most of the coal

∧
Colonial oven included as part of the kitchen range at Totaranui House, built in Palmerston North in 1875.
E. Creamer photograph, 1981, Creamer Collection, Manawatū Heritage image, 2010N_Bur194_3090.

sourced in New Zealand was sub-bituminous or lignite.[41] People living in the bush could substitute wood for coal.[42]

Henry Shacklock was one of the settlers inconvenienced by these imported stoves. A young ironmoulder from the English Midlands who arrived in New Zealand in 1862, Shacklock worked in Oamaru for brief periods between 1863 and 1871 then moved to Dunedin, where he established the South End Foundry on a small piece of land on Crawford Street.[43] For the first two years of operation the foundry produced items such as grates and colonial ovens, but at some point in the first eighteen months Shacklock was approached by fellow Midlands colonists who suggested that he should make a coal range based on the model seen in their home counties.[44] He began experimenting, and the result was the

Salesmen for E. Buxton & Co. Ltd with a selection of Orion ranges, purported to be 'the best colonial-made range in the market', c. 1905. Louis Daroux photograph, Tyree Studio Collection, Nelson Provincial Museum, 70819.

Orion Portable Coal Range No. 1; the prototype was produced in 1873 but it was not patented until 1882.[45]

The Orion was designed with New Zealand consumers in mind, taking into account the economic conditions and resources available in the colony at that time. Although it was not freestanding, the Orion did not need to be 'built in' because the flues were enclosed in the cast-iron casing, so purchasers were not reliant on a bricklayer for installation.[46] In addition, it was 'SPECIALLY DESIGNED for burning New Zealand Coal', a feature emphasised in subsequent advertising.[47] Lignite needs a fire to draw well in order to burn properly, so Shacklock designed a wide, shallow firebox that drew in more air than other ranges, and designed the flues to encourage the flames to travel further.[48] The Orion could also burn peat or wood, and had an attachment that allowed logs up to 60cm in length to be burnt: 'a manifest advantage in up-country districts'.[49] Shacklock seems to have had rural customers in mind when he designed his ranges, as he advertised directly to farmers and described the ranges as being 'very suitable for Shepherd's Huts, Sheep Stations, Farms, Hotels and Dwelling Houses'.[50]

Later, as the business grew and a greater variety of ranges were introduced, the advertisements became more expansive, and alerted customers to the efficiency and economy of Shacklock products. An advertisement in the *Wanganui Herald* in 1888 announced: 'The cost of cooking for ten persons in a No. 1 Orion Range is about 3s a week', and '[t]he comfort, convenience, and cleanliness attained are such that cookery becomes a pleasure, and persons using these ranges will find them divested of all those too familiar "disagreeables" inseparable from nearly all ordinary cooking ranges.'[51] Customers, both rural and urban, must have agreed with this assessment, as by 1894 the business had expanded and was employing between thirty and forty hands.[52] It is difficult to know exactly how many of New Zealand's 'Favourite Kitchen Range' were being sold at this time, as the figures varied markedly in different advertisements.[53] In 1903 alone, various Shacklock advertisements testified to sales of 19,000, 27,000 and 45,000 ranges.[54] This inconsistency aside, the fact that the Orion remained the company's flagship product, almost unchanged, for over five decades is testament to its popularity and success.

The Shacklock Orion in 1891. Advertisements, *Wanganui Herald*, 11 June 1891, p. 1, National Library of New Zealand.

Although H. E. Shacklock Ltd was the best known, it was not the only New Zealand company producing cooking ranges for local conditions, and by the turn of the century firms such as Scott Bros (Christchurch), Brinsley & Co. and Barningham & Co. (both in Dunedin) were well established. As John Angus suggests in *The Ironmasters*, his study of H. E. Shacklock Ltd, the period from 1900 to 1939 'was the epoch of the coal range', and Barningham's Zealandia model, Brinsley's Champion, and the Scott Bros' Atlas were all popular.[55] These companies also emphasised the convenience, fuel economy and versatility of their products, while promising customers that cooking with their appliances would be a pleasure (see page 94).

In her autobiographical sketch Alicia Chitty (née de Vere Hunt), who lived on a mixed crop–livestock farm near Hamilton, remembered it as a 'red letter day' when a Shacklock stove became available in the 1880s, freeing her from the rigours of the colonial oven.[56] Winifred Carson recalled the excitement that came with the installation of a wood stove: she wrote that her father 'built an alcove off the kitchen with an opening in the kitchen wall. It had an ordinary black woodstove at the back of the small building. A real dinky little stove house which must have been a wonderful provision for cooking and heating water kettles without all the lifting over the hot open fire, and a real labour saver for Mum with her growing family.'[57]

The coal range became an enduring feature of rural Pākehā kitchens, and the 1945 census found that they were still the sole means of cooking in 59.8 percent of rural Pākehā households (compared with 24.9 percent of urban dwellings, in which gas and electrical appliances were more popular).[58] The question was not put to Māori households in the 1945 census, but housing surveys carried out in 1937 in relation to the Native Housing Act do give an indication of the cooking technologies used at that time. The surveys show considerable variation within and between settlements. In Tintown (Ruatōria), for example, all of the houses surveyed had a stove, while in Makarika and Anaura Bay (both in Gisborne) half of the households surveyed cooked over an open fire.[59] There was some evidence in the surveys, too, of a continued preference for separate cooking and dwelling spaces, as in Makarika, where a mother and son lived in a 'new "wharepuni" with a detached tin Maori kitchen'.[60]

ORION RANGES,

The Most Economical Self-Setting Range Made.

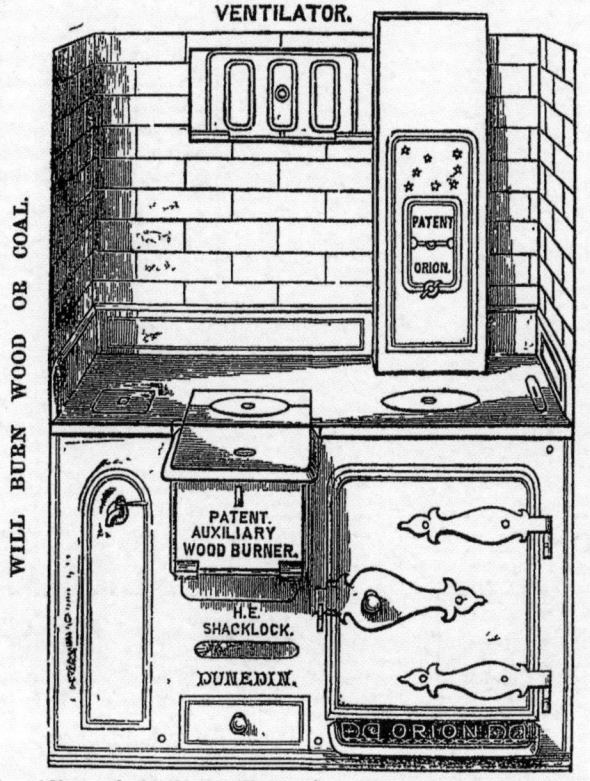

Several Sizes made for Burning Wood in Long Lengths, and are Specially adapted for the Country. They are fitted with

CAST IRON OR INTERNALLY TINN'D COPPER BOILER.

Upwards of

4000, 4000, 4000

are in Use in Various Parts of New Zealand.

The OVENS keep a GOOD REGULAR HEAT.

THEY ARE GOOD BREAD BAKERS.

The OVEN BOTTOMS heat well. Pastry may be Browned and Liquid Substances such as a Pie or Rice Pudding may be BOILED on the OVEN BOTTOM.

If you are about to Build a New Kitchen Chimney, be sure and have it fitted with the Patent Take All Flue and Ventilator, it gives a Cool and Pure Atmosphere. No Steam Heat or Effluvia. No Headache.

Consult your Architect about it.

J. THAIN & CO.,

AGENTS.

> An advertisement for Shacklock's Orion cooking ranges, appealing directly to farmers. Business Notices, *Otago Witness*, 6 January 1883, p. 5, National Library of New Zealand.

∨ Advertisement for Brinsley and Co.'s 'Champion' closed-fire range. Advertisements, *Oamaru Mail*, 18 August 1899, p. 1, National Library of New Zealand.

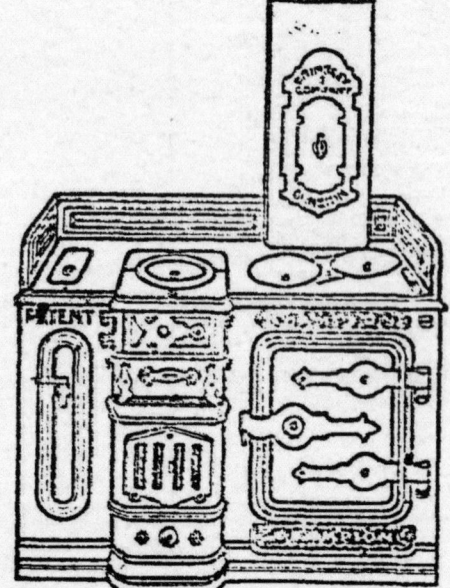

Where new housing was to be constructed, the installation of an Orion wood- or coal-burning stove was recommended.[61]

Using a coal range was not without its trials: it took some skill to be able to gauge the temperature of the oven and position the dampers correctly for different recipes, and learning to control the temperature was often a matter of trial and error. Amy Tremenheere Yorke arrived in New Zealand from India in 1930, and she and her husband worked as farm labourers in the Waikato. Although she was unaccustomed to cooking, Amy was expected to help in the house as well as on the farm, and she later recalled the difficulty of learning to use the stove.

> On one unhappy occasion, the sharemilker's wife asked me to mind the baby and keep an eye on the roast that was cooking in the oven while she helped with the milking. She said that the roast would take care of itself so long as I kept the fire stoked up and that the baby would probably sleep until she got back. She evidently thought that even I could hardly mess up so simple an assignment. How little she knew me! The baby was asleep in his cot, so, thinking that I had landed a really cushy job for once, I laid in a stock of firewood and settled down to read a book between stoking operations. I certainly kept the fire well stoked – when the poor woman returned the whole stove was glowing red and the roast was burnt to a cinder.[62]

Amy did eventually learn to gauge the temperature of the stove by sprinkling flour onto the oven slide and timing how long it took to turn brown – a common strategy.[63]

Unlike later enamelled stoves, the early versions of the coal range required regular cleaning and polishing. Housewives were advised to plan their working weeks and create an efficient, orderly system, comparable to the structures of paid employment: Monday was invariably washing day, Tuesday was for ironing, and one day a week was scheduled for cleaning and blacking the stove.[64] Sophie May Johnstone-Smith gives a detailed description of this 'unenviable task' in her account of life in rural Waikato around the turn of the century.

This wooden blacklead brush with natural bristles was used to apply polish to the kitchen range and keep it from rusting. 80mm high, 260mm long, 65mm wide. Unknown maker, Owaka Museum, CT81.1504d.

Three 'extras' came with the stove, a flu [sic] brush, a poker and a scraper. From the door in the front of the chimney the flu brush was pushed up and down, thus bringing down the soot which was drawn out from below the oven with the scraper. Now watch it, all doors and windows must be closed, or a puff of wind or a draught would send the lot flying, so wrap it up very carefully, then bury it. If you think you have done with the stove, you are sadly mistaken. So far only the inside has been cleaned, the worst is yet to come. That great big bulk has now to be polished, the dirtiest job of all. Place a cake of 'black lead' in a shallow tin of water, wait until dissolved, then with a brush, paint the whole face of the stove. Now with a dry brush, similar to [a] boot brush with a handle, polish until a satisfactory shine has been achieved, by which time the whole kitchen is filled with dust.[65]

Angus suggests that the range-cleaning ritual became part of the cultural patterns of the late nineteenth and early twentieth centuries.[66] That may be so but, as Joan Millar (née Tait) learnt during her childhood in Hindon, the family should 'keep well away' on stove-cleaning day and avoid the disgruntlement that accompanied this dreaded task.[67]

A stove flue brush, used to bring soot down from the chimney. Twisted heavy wire forms the handle and secures the black bristles at one end. 870mm long. Unknown maker, Collection of the Cromwell Museum, CR1977.516.

Radiation NZ Ltd (now in control of the Champion Brand) threw the weight of science at the problem of dusty, rusty ranges with its colourful enamelled models. In an advertisement in the *Dairy Exporter* in 1939 it told readers:

> City folks need not have all the good things in life. Country kitchens have been modernised too; science has come to the aid of the household manager and transformed a dull, prosaic kitchen range into a thing of beauty and a joy to cook with.
>   No longer need black-lead brushes be the bane of existence – no longer need the country dweller spend hours of unending toil stoking in a hot kitchen and everlasting polishing and cleaning flues. Expert engineers have now designed a coal and wood range that is the acme of perfection . . . it is called the Champion De Luxe Streamlined Coal and Wood Range.[68]

Other advertisements for the Champion De Luxe boasted additional features such as temperature control and oven insulation technology, and assured farmers' wives that the 'streamlined beauties' would give them beautiful kitchens comparable to those of their urban counterparts (see page 98). A fuel saving of 25 percent was also promised, which must have been enticing, given that obtaining fuel could be costly and labour-intensive.

HAVE LOVELY KITCHENS NOW

25% SAVING IN FUEL

PERFECT OVEN CONTROL

Look at this lovely Champion De Luxe Coal Range! This streamlined beauty turns a kitchen into as smart a room as any. This De Luxe Champion is the greatest advance in coal and wood burners yet devised.

25% Fuel Economy: Champion engineers have devised a unique scientific method of oven insulation, which actually **stores the heat** and saves 25% in fuel.

Colour in the Kitchen: Lovely colours to harmonise with any room. In cream and green ... cream and blue ... and cream and red, porcelain enamel finish. No crevices or corners to harbour dust — a mere whisk with a cloth and it gleams like a jeweller's window.

Oven thermometer for perfect oven control for every kind of cooking. Range fits into recess now occupied by your old range.

See the new "Champion" Coal and Wood Ranges in popular colours at any hardware merchants, builder suppliers, plumbers, or Champion Depot, 283 Victoria Street West, Auckland, from any of whom residents in the Auckland District may procure descriptive literature. Residents in other parts of the Dominion should write to the makers: Radiation (N.Z.) Limited, Brinsley Works, Dunedin.

1939 *Streamlined* CHAMPION COAL RANGE

Electrical appliances

From the 1920s there was another solution to the fuel problem, as this rural woman discovered to her joy in 1938:

> Some months ago there appeared in 'Between Ourselves' a par by some poor harassed Mrs. B whose husband simply would not keep her supplied with wood for the range, and having a Mr. B myself with the same little failing, I was most interested in her rather drastic remedy, i.e. serving the Sunday roast, garnished with vegetables, etc., all quite raw. Plucking up sufficient courage one day when everything went wrong from sunrise, I did the same thing – but not with the same results. My Mr. B solved the problem in quite a different way – no filled wood bins. He has ordered me an electric stove![69]

One of the earliest electric stoves manufactured in New Zealand, echoing the name of Shacklock's original coal range, was a trusty Orion (No. 52), which went into production in 1926.[70] Scott Bros also produced electric stoves as part of their Atlas range, as did companies such as the National Electric and Engineering Co. Ltd (NEECO) of Wellington. However, the best-selling electric stove in New Zealand was produced by Moffat, a Canadian company that was able to produce cheaper and more modern stoves than those available through local firms.[71]

An advertisement for the Champion De Luxe Coal Range, suggesting that farmers' wives can now have lovely kitchens. Advertisement, *New Zealand Herald*, 14 January 1939, p. 7 (Supplement), National Library of New Zealand, reproduced courtesy of NZME.

< Moffat electric stove, mid-1920s, 1000mm high, 697mm wide, 540mm deep. Acquired 2018, Museum of New Zealand Te Papa Tongarewa, GH025308.

Electric era

Full-size electric stoves were scarce in New Zealand until 1924, but by the end of that year three models of Moffat electric stoves were available, followed quickly by six McClary models, also produced in Canada. With its gleaming white enamel door and elegantly curved cabriole legs, this Moffat stove must certainly have been an object of pride for its former owner – although its exact provenance is unknown.

The stove has three elements on the cooktop and two inside the oven – one at the top and one at the bottom. These elements supplied the heat but the cook still had to regulate the temperature in the oven – which could be read off a thermometer in the door – by adjusting the power supply. Very few electric stoves in the 1920s had thermostats.[72]

Every new stove came with a recipe book and instructions for use. One such book, probably from the 1930s, explains that for baking, the cook should preheat the oven to the desired temperature by turning the top and bottom elements to high, then turning the top element off and the bottom element to low before putting the baking in the oven. Roasting used a similar technique, although the book suggested searing the roast in the hot oven before lowering the temperature.[73] According to Helen Leach, this was still the rule of thumb for those who learnt to cook in electric ovens in the 1950s.[74]

The market for electrical appliances expanded quickly in middle-class New Zealand homes in the 1920s, fostered by the rapid extension of the national power grid. Before 1910 the development of electricity supply schemes had been considered a local rather than national concern, and the use of electricity was largely restricted to public buildings, streets and factories in centres such as Auckland, Wellington and Dunedin.[75] In 1910, however, the government decided that the economic benefits of electricity warranted the state's involvement, and the Public Works Department began work on a hydroelectric power station at Lake Coleridge on the Rakaia River in Canterbury. Encouraged by the success of the scheme, the state officially assumed primary responsibility for electricity generation with the 1917 State Supply of Electrical Energy Act, and in 1918 introduced the Electric-power Boards Act to manage retail distribution. Power boards were elected by ratepayers to oversee the supply and distribution of electrical energy to local districts, including both town and country localities.[76] The idea was that the cost of supplying power to areas of low population density would be subsidised by returns from urban areas with high consumer densities. The expansion of the system was not without difficulties, but it did result in a rapid increase in the number of rural consumers. Whereas in 1920 less than half of the population had access to electricity, by 1938 it was accessible to 93.3 percent.[77]

Some have suggested that New Zealand had the most advanced programme of rural reticulation in the world by 1935, as 80 percent of New Zealand dairy farms were electrified while in the United States only one in ten farms had electricity.[78] It is worth noting, however, that because they had to be able to deliver to a factory at least once every two to three days, dairy farms tended to be located closer to population centres than sheep and beef farms, so they benefited more immediately from the development of electricity infrastructure. In addition, although the state had responsibility for building the electricity generating system, distribution was left to local authorities, and the price paid for power varied greatly between districts.[79] Where urban electricity returns did not cover the cost of installing rural powerlines, customers had to guarantee a minimum annual payment, reassuring the authority that the line would eventually pay for itself.[80] By the end of the 1930s there was still a proportion of the rural population in the 'backblocks' who had no access

Walles Tivie stands by her Moffat electric oven, location unknown. Walles used the stove from the date of purchase in 1930 until 1980, when this photograph was taken. Unknown photographer, Central Stories Museum and Art Gallery, Alexandra, 01.41.

to electricity, and who had to rely on coal, wood and kerosene (which was in fairly general use for lighting) until after the Second World War.[81]

The Rural Electrical Reticulation Council was established in 1945 to connect the remaining 7 percent of the population. The council imposed a levy on gross revenues from the sale of electricity and used this to subsidise the building of lines in sparsely populated areas.[82] Still, some rural areas were without electricity into the 1950s. In April 1949 a Mr H. C. Reynolds of Tūtāmoe–Waimatenui District wrote to the North Auckland Power Board that although Tūtāmoe means 'standing asleep', the people of the district 'have wakened up, are power-hungry, and if our appetite is not soon satisfied we will howl so loudly that it will be heard all over the country'.[83] A group of farmers in the district promised a cash guarantee and offered to supply their own tōtara power poles, and their application was approved in June that year.[84] Also in 1949, Prime Minister Peter Fraser attended a meeting at the marae in Kaikohe and was told that Māori farms at Waimā still did not have power despite electricity being connected to the east and west of them.[85] Later that year the local power board noted that there were a number of places in Northland still without power, and that they would likely need to apply for subsidies from the Reticulation Council to construct the lines.[86]

One of those places was Panguru, which did not get electricity until 1957. Even if it had been available, though, we can't assume that people would necessarily have changed the technologies they used in their homes. For Raiha and Eruera (Buck) Tipene, who moved from Panguru to New Lynn in 1958, 'back home experiences' were more important than pressures to modernise in how they set up their new home. They chose to install a wetback – a range with a coil at the back of the fire that feeds hot water to a nearby cylinder – rather than an electric stove, and initially the only power they used was for lighting.[87] This reduced the family's energy costs and also gave Raiha time to evaluate new appliances. Her son Chris recalled that Pākehā machines had to prove their worth, and it was only when Raiha was certain the agitator washing machine would do a good enough job that she abandoned the laborious system of boiling the clothes in the copper and scrubbing them on the washboard.[88]

The extension of electricity meant some rural people could enjoy a variety of new appliances, and electric irons, toasters, grills and kettles

were produced in large numbers from the early 1920s.[89] Perhaps the most coveted item was the domestic refrigerator, which, for the farmer's wife especially, was considered 'an all-the-year-round NECESSITY . . . not a luxury. For she knows by experience how much meat, vegetables, milk, cream, butter and other perishables are wasted every day of the year.'[90] Necessity or not, if W. T. Doig's 1937–38 survey of dairy farms is indicative, it seems that very few rural women could afford a refrigerator before the Second World War: only eighteen of the 462 households surveyed (3.9 percent) had one.[91] Most homes instead used a food safe (a wooden box with mesh air vents), which was placed in a cool spot outside with good air circulation to keep the food fresh as long as possible. Rural people used a wide range of strategies to preserve food and ensure the family was well provisioned year-round, but these were time-consuming and inconvenient (see chapter 3). It is not surprising, therefore, that when the cost decreased postwar, the number of refrigerators in homes increased dramatically.[92]

>
Two men assembling a refrigerator at the General Motors Assembly Plant in Petone, c. 1936.
Ken Niven photograph, Gordon H. Burt Ltd., Museum of New Zealand Te Papa Tongarewa, C.002298.

A Depression-era food safe (two views) made from recycled packing cases, c. 1930, 1160mm high, 675mm wide, 590mm deep. Unknown maker, purchased 1997 with New Zealand Lottery Grants Board funds, Museum of New Zealand Te Papa Tongarewa, GH009103.

Keeping cool

The heat emanating from a coal range in the kitchen made it necessary to store food in a separate space in order to keep it from spoiling.[93] Many homes had a pantry for dry goods, and meat safes like this makeshift example from the 1930s were often built into outside walls or kept on the porch.

Another solution to the problem of keeping food cool in the absence of a refrigerator was to hang perishables in or above a creek or other body of water; and Maisie Dalbeth (née Ford), who lived with her mother in Ngongotahā in the 1920s, recalled that you could cool cream or set a jelly by that method.[94] Dorothy Davidson of Ōrātia kept milk fresh in summer by setting her full milk jug on a brick in the middle of an enamel dish filled with water. She would then drape a clean teatowel over the milk jug and ensure that the corners dangled in the water. As long as there was water in the dish, the milk would not sour.[95]

Enterprising though these solutions were, it is no wonder that rural women coveted domestic refrigerators.

∧
A girl sitting on the doorstep of a weatherboard cottage, with a food safe on the verandah in the background. Laingholm Bay, c. 1920. Unknown photographer, J. T. Diamond Collection, Auckland Libraries Heritage Collections, JTD-09A-04412.

Switching to electrical appliances did not necessarily reduce the burden of domestic chores. US historian Ruth Schwartz Cowan suggests in her groundbreaking 1983 book *More Work for Mother* that one of the great ironies of the industrial age was that '[l]abor-saving devices were invented and diffused throughout the country . . . but they reorganized the work processes of housework in ways that did not save the labor of the average housewife'.[96] Every household chore, Cowan argues, is actually a series of definable and interconnected tasks that constitute a work process. Almost without exception, industrialisation altered household work processes in ways that eased the work of men and children but left women with just as much work as before.[97] Using the work process of cooking as an example, Cowan points out that of the three main parts of the process – supplying fuel, tending pots, cleaning the appliance – only the first was eliminated by the introduction of electrical or gas appliances, and this tended to be the part traditionally assigned to men and children.[98]

Articles and advertisements in magazines such as *New Zealand Farm and Home* informed rural women that modern science had 'robbed the housewife of half her labours', but some women rejected this rhetoric.[99] In fact, the idea that a vacuum cleaner or electric range exonerated women from domestic work could be a source of resentment.

'A brand-new house!' I heard her murmur,
'There can't be much for you to do;
Perhaps, next wool-clip (if I'm firmer)
Jack may consider building too.'

'Your modern home's a perfect treasure –
Such endless gadgets saving you –
I only wish I had some leisure –
Whatever do you find to do?'

I shook my head and answered gaily;
Spoke to her as I speak to you:
'We still must eat, you know, thrice daily
And even though the house is new.

> The pies won't bake, the peas won't shell,
> The mint won't chop, the jam won't jell;
> The cakes won't mix, the lamb won't fry
> Unless, of course, I'm standing by.
>
> And what is more no brass will shine,
> No clothes will wash, no wash will iron,
> No beds will make (you understand)
> Unless I'm there to lend a hand.'[100]

Two months later another woman wrote to the same magazine in which this was published, thanking the contributor for submitting the poem. She framed it so that when someone remarked on her abundant free time, she could just hand the poem over.[101] These assumptions of leisure and domestic ease presupposed not only that new technologies eliminated labour, but also that rural women only had to undertake work within the house – a middle-class, urban ideal that was simply not a reality for most.

Variations in cooking techniques and technologies

This chapter has charted the introduction of cooking technologies, from open fire and earth oven to coal range and electric oven in roughly chronological order. In fact, a variety of cooking technologies – some ancient, some modern – were used in rural New Zealand at any given time, and none was completely supplanted by later developments. The introduction of the colonial oven did not eliminate open-fire cooking, just as the introduction of the electric stove did not signal the end of the coal range. The reasons for this are economic, personal and practical as much as technological, and bear further consideration for the insights they can provide into rural life.

The rural economy and the rural kitchen

The popular image of rural Pākehā New Zealand tends to be one of stability, of families who farm the same land for generations, close-knit communities with enduring rhythms and rituals, and hard-working individuals who, by repeating a seasonal cycle of tasks year after year, eventually hope to prosper.[102] This vision is largely a product of the early twentieth century, when small-scale, intensive farming became commercially viable and a small dairy farm or a mixed wool and fat-lamb farm could earn a surplus. These smaller units were usually family farms and hired little or no outside labour.[103] Nineteenth-century New Zealand, however, was characterised by 'hyperactive movement', and transience 'was to varying degrees normal to all strata' of society.[104] The developing rural economy produced an extraordinarily mobile and unstable labour market, and every year thousands of itinerant labourers took to the road in search of seasonal work.[105] In the 1890s some three-quarters of land in private ownership was held in pastoral stations and mixed crop–livestock estates of 1000 acres or more, and these farms between them employed more than 40,000 workers during the summer season – 20,500 permanent workers and 20,000 seasonal workers.[106]

For itinerant labourers such as those working in plough camps (camps of portable huts used during large-scale ploughing operations), mustering gangs, or walking from job to job 'on the swag', open-fire cooking was the only option available, and utensils were limited to what they or their 'packer' could carry.[107] The packer or packman travelled with the mustering team, delivering gear and cooking meals. A 1908 article in the *Press* on the life of the packman described the mobile kitchens built during musters that often lasted several weeks:

> To see him at work one would need to rise early – sometimes not long after midnight. Four tents are standing on the verge of a belt of bush, not far from a creek. From one of them issues a sleepy form, which walks to the rude galley beneath the big totara, where two forked sticks and a cross-bar constitute a kitchen. There is the scrape of a match and a rush of flame as the packman sets a light to his dry scrub kindling; the light shows a billy hanging from a

pot-hook ... Next a camp-oven full of chops is swung into the blaze, with perhaps a satellite frying-pan; before long their contents begin to inform the senses both of smell and hearing that they are nearly ready, and 'packy' as he is familiarly called, sets about rousing the sleeping camp. Soon a dozen men are standing and squatting round the fire, consuming chops, bread and tea.[108]

Cooks at plough camps, harvest camps and threshing mills probably worked in similar conditions, although on larger estates some camps had the use of a mobile cookshop (see frontispiece). By the early twentieth century the increased emphasis on intensive farming, the subdivision of many large stations and estates into smaller units, and the introduction of technologies such as the reaper-binder and the mechanical shearing machine had diminished the need for seasonal workers and increased the local labour pool in most rural areas. Fewer labourers moved from place to place in search of work, but there was still seasonal employment available for contractors such as shearers, musterers and harvesters.

Open-fire cookery and cast-iron camp ovens were also used as 'stop-gap' solutions by subsistence farmers while they were establishing homes and farms. In the early days of Pākehā settlement, most small landholders had to clear their sections of bush before they could work the land, and they eked out a living through subsistence activities and contract work. For most, cash was scarce and conveniences were few. When Helen Wilson (née Ostler) and her mother moved to a 20-acre block of land in Levin in 1888, they had a colonial oven but nowhere to install it; instead they used it as a sideboard in what Helen described as a 'charming' outdoor dining room, and did their cooking over an open fire.[109]

Even in the twentieth century, as subsistence farming declined and small units became commercially viable, individuals and families were not rooted to their smallholdings.[110] One commentator reported in 1936 that in New Zealand 'there is a readiness to move about the country to a degree [that is] astonishing to a visiting observer of our manners'.[111] Although the preference for small farming was already deeply entrenched, many family farms proved too small to be profitable. New settlers, such as those granted land and offered cheap credit under the Discharged Soldiers Settlement Act 1915, were often burdened by massive mortgages.

A PACKMAN PREPARING A MEAL IN A MUSTERERS' CAMP ON ST. HELEN'S STATION. G. S. Buckley.

This tendency to move from place to place often resulted from the difficulty of turning a profit on marginal properties, or the search for better prospects, and meant material conditions in the home improved only slowly. As John C. Weaver and Doug Munro suggest in their study of rural suicides between 1900 and 1950, '[p]eriods of extraordinary rural expansion and prosperity papered over acute and chronic rural troubles'.[112]

The Māori population at this time was still fairly mobile, partly because people needed to travel to find work but also because traditional food-gathering skills were still greatly valued.[113] Ariana Rene (Ngāti Toa, Ngāti Koata, Taranaki, Ngā Puhi), born in Nelson in 1918, recalled that people of her parents' generation travelled constantly for work and to maintain links between iwi. People from the Wairau Valley would come to stay with her whānau on Rangitoto ki te Tonga D'Urville Island and catch fish, and her whānau would in turn travel to the Wairau to catch whitebait and gather walnuts. Busloads of people from Te Tau Ihu the northern South Island crossed over Te Moana o Raukawa to go shearing in Porirua, and men from Porirua worked in the Wairau at haymaking and harvesting times.[114] In Tairāwhiti, extended whānau groups were employed for shearing, shedhand work and cooking. Hei Ariki Algie (née Smith; Rongowhakaata) recalled that when working with her father running a big shearing gang in the 1940s, she had to cook for about eighteen people, 'all over a smoky fire!'.[115]

In communities where land had been alienated, Māori became a cheap labour force for Pākehā, supplementing their income by working as shearers, fencers, bush fellers, ditch diggers and shepherds.[116] In these situations the cooking and living facilities were often very basic. North Island runholders, for example, commonly supplied little or no accommodation for their Māori shearers, and according to John Martin these conditions meant that the mortality rate for Māori shearers was particularly high during the 1918–19 influenza epidemic.[117] In Te Tai Tokerau, Māori families and communities left their settlements to work on gumfields alongside thousands of immigrants from China, Britain, Dalmatia and elsewhere.[118] In some cases families camped on the fields for up to nine months at a time, living in huts with walls and roofs of sacking and chimneys made of sod.[119]

Packman preparing a meal for musterers on St Helens Station in 1923, using equipment that would have been very familiar to his nineteenth-century counterparts: a camp oven, billies and a frying pan (see Martin, *The Forgotten Worker*, 143). G. S. Buckley photograph, *Weekly Press*, 13 December 1923, p. 31. Christchurch City Libraries Collection, reproduced with permission.

Where land was kept in Māori ownership some individuals and iwi groups were able to develop large-scale sheep runs, as for example Ngāti Porou did in Tairāwhiti.[120] Most Māori communities, however, did not have the finance, infrastructure or access to training that would have enabled them to take advantage of the burgeoning pastoral economy; instead they leased or sold parts of their land in order to live on and develop what remained.[121] Government officials assumed that Māori farming would be mainly subsistence agriculture, and did not provide the support that would have allowed for housing improvements or household conveniences.[122] Heeni Wharemaru (Tainui), who lived on a small farm at Kamate (near Mōkau) from 1912 to 1927, describes the house her whānau lived in:

> [It] had a mud floor and was built from the trunks of ponga ferns. It was rectangular, not too wide but fairly long. One area was designated for eating, one for sleeping and one for important discussions, which were often held at our house.
> The eating area was the main one, down at one end of the house where there was a fireplace and a chimney stack made of galvanized iron. Around the fireplace hung a big kettle and other pots; this was where all the cooking was done. We had one table, but no chairs.[123]

At Te Kao the government financed the development of dairy units as an alternative to gumdigging, but the Department of Maori Affairs held on to the profits and paid the farmers a salary little above subsistence level.[124] In 1936 members of the community wrote to the prime minister: 'our houses are shacks made of rusty iron used many times over and badly holed. They are not fit for human beings to live in. . . . If by working long hours we earn more than sufficient for food and clothing, we would use the balance cash to pay for new cottages.'[125]

Unlike Māori farmers, Pākehā farmers were given support to develop commercial enterprises through ready mortgages and development loans. The government encouraged agriculture by sponsoring research into soil fertility and stock practices, setting up marketing boards, promoting intensive farming and providing cheap credit. However, as Brooking argues in his analysis of economic transformation around the turn of the century, '[t]he apparent beneficence of successive governments was frequently tinged with an almost cynical disregard for economic reality'.[126] Farmers had enjoyed relatively good prices and a guaranteed market for primary products during the First World War, as the British government agreed to purchase the entire national output (beyond domestic requirements) of commodities such as meat, cheese, butter, wool and sheepskin.[127] When the commandeer system ended in 1921 and export prices fell, however, many farmers struggled to meet their financial commitments. While the state was generous in assisting those who wanted land, there was little support available for farmers whose land proved unsuited to farming or uneconomical.[128]

Investment in improving the land often required a great deal of sacrifice on the part of rural women. The president of the WDFU highlighted the impact these policies had on individual families in her monthly message for January 1934.

> Most of us are rather tired of being reminded of farmers' 'Good times', knowing as we do that for the majority of farmers there were no really good times. Prices were high, but costs were high also. . . . More scientific means of farming were advocated. Top dressing was believed to be a possible way out, and farmers thought that at last there was a chance of attaining that position in which their income would cover their costs and leave a living wage. . . . For several years every penny that could be spared was put back into the land. Then came the slump, and farmers wished that they had not listened to the slogan 'Produce more.' They realised when it was too late that all had gone for nothing. They regretted that their sons had had no wages, and that their wives had sacrificed to no purpose. They found themselves in the grip of a calamity as irresistible as an earthquake.[129]

And as Helen Wilson reported, 'It was sometimes easy to detect signs of resentment against husbands who had refused amenities in favour of ploughing a new paddock or buying more stock. Now these things had been proved useless women felt they had pinched and denied themselves for nothing.'[130]

The mechanisation of farm work and the improvement of land were often prioritised over improvements to the material conditions of the home, reflecting a gendered hierarchy that valued men's 'productive work' above women's. Rural women maintained farm households through their domestic work, production of primary products, and unpaid farm labour, but often had little say in how farm funds were allocated and priorities set. They were not blind to this hierarchy, as the example of Jean Boswell (née Smith) shows. Born in 1893 at Mangawhare near Dargaville, Jean noted in her autobiography that although her mother Jenny never complained, she did hear other women complaining about the inequalities in their homes and marriages.

> We [as children] never thought of the inconveniences and hardship that the many primitive make-shifts made for Mother, I suppose because we heard no grumbling. In fact, all our sympathy was for the men of the settlement, who made no bones about grumbling over *their* lack of farm conveniences, and I was twelve years old before I knew what the women thought about it all. It was through hearing a conversation between my mother and a visiting neighbour.
>
> 'Yes,' said the woman, wearily, 'we can slave our soul-cases into carcasses, with scarcely a convenience of any sort to help us. It's all "the farm, the farm, the farm."' And then they try to tell us that it's only us they're really thinking of; that it's all for our comfort eventually. Pah! It makes me sick! By the time there's anything left over from the farm for us we'll be done to death, and some other woman will get what we drudged for!'[131]

Living in a bush settlement in the last years of what became known as the Long Depression (1885–1900), these women eked out a basic subsistence, but comforts must have been few. It was under these conditions, when the economy failed and dreams for the future seemed unattainable, that the drudgery occasioned by a lack of conveniences seemed particularly unbearable. In good times there might be money available for some small luxuries, although as Sally Parker notes of the 'Golden Age' of farming in the 1950s, rural women still 'enjoyed only a small slice of the farm's increased profits, which their husbands preferred to invest in machinery and additional stock rather than in home comforts and a more expansive life-style'.[132]

Custom and convenience in the choice of appliances

Factors such as the mobility of the rural labour force, the economic instability of many small farms, and the use of farm profit for land improvement rather than domestic improvement all had an impact on the uptake of new domestic technologies. However, cultural and social factors were also important in shaping how cooking techniques have endured or changed. In Māori communities, traditional cooking techniques such as hāngī were so integral to the maintenance of culture that they continued to be used throughout the twentieth century – and into the present. The preparation for and laying of a traditional hāngī is a collective effort, encouraging a sense of community and a sharing of knowledge and stories. It also sustains close connections with whenua – the earth in which ingredients are both grown and cooked – as a successful hāngī requires an understanding of the land and how it will hold heat, the right types of wood and rocks to use, and the foods that can be gathered or grown in the local area.[133]

Some aspects of the hāngī have changed, for example in the use of wire baskets to hold food and, more recently, the use of artificial hāngī cookers. In fact, some now consider that the hāngī is not so much a specific cooking technique as a gathering of people in a Māori cultural environment: the method of cooking is less important than the socialising, with all sharing a commitment to te ao Māori and the spirit of manaakitanga.[134]

Pākehā, too, sometimes opted for the old ways out of preference, habit or custom. Advertising for cooking appliances and kitchen gadgets invariably targeted women, attempting to lure consumers with promises of domestic convenience and modernity,[135] but not all rural women welcomed the new technologies. As Susan Strasser explains in her history of American housework, domestic labour without modern conveniences had its compensations: homemaking, although it was often gruelling, offered women 'satisfaction in their craft, intimate connections with their families and with other women formed through work, and the sense of value derived from work done for love, not money'.[136]

Elizabeth Hollard (née Robinson) looks back on the years she spent at Tauherenīkau in the 1860s and 1870s with a sense of pride in her domestic skills. 'I was not exactly fitted for the role of farmer's wife either in physique or by training: but I may say, with modest pride, that I held my own in that capacity a good many years. Devices that lighten the housekeeper's task now, were then unknown; and work that is now performed at the milking shed and the butter factory, was then counted among the legitimate duties of the farmer's wife.'[137] Gwen Wingate Mackenzie describes her mother Gertie's duties on their sheep farm near Palmerston North in the 1930s, and recalls that once she had learnt to 'hold her own' in the role, she was reluctant to change her domestic routine: 'Mother never stopped using the old coal range even when Dad bought her a Moffat electric stove. She didn't like the electric oven, but she was confident of always producing an award winning sponge cake using her tried and true range.'[138] And Stephanie Tuhoro recalls that her Nanny Te Uruhina Kameta (Ngāti Raka) made delicious rēwena potato bread in a wood stove, and although her husband Te Toiroa Charles Kameta later bought her a 'flash new electric stove . . . her rewana just wasn't the same so she went back to cooking in her old wood stove'.[139]

Women had other, more pragmatic reasons for continuing to use older appliances, which were often more convenient and more fit for purpose than modern alternatives. Anne Duncan (née Taylor) of Conroys Gully, Central Otago, noted in her 1996 oral history that the old coal range had other advantages besides cooking functions: it heated the water and it dried the laundry on a 'great big clothes horse' hanging from the kitchen ceiling.[140] Anne's mother later had an electric stove installed, but the coal range still 'had its purpose' and was used often. Similarly, when Irene Staples moved to a sheep station in the 1950s she tried cooking meals in summer without lighting the coal range, but she found that the electric oven was often too small to hold all the pots and pans she needed; and besides, the coal range, while it belted out intense heat, had a big expanse of tiles around it where she could keep the food warm until the workers came in for their meals.[141]

Hot water laid on

In *Looking Backward*, Ann M. Easy (née West) suggests that 'one of the greatest hardships the early settlers had to face was the lack of any kind of water supply'.[142] Ann grew up in Ormondville, 30 miles (48km) from Waipukurau, around the turn of the century, and because her family's house was not handy to a stream they had to draw water by hand from a well on a nearby hill. '[W]e drew it up with a bucket on a fairly long rope which wasn't as simple as it sounds. If you just let the bucket down it would stay on top of the water. There is quite a knack to giving the rope a twitch so that the edge of the bucket goes under water. . . .

. . . With several small children to keep clean, and we were kept clean, and the butter making, I've wondered how many buckets of water a day my mother carried down that hill.'[143]

Until the mid-1800s most households, rural and urban alike, took their water from streams or wells, or collected rainwater in barrels.[144] In the 1880s large, inexpensive corrugated-iron tanks came onto the market that were large enough to store water for all of a household's needs, and by the early 1900s these tanks, sitting on a wooden tankstands, were a feature of most backyards.[145] Ann remembers vividly 'the day the plumber arrived with a big 800 gallon tank and put it up with a pipe through the wall so that we didn't even have to go outside for a bucket of water. That was another red letter day.'[146]

Not all houses with a tank had the water piped directly inside, however – Lily Winter (née Manson), born in 1916, wrote that in her childhood home the water was collected from the roof into a tank but that all the water they used 'had to be carried where it was needed'.[147] And not all houses had a rainwater tank: in some Māori households rainwater was considered tapu because it had come off the roof above people's heads. Sophie Kaa (née Whaanga; Ngāti Kahungunu, Ngāi Tahu Matawhaiti, Rongowhakaata, Te Aitanga-a-Māhaki) told historian Judith Fyfe that when she was growing up, her family collected water from a well for this reason.[148]

The coal or wood range was especially useful for heating water for washing. Before the introduction of the coal range with a boiler attached, water was heated in kettles or in a large copper vat with a capacity of about 60 litres, set on a brick or concrete base. The copper was extremely versatile: as well as boiling water to do the laundry, it was used for boiling puddings, scalding a pig carcase to remove the bristles, brewing beer and making soap.[149] It had its disadvantages, though: it had to be lit very early in the morning, and it required setting a separate fire to that used for cooking or heating. The benefit of the hotwater tank on the coal range was that, so long as you kept it full and kept the fire stoked up, you had your 'hot water laid on'.[150]

Hot water for doing the dishes or filling a bath was drawn from a tap on one side of the coal range. Nessie Krippner (née Karl) of Rotorua remembered that 'the first job every morning before the fire was lit was to pump water into a kerosene tin and fill the boiler attached to the stove'. In households where the tank was connected to the main water supply, the boiler

would refill automatically as hot water was drawn off.[151] The wetback was a later development that heated water and fed it into a hotwater cylinder.[152]

 The wood or coal range was thus a relatively economical way of cooking food, warming a room and heating water all at once, and it still had a place in many rural – and some urban – kitchens long after more streamlined, modern alternatives were available.

∧
This photograph by Hubert Vaile shows a small girl, possibly Marjorie Vaile, stirring a wood-fired copper. Broadlands, Waikato, 1910. Auckland Libraries Heritage Collections, 2-V0472.

Some rural Pākehā commentators viewed the introduction of electrical appliances with a certain moralistic disdain. The editor of *New Zealand Farm and Home* wrote in 1932: 'with the rush of modern inventions we farming folk have been simply swept off our feet. They found us in our quiet backwaters unprepared. We forgot our high estate, followed the crowd, lost our sense of proportion, and took on the city folk's mentality, and all those fine sweet things that had given poise and dignity to our lives were as though they were not.'[153] A School Publications Branch booklet titled *Washday at the Pa* was published in 1964 to considerable controversy, but some Pākehā readers found in Ans Westra's photographs of a rural Māori family living in Ruatōria evidence of familial warmth and happiness that did not rest on 'the acquisition of revolving clothes lines, washing machines, and spin driers'.[154] This nostalgia was not shared by members of the Māori Women's Welfare League or the Māori Council, who objected to false sentimentality about the 'old days' and attempts to fix Māori identity in the rural past.[155] These organisations fought for Māori to have access to the same types and standards of housing and amenities as Pākehā enjoyed, and rejected the type of nostalgia that might have undermined Māori rights to equality in living standards.[156]

In her 2011 book *If Walls Could Talk*, Lucy Worsley suggests that 'kitchens are conservative spaces. Cooking involves routine [and] cooks are the guardians of traditions. Their recipes order the world.'[157] At first glance it might appear that the incremental uptake of cooking technology in rural New Zealand supports that view, confirming an entrenched conservatism in domestic spaces. Analysis of personal manuscripts, however, reveals that a whole host of economic, cultural and personal factors influenced rural people's access to technology, and that, in fact, most were not wedded to timeless traditions. Rural New Zealand in the nineteenth century and even, in some parts, into the twentieth was not an ordered world, and kitchens in their multiple and diverse forms reflect that lack of uniformity. Some people did uphold traditions, while others embraced new technologies and enjoyed the trappings of modernity. In many cases, though, cooking techniques evolved organically as a series of 'shifts and makeshifts', and were altered or updated as necessary or as resources allowed.[158] Pragmatism, rather than conservatism, was usually the overriding concern. Cooks may have been the guardians of tradition, but they had to reconsider and reconfigure those traditions in response to complex social, cultural and economic changes.

3
Rēwena and rabbit stew:

Provisioning the rural kitchen

This chapter traces the introduction of new land use systems in rural New Zealand in the nineteenth and early twentieth centuries, and considers how the making of Pākehā rural worlds impacted on the making of meals. It examines the foods that rural Māori and Pākehā had access to, how they prepared and preserved their ingredients, and how those processes changed as the environmental and economic landscape changed.

In an account of her family history and her mixed Māori and Pākehā identity, Helene Connor (Te Āti Awa, Ngāti Ruanui) considers the importance of manaakitanga in the lives of her grandparents and parents. Her grandmother Lulu Skelton (née Coulter), who lived with her husband Leslie (known as Mick) on a dairy farm in Motunui in the mid-twentieth century, 'held on to the Māori traditions embedded in manaakitanga'.

> Anyone who visited the old farmhouse would get a warm welcome. She was the life and soul of the whānau (family).... She grew a huge vegetable garden, which fed her large family and many others. She also kept chickens for eggs and poultry and prepared traditional Māori kai (food) using food preparation practices she learned from the women in her family. Lulu's mother and beloved aunt Tangiora, her mother's sister, taught her how to cook fresh kaimoana (seafood), which was collected from the local beach, including kōtoretore (red sea anemone), which were found in rock pools that were slow cooked for several days. Another time-intensive dish was karaka berries, which can be poisonous unless cooked correctly. The preparation involves days of soaking and endless boiling and straining.[1]

Lulu placed great importance on being able to welcome and feed visitors, and she drew on a range of strategies and resources to provide 'endless meals' for friends and whānau. Vegetables from the garden, eggs from the chookhouse, seafood from the beach, berries from the forest, as well as sugar, flour and other staples from the store were brought to the kitchen and prepared using new and old techniques, adapted to suit the coal range. For Lulu and Leslie, as for so many other people in rural New Zealand, domestic provisioning involved a complex network of market and non-market forces that were specific to their location, economic situation and cultural background. This chapter traces the food paths trodden to and from rural Māori and Pākehā kitchens, and considers how food was produced, distributed, acquired and consumed.

New Zealand historian Tony Simpson writes in *A Distant Feast*: 'Hunger, in one form or another, drove our European ancestors out of Britain.'[2] Some hungered for land, others for freedom and opportunity, and some sought escape from the hunger of constant malnourishment, of lives spent toiling and barely scraping by. Massive population growth, coupled with crop failures in Europe from the mid-eighteenth to the mid-nineteenth century, had resulted in regular and serious famine; what one historian called 'the century of hunger'.[3] New Zealand, meanwhile, was seen as 'the country for living – [with] beef, mutton, butter and eggs, and everything that else that is good'.[4] Settlers came to this country determined never to starve, and in order to achieve that security they implemented their own systems of land use, disrupting or completely destroying Māori provisioning systems in the process.

Māori food paths had been built on centuries of experimentation and generations of accumulated environmental knowledge. Plants, techniques and tools brought from Polynesia were adapted for use in Aotearoa, and food economies developed based on complex systems of land rights and highly regulated distribution practices. In parts of the North Island and the upper South Island agriculture was practised extensively, while in the colder districts of Te Wai Pounamu the lifestyles of Ngāi Tahu communities were based primarily on hunting and gathering.[5] Some iwi relied chiefly on resources from the forest, others on seafood or freshwater resources, but nearly every district yielded a variety of food products that were carefully tended, hunted and harvested on a seasonal cycle.[6]

The food paths laid down by European settlers in New Zealand were initially oriented towards small-scale production for domestic consumption.[7] Almost everyone with access to land kept livestock of some sort – chickens or pigs and sometimes a house cow – and grew vegetables and fruit. This provided most of their subsistence needs, and surplus eggs and butter could be traded for flour, sugar and tea. It was an effective system built through hard work and experimentation, and it insulated small-scale farmers from the most severe effects of economic instability. It also fed into systems of meaning and identity that placed great weight on self-sufficiency and the ability to make do. The making of rural New Zealand as we know it today involved dispossession and displacement as well as industry and innovation, and all of these factors are evident in the history of food production and provisioning.

Implicit in the development of rural New Zealand, and evident in all British settler colonies, was 'an aggressive will to possess and alter land'; to impose patterns and grids on the landscape so that it might better serve human needs.[8] As Hugh Campbell notes in his history of rural worlds, while the majority of settlers had little to do with the establishment and implementation of colonial infrastructure at the government level, farms and farmers were the 'primary agents that first pushed back the frontiers of indigenous land-use and indigenous ecologies, unleashed chaos, before starting to create enclaves and then entire new landscapes within those chaotic ecological and social crises'.[9] Settlers had travelled across the world determined to own land and achieve a modest self-sufficiency, so when their interests came up against those of Māori, they would not surrender their claims.[10]

Competing systems of land use

Food paths are the processes, people and goods needed to make food available to particular domestic groups. These paths are defined by access to land and other means of production (such as capital or credit), knowledge of the environment and its uses, distribution patterns and practices, and cultural norms around food consumption. By exploring food paths in particular historical settings, we can more clearly understand social differentiation, systems of meaning and identity, and the reproduction of social and economic structures.[11]

Over centuries of settlement, Māori communities had developed complex systems of land use based on overlapping tenure and resource rights. Land was not owned in the sense that it was a commodity to be bought and sold; rather, whānau members would have rights of residence in a certain place or places, while use rights were granted for mahinga kai, either at individual, whānau, hapū or iwi level.[12] Different groups could have rights to the same piece of land – for example, one group might have rights to catch birds in the trees while another had rights to garden the adjoining land – and these rights were constantly being renegotiated.[13] Seasonal use rights were a cornerstone of Māori provisioning systems, and resources such as tī, aruhe, weka, tītī, tuna and kaimoana, harvested at mahinga kai, were essential to the sustenance of Māori communities. Basil Keane offers this proverb as a way of encapsulating the importance of land to Māori: 'Te toto o te tangata he kai. Te oranga o te tangata he whenua (the lifeblood of a person is derived from food; the livelihood of a people depends on land)'.[14]

Use rights came with obligations to the rest of the community – such as assisting with the repayment of gifts or hosting visitors – and could be lost through neglect or relocation. E. T. Durie explains that 'while individuals or particular families had use rights of various kinds at several places. . . . the land of an area remained in the control and authority of an associated ancestral group, and . . . neither the land as a whole, nor a use right within it, could pass permanently outside the bloodline. Land and ancestors were fused.'[15] Consequently there was no existing concept of land sales, and the idea that an individual could accrue total land-use rights in a particular area, freed of specific obligations to the ancestral group associated with the land, was foreign.[16]

European settlers brought very different attitudes to land, and emphasised individual land ownership as the means of achieving economic and social independence. Although the export economy was founded on extensive pastoralism and squatters grabbed early positions on the land with less-than-absolute property rights, by the end of the nineteenth century small, family-owned farms had come to dominate the colonised landscape.[17] These farms anchored very particular economic and emotional worlds. Farmers brought stability to the chaos of the colonial frontier by dividing land into blocks that could be privately owned and scientifically farmed. This generated a set of beliefs about rural life that emphasised autonomy and self-reliance, linked family and kinship ties to the boundaries of the farm, and attempted to assimilate Māori into European farming and erase other types of land use.[18]

Brooking explains that the emphasis on privately owned farms incorporated a variety of ideologies which, when taken together, created a broad-based consensus among the settlers in favour of closer settlement.[19] Biblical injunctions to bring civilisation to the wilderness and make the land fruitful added a moral dimension to the discourse, while also contributing to the critique of land monopoly that had emanated from village Britain.[20] Furthermore, most settlers adhered to a set of attitudes known as ruralism, believing firmly in the moral and social superiority of rural life. This cluster of ideas created a very strong belief that the small farmer should be the central figure of the ideal society, and that one of the primary purposes of the state should be supporting individual initiative in this direction.[21]

There were small farms in New Zealand from the beginning of European settlement, but these often yielded little more than the household's subsistence needs. The development of refrigerated shipping in the 1880s enabled a transition from land-extensive pastoralism for wool to land-intensive farming for wool, meat and dairy products, and small farms were gradually integrated into the export economy.[22] Small-scale subsistence activities continued for household provisioning, with home-grown vegetables, home-killed meat, hand-churned butter and farm eggs. W. J. Gardner wrote in an essay on New Zealand's colonial economy that 'the spread of small farming after 1900 had its roots deep in the subsistence farming before 1890', and historians of rural economies elsewhere have noted similar trends.[23]

The state, for its part, was quick to offer support to Pākehā small farmers, and successive governments implemented legislative and structural measures to facilitate closer settlement. The forested areas of the North Island, for example, were opened for settlement by the extension of railway networks, while land formerly leased by pastoralists was made available through policies of compulsory subdivision. Most significantly, various mechanisms for alienating Māori land were introduced, including crown pre-emption, by which about two thirds of the total land area of New Zealand was purchased cheaply between 1840 and 1865; land confiscations in the wake of the New Zealand Wars; and the Native Land Court, which enabled the conversion of customary title to freehold and made it easier for Pākehā to purchase Māori land.[24] As a result, 34.5 million acres of the South Island had been purchased by 1864, and in the North Island, Māori-owned land shrank from 23.2 million to 2.8 million acres between 1860 and 1939.[25]

With the land that remained, some Māori groups and individuals were able to farm profitably.[26] In general, however, Māori found it very difficult to participate in the export economy. Dairy factories, freezing works and transport links were not conveniently located, lenders would not advance capital on land in multiple ownership, and Māori were not offered the same access to training and development assistance as Pākehā farmers.[27] Many Māori communities adopted a more mixed form of subsistence agriculture, supplemented by seasonal wage labour and the harvesting of customary resources.[28]

The Waitangi Tribunal's *Te Tau Ihu o te Waka a Maui: Report on Northern South Island Claims* notes that in the early 1900s Māori in Te Tau Ihu began producing a wider range of foods, including mutton, beef, poultry and vegetable crops, in order to replace some of the resources they had lost.[29] Chris Love reported in evidence to the Waitangi Tribunal on behalf of Te Āti Awa that his father 'was as skilled at slaughtering a mutton as he was at being able to supply kina, wet fish or crayfish to the kai tables'; and Luckie Macdonald suggested in evidence on behalf of Rangitāne that chickens were such a staple that they became one of the foods for which the Wairau was noted.[30] Many of the contributors to *Ngā Mōrehu: The Survivors*, which documents the lives of Māori women from small rural communities in the Bay of Plenty, Te Urewera and Tūranganui a Kiwa Poverty Bay in the early twentieth century, recall that a range of foods were produced by their whānau and hapū to supplement customary resources. Heni Brown (née McDonald; Ngāi Tai) and her family had cows, pigs and acres of kūmara and potatoes; and Reremoana Koopu recalls that although maize and pigs were the main focus in her community, they also had potatoes, kūmara, fowls, pork and beef.[31]

From the 1930s a long-awaited government scheme for Māori land development, established in 1929 by Apirana Ngata as minister of native affairs, was set in motion. The scheme included various mechanisms for title reform, and enabled Māori Land Boards to finance all aspects of land development.³² This funding supported participating communities through the Depression and the Second World War: it provided modern homes and a reasonable living but, as Aroha Harris notes, it was 'never a cure-all for poverty'.³³ Māori farmers continued to supplement their incomes with casual labour and regular social security payments, and customary hunting, fishing and food gathering were still vital provisioning strategies.³⁴ By 1940 it was clear that the land remaining to Māori would afford economic independence to only a fraction of the population; many of the younger generation were forced to look for opportunities in towns and cities.³⁵

The making of rural New Zealand was, according to Hugh Campbell, a 'cataclysmic meeting and rupturing' of worlds. The world that had existed – 'a settled land of cultivation and food gathering' – was pushed aside by settlers who arrived in New Zealand and saw a potential farm, blind to the fact that Aotearoa was already a productive garden.³⁶ The competing systems of land use brought to bear in rural New Zealand were, in large measure, oriented towards food production, so by studying food paths as they shifted and changed over the nineteenth and early twentieth centuries we gain a better sense of that cataclysmic meeting.

Hunted and gathered

The provisioning practices used in rural New Zealand varied greatly across the country, but can be broadly separated into three categories: wild foods hunted or gathered; domesticated foods grown or reared; and consumer goods traded or purchased. The ancestors of Māori who arrived in Aotearoa enjoyed an abundance of wild animal foods in the form of fish, marine mammals and flightless birds; and they used processing techniques already familiar to them to make wild plants safe to eat and palatable.³⁷ When the 'protein boom' ended – with the moa extinct and the most accessible seal-breeding rookeries hunted out – a broader range of provisioning processes were needed. As James Belich put it, 'an all-year-round living could be wrested from New Zealand nature, even in the absence of game or gardens, but it took immense effort and organisation, aimed at a wide range of targets'.³⁸

> A selection of fishhooks in the Te Papa collection, from several different iwi. Michael Hall photograph, 2003, Museum of New Zealand Te Papa Tongarewa, MA_I.006400.

Saltwater and freshwater resources

Fish has always been a major food source for Māori communities, according to Māori oral history, archaeological records, and observations by early European explorers.[39] The crew of the *Endeavour*, which visited New Zealand in 1769–70, observed fishing activities up and down the coasts of Aotearoa, and Captain Cook wrote of Māori fishing in the Bay of Islands that 'some few [fish] we caught our selves with hook and line and in the Saine but by farr the greatest part we purchass'd of the Natives and these of Various sorts, such as Shirks, sting-rays, Breams, Mullet, Mackarel and several other sorts'.[40] Māori used a range of equipment to catch fish, including kupenga, aho, matau and pātia (spears).[41] These tools were Polynesian in origin but adapted for use in Aotearoa, for example by using bone, stone and pāua shell in place of pearl shell, and adapting the shape and construction of fish hooks to suit the available materials.[42]

As well as fish, the sea also offered an extraordinary array of shellfish, gathered as part of the seasonal provisioning cycle. Evidence from middens shows that in addition to the species still gathered and eaten today, such as tuatua, pipi, pāua, tuangi and tio, Māori gathered numerous other types of kaimoana.[43] This was usually the work of women, who used various tools to scoop or dredge the shellfish out of the sand or prise them from the rocks.[44]

Large-scale tribal fishing declined from about 1885 as introduced crops and livestock reduced Māori dependence on fish, and as new laws restricted Māori access to fisheries.[45] Still, individuals continued to fish and gather kaimoana to sustain family livelihoods, and as oral testimonies presented to the Waitangi Tribunal make abundantly clear, many coastal hapū continued to rely on their fishing and shellfish-gathering practices into the twentieth century.[46] Edward Birch of Waipōua valley (South Hokianga) commented in evidence for the claim of Te Roroa:

> When I think back to the resources that used to abound in Waipoua I have to also think of the sea. It was a major part of our life style back then. . . .
> . . . These resources to us were essential we could gather our paua, kina, mussels, toheroa which were very common from

∧
Men fish for kahawai using a long scoop net called a kupenga koko kahawai, Waiapu, 1923. As Te Rangi Hīroa notes in *The Coming of the Maori*, many types and sizes of nets were in common use, including baited bag nets with sinkers, funnel-shaped set nets, and seine nets (212–16). James McDonald photograph, Museum of New Zealand Te Papa Tongarewa, MU000523/006/0030, reproduced with permission of Tā Selwyn Parata KNZM, Ngāti Porou.

> Ngati Tiiheru to Waikara approximately 10 miles of beach. There was enough Kaimoana in this rich and beautiful coastline to feed all the other settlements as well as our own.[47]

Kelly Russell Wilson of Arahura wrote in his evidence for the Ngāi Tahu claim:

> Maori people had [a] great resource ... the sea. It was not only a garden that provided much of the food. It was also a highway by which we travelled up and down the country. The Coast and the coastal fishing grounds were identified like the land, marked off in tribal boundaries just as the land was. ... The importance of Kai Moana was very great as it is today. Seafood was the staple diet of Maori people.[48]

As these extracts suggest, and as was also discussed in the Tribunal report for Te Tau Ihu, fishing and shellfish-gathering were necessary for survival in some communities, and this ensured the transmission of these practices from generation to generation.[49] The sea was a great provider, a 'veritable food basket',[50] and it likely saved a number of communities from deprivation.[51]

The main method of preserving fish was to dry it in the sun or over a slow, smoky fire; and shellfish were strung up to dry for a few days before being pounded flat and left to dry completely.[52] Mihipeka Edwards (née Davis; Waikato, Te Arawa, Ngāti Raukawa, Ngāti Maniapoto) recalls that shen she was growing up in Manakau (in the Horowhenua district) in the 1920s, a group of her whānau members would take an annual summer trip to the sea, where they would set up a smokehouse to preserve the catch for winter. Then, at the end of each week 'the rest of the family, who were left at home, would come on drays and take back the goods already caught and prepared by us; they would take them back, store them in the pataka and kauta'.[53] Ruku Arahanga (née Tuatini; Te Āti Haunuia Pāpārangi, Ngāti Hauiti, Ngāti Tūwharetoa, Ngāi Tahu, Ngāti Māmoe, Ngāi Te Ruahikihiki) did not have a pātaka at her childhood home in Raetihi, but they did have a storeroom at the back of their house where Ruku remembered bacon hanging. 'It had just been regularly smoked and it was there as food for our family during the winter months. The tuna pāwhara [dried eel] hanging up in the same little house and also many other kai that he [her father] grew in his garden was all stored and ready for his family so they wouldn't go without.'[54]

Tuna were found in creeks and rivers throughout the country and were a particularly useful food source because they were available year round, although they were usually caught in large numbers from February to April when they were migrating back to the sea.[55] They could also coexist quite successfully with introduced trout.[56] Tuna were caught en masse using a pā tuna or weir (see page 138).

> The pa consisted of a v-shaped wooden race, into which the tuna would swim, narrowing at the downstream end, where a hinaki (basket or trap) was attached. Once inside the pa, the force of the current prevented the tuna from swimming upstream and escaping, but the hinaki had a small opening at the downstream end for smaller tuna to pass through.[57]

If only a small number of eels were needed for immediate consumption, they could be caught by hand, with a spear, or a bob – a flax line with a bundle of worms tied at one end.[58] Various claimants to the Waitangi Tribunal recalled the importance of tuna in their diet, such as Rawiri Te Maire Tau (Ngāi Tahu), who noted: 'The eel was a principal source of nourishment for the South Island Maori.'[59] Dot Davis (Ngā Paerangi, Ngāti Porou, Ngāti Kahungunu) of Kaiwhaiki (Whanganui River) recalled that in the 1920s and 1930s her whānau survived on eels: 'Mutton was a delicacy so we didn't know what it was to have meat like that. Eels, fish flaps and fish heads were it.'[60] Unable to produce enough food to sustain them on the land left to them, this family relied on what they could catch or gather using traditional practices, perfected over centuries.

Wetlands were also important mahinga kai, as they were breeding grounds for fish such as īnanga, kōaro and kōkopu (types of whitebait) and waikaka (mudfish), and a habitat for birds such as weka, pūkeko and whio.[61] The destruction of wetland environments and the gradual restriction of fishing rights (overseen by local authorities) were therefore very significant aspects of the colonial experience.[62] Just as Māori and

Three young women sitting on a beach shelling toheroa from two large kete into kerosene tins, Northland, early to mid-twentieth century. Arthur James Northwood photograph, Northwood Brothers: Photographs of Northland, Alexander Turnbull Library, 1/1-026522-G.

Pākehā had fundamentally different conceptions of the utility of land, they disagreed also over the value of waterways and wetlands. In his 1857 publication *New Zealand or Zealandia*, Taranaki settler Charles Hursthouse described wetlands as 'the bittern's dank domain, fertile only in miasma'; but he noted that, once drained, 'the plough converts them into wholesome plains of fruit, and grain, and grass'.[63] For him, a swamp had no inherent value: it was merely an impediment to settlement that must be dealt with before the land could be brought into cultivation. Most of his countrymen no doubt shared his opinion, for they set about draining wetlands at an alarming rate. Since the beginning of European settlement, 85 percent of New Zealand's wetlands have been destroyed.[64]

From the forest

Māori harvested a wide range of resources from the forest, including birds such as kererū, kākā and tūī, various fruits and berries, fern root, and plants for medicine, building and weaving.[65] The main bird-harvesting season was from May to July, although kererū were caught in summer when they were eating tawa berries, and Ngāi Tahu fowlers began catching weka in April. Bird-catching was timed for when the birds were plumpest, and Māori used a variety of snares, spears and traps depending on the type of bird being hunted and the type of tree they were in.[66]

Birds such as kererū were preserved, partially cooked, in their own fat. Historian David Burton describes the process: 'The birds were roasted on a spit over a fire and the fat was collected in a trough below. . . . The hot fat was then poured over the bird in the container. In the case of birds other than muttonbirds [which were kept in kelp pōhā], this container was usually a hollow gourd decorated with a carved wooden mouthpiece and a few of the bird's feathers for identification.'[67] In the nineteenth century this process was adapted to suit new meats such as pork, mutton and rabbit, and in the twentieth century the hollow gourd was replaced by the ubiquitous kerosene tin.[68] Heni Sunderland (née Brown; Ngāi Tāmanuhiri, Rongowhakaata), who grew up in Muriwai, remembered that her father 'would make us miti tahu, cut up the pork and partly cook it, and then throw it into a camp oven of boiling, boiling fat. Probably kept it air tight and the meat used to keep indefinitely.'[69]

Poutama Te Ture, his wife and others, smoking eels at Koriniti in 1921. James McDonald photograph, Alexander Turnbull Library, PA1-q-257-79-1, acknowledging Koriniti marae, Ngāti Pāmoana hapū.

Pā tuna (eel weir) on the Whanganui River, 1921. James McDonald photograph, Museum of New Zealand Te Papa Tongarewa, MU000523/005/0456, acknowledging Ngāti Kura of Pipiriki.

In evidence to the Waitangi Tribunal for the Ngāi Tahu Land Claim, Rakiihui Tau remarks on both the importance of the forest as a source of food and rongoā well into the twentieth century, and on the increasing scarcity of those resources.

> By the time I was a teenager the birds which our people had relied on for food, had largely disappeared so there was not much birding. ... Today almost all of [the bush around Banks Peninsula] has disappeared. We would catch the odd Kereru (wood pigeon) which could be found in odd pockets of bush in the Waipara area or among the cherry trees at Lowburn. I was grown up before anybody told me that it was illegal to catch the Pigeons. ...
>
> It is important to stress that the Kai which we got in this way formed the basis of our diet. It was not a case of catching food to supplement what we could buy, rather it was the other way round; we bought food to supplement what we caught. This practice was unquestioned among my family, it was the way my parents and their grandparents had always lived.[70]

By the time Rakiihui was born in the early 1940s, the forests of Aotearoa had already been reduced to a fragment of their former extent. Pre-European Māori burnt large areas of lowland forest, virtually eradicating the forests of the eastern South Island by 1450 and leaving only remnants in Murihiku Southland, the Catlins, Banks Peninsula and some of the eastern ranges.[71] The arrival of European settlers heralded another wave of deforestation, focused on burning, logging, draining and clearing the remaining forest to make the land suitable for farms.[72] This process began in earnest in the 1870s, with areas of seasonal bush-burning radiating out from a growing network of roads and railways.[73] Once begun, the assault on the bush proceeded apace, and by 1905 there were 414 timber mills operating in New Zealand.[74]

At the start of the twentieth century it became clear to Māori and Pākehā alike that birds of the forest, particularly the kererū, were in danger of extinction because of habitat destruction, and yet in 1913 a royal commission suggested a 'broad principle' whereby 'no forest land ... which is suitable for farm land, shall be permitted to remain under forest'.[75]

The government's solution to the vulnerability of bird populations was to ban people from hunting them – a measure that caused lasting resentment. Alfred Elkington, who grew up on Rangitoto ki te Tonga D'Urville Island in the 1930s, reported to the Waitangi Tribunal:

> The kereru is another resource taken out of our control. From my understanding the prohibition against taking kereru was not put in place because we were killing the kereru off, but because there was a lack of food for them as a result of farmers cutting down trees, and because of the detrimental effect of possums. The kereru did not need protection from us – we had a long tradition of protecting the kereru.[76]

Poultry provided an alternative to forest birds, waterfowl and weka, but it could never substitute for the culturally specific value of these wild species – described by a claimant for Ngāti Koata as 'soul food'.[77]

'Wool not weka. Mutton not muttonbirds'[78]

In their dramatic transformation of the land, European settlers destroyed or diminished traditional food sources, and although rural Māori communities continued to utilise customary foods, the range and variety of those foods had decreased markedly. Rakiihia Tau made it clear to the Waitangi Tribunal that although he tried to be objective and unemotional in giving evidence, he 'would not like to leave the tribunal with the impression that the Mahinga Kai issue is just that'.[79] He expressed a 'deep sense of outrage' at the desecration of mahinga kai. This is also evident in the testimony of Emily Paniora for the claim of Te Roroa:

> This is all ancestral land, rich in our history, of the lives of our Tupuna. It is land which, like Pakeha history books, tells us where we came from and where we belong in the Ao-Marama. It defines us as a people. It is land which vividly brings history to life for us. The location and stories of the Wahitapu, kainga, mahinga and pa remain known to this day. These places form an essential part of tangata whenua, part of the landscape of our hearts and minds.[80]

The arrival of Europeans disrupted many of the locations and stories associated with mahinga kai, so while Māori could not participate on an equal footing in the European economic system, neither could they continue to rely on their own systems of resource use. As Rawiri Te Maire Tau put it, in relation to Ngāi Tahu communities in Canterbury: 'In essence an existence in the traditional world and the European world was declined. Ngai Tahu lived a vulnerable existence in both worlds and yet belonged to neither.'[81]

Despite these devastating changes, this is not altogether a story of loss. As revealed in Waitangi Tribunal reports and in personal manuscripts, Māori continued to harvest customary resources well into the twentieth century, and in some cases – notably the harvest of tītī in southern New Zealand – customary rights are still observed. These activities not only provide physical sustenance, they are also acts of resistance. As Bill Dacker explained, in relation to the Ngāi Tahu communities of Otago: 'During the preparation for the season concerned, the expedition itself, and the return, elements of taha Māori remained strong that no longer existed in other parts of the lives of an increasing number of those involved.'[82] Similarly, the Tribunal Report for the upper South Island states: 'Customary gathering of kai and rongoa was required for physical survival for much of the twentieth century. As a result, core aspects of the tangata whenua's way of life in Te Tau Ihu resisted acculturation from the surrounding Pakeha majority.'[83]

As evidence for this point, the report includes extensive testimony from Ropata Stephens, who detailed the life of his grandfather, Warren Tiwini, in Motueka in the late nineteenth century. Ropata told the Tribunal: 'My grandfather faced the pressures of two worlds in which he had been brought up and in which he lived. On the one hand, he was definitely Maori. He spoke te reo, gathered food from the landscape in accordance with traditional practices and occupied papakainga land.'[84] However, the social pressure Warren faced to be like his Pākehā neighbours must have been intense, for he never spoke Māori in front of his children, he did not allow them to learn the language, and he did not assert his 'Maoriness' in public. He did, however, continue to gather customary foods, despite facing ridicule from others in the community.

> The community knew when they saw my grandfather with his whanau heading in [the direction of the beach], the time must be close to low tide, as this was a regular activity. A pakeha called mockingly from the footpath in a big booming voice 'Hello Warren, going down to the old Maori butcher shop eh'[.] My father could sense the sarcasm in the voice of the pakeha and willed his father to answer him in the same contemptuous manner.... But being the gentleman he was, my Grandfather replied 'Yes Mr Smith, when the tide is out, the table is set.'[85]

For Warren Tiwini, Māori and Pākehā customs seem to have existed in opposition, and the maintenance of traditional food-gathering practices provided an opportunity to resist acculturation by the 'surrounding Pakeha majority'.

Historian Michael Stevens suggests, in his study of muttonbirding in Murihiku, that the continued utilisation of mahinga kai in the twentieth century, rather than representing a rejection of modernity in favour of timeless tradition, in fact allowed Ngāi Tahu whānau to modernise their practices on their own terms.[86] Muttonbirders embraced new ideas and innovations and incorporated them into the practice, but 'the nexus between whakapapa and access to natural resources continued to be a defining aspect of Kāi Tahu life'. By combining tradition and modernity, Ngāi Tahu 'fashioned a new way of being in the world; a way of being they understood as being authentic and meaningful'.[87]

Hunting and fishing by European settlers

European settlers incorporated wild fish and game into their diets, too, and in fact in the early years of settlement hunting was often what kept food on the table.[88] Kate Hunter notes in her history of hunting in New Zealand that before agriculture was well established, introduced livestock were too valuable to eat, so settlers, surveyors and bushmen relied on the forest for food, supplementing produce purchased from Māori with wild pork and native birds. In more remote areas hunting was still a vital provisioning strategy into the twentieth century, although as agriculture expanded most families were able to use farm produce for their basic sustenance with game as a welcome variation.[89]

Two men in the Far North displaying their catch, 1920s. They also have fish drying on wooden branches beside their tent. Northwood Brothers photograph, Photographs of Northland, Alexander Turnbull Library, 1/1-006326-G.

There is some debate as to how much fish featured in the diet of Pākehā New Zealanders in the nineteenth and early twentieth centuries. Official statistics show a low level of fish consumption: a 1912 report on the cost of living suggested that the practice of catch limitation and the high cost of distribution 'are responsible for the fact that fish as a commercial article of diet is beyond the reach of the bulk of the population'.[90] Tony Simpson also suggests that fish consumption was low: he argues that in the settlers' home culture, 'eating fish was a mark of low status and that status was precisely what they had come here to escape'.[91] Anthropologist David Veart wrote from his own experience in *First Catch Your Weka*: 'Coming from a family that has assiduously fished and gathered for at least three generations, I have wondered whether the official figures hide a truer consumption based not only on this personal fishing but also on a form of suburban gift exchange.'[92] Food historians Ray Bailey and Mary Earle also warn against unqualified use of the statistics: 'This apparent low fish consumption during the 1900s was, no doubt, modified by amateur harvesting of the plentiful in-shore fish.'[93]

Sources suggest that rural New Zealanders enjoyed eating fish if they could get it, either by fishing themselves, trading with neighbours, or purchasing from a merchant. Margaret Trotter of Ōtāpiri, Southland, wrote in her recollections: 'We did have fish from the river although Dad was not a fisherman. Andy Henderson, a great fisherman, always made for the river when the family visited and left a trout for us. We would have trout for tea – and enjoy it too.'[94] George Welch of Masterton was a keen fisherman, and either he or his son Kemble would go fishing for trout regularly during the summer. This added welcome variation to their usual menu of pork and mutton, a novelty which, as George noted in his diary, he 'enjoyed . . . muchly'.[95]

Rabbit was available almost everywhere; in fact, in semi-arid parts of the open country they reached almost plague proportions in the late 1800s, destroying vegetation cover and triggering soil erosion which in turn caused a rapid decline in the productivity of the pastoral stations.[96] The carrying capacity of Earnscleugh Station in Central Otago, for example, was almost halved between 1879 and 1897, causing the runholder to abandon his lease. When it was taken up again in 1902, the new owner hired thirty-two rabbiters who killed over 250,000 rabbits on the property in five months.[97] But for all the environmental and economic damage they caused, rabbits provided a food source for the less affluent small farmer. Christina Drake (née Webster), born at Moa Creek in 1913, recalled that her family regularly had a meal of 'underground mutton'.

> [We] used to stuff it, and just slit across the back and fold the back legs over the front and tie it that way, very often pot roast it, that was quite nice, and sometimes stewed. If you cut the lower part of the legs off to the mid joint and the tail piece, that gets rid of that rabbit flavour. That could be very nice eating.[98]

← PAGES 146–47
Wining's Wairau NZ April 1851. This painting by Charles Emilius Gold shows a Pākehā man – probably James Wynen – and a Māori woman, sitting in a house or hotel at Wairau and warming themselves by an open fire. Various meats including duck, pūkeko and fish hang from the thatched roof, as well as drying ears of corn. Charles Emilius Gold, Alexander Turnbull Library, A-447-002.

\>
A man and woman preparing food outdoors, while a young girl watches on. The man is skinning a rabbit. Unknown location, c. 1905. Unknown photographer, Hardwicke Knight Collection, purchased 1991, Museum of New Zealand Te Papa Tongarewa, A.009904.

Albert Gordon Duff, who grew up on a family farm at Rimu, just out of Invercargill, recalled in his 2011 interview for the Southland Oral History Project that his grandmother loved eating hares, particularly in soup, and before cooking them she would hang them up until she could pull the hair from their bellies; he reckons that 'they must have been damn well stinking then'.[99]

The idea that anyone with a gun or a rod had at their disposal a bounty of wild foods was one that Pākehā New Zealanders held dear, not only because it fitted with notions of New Zealand as the promised land of plenty, but also because in Britain the right to hunt had been the prerogative of the upper classes.[100] However, wild foods were rarely the main source of sustenance available to Pākehā families, whereas for Māori, access to customary food resources was culturally and economically vital.

Grown and reared

In addition to wild foods, domesticated plants and animals were cultivated and farmed for food. In parts of Aotearoa where the tropical plants they had brought from the Pacific grew successfully, early Māori communities invested a great deal of effort in cultivating, harvesting and storing them correctly. European settlers came with a food culture centred on small-scale food production: everyone who was able to kept a garden and livestock of some sort.[101] They introduced plants and animals to replicate British food traditions, and developed subsistence agriculture alongside large-scale commodity production for export.

Fruit, vegetables and grains

The Polynesians who settled Aotearoa from 1250 to 1300 CE brought an ancient gardening tradition and a number of tropical plants, including kūmara, taro, uwhi, hue, tī pore and aute. Of these, kūmara was the most extensively cultivated Polynesian cultigen, although it did not grow south of Te Pātaka o Rākaihautū Banks Peninsula; and uwhi, taro and hue were grown to a lesser extent.[102] In most parts of tropical Polynesia kūmara is of relatively minor importance as a food crop, but its advantages in

Aotearoa were that it can tolerate cooler conditions, and it has a relatively short growing season. Even in the most suitable regions, however, the supply of kūmara fluctuated, and horticulture could not guarantee a year-round carbohydrate staple.[103] As evidence of the struggle for existence, historian Hazel Petrie points to the many waiata mō te kai kore (songs for those lacking food) and laments for ruined gardens that have been recorded in Māori oral history, as well as to the fact that rangatira assumed primary responsibility for maintaining an ample supply of food.[104] Nevertheless, the survival of Polynesian cultigens indicates that horticulture has been carried out successfully in New Zealand since first settlement.[105]

In Polynesia, where kūmara grows year round, it is propagated by planting shoots, but in Aotearoa kūmara grows only in summer and must be grown from tubers.[106] It was therefore essential to devise an effective storage facility which would keep the kūmara fresh through the winter and allow for re-planting in spring, a facility which took the form of a roofed, drained and sealed pit (rua).[107] These were best classified as semi-subterranean storehouses, made by excavating a large section of ground and then covering the space with a sloped roof. Often this was covered with earth, while inside small drains were built to carry off stormwater.[108] Once built, fronds would be placed on the floor of the pit, and the kūmara or potatoes stacked with great care. As Tom Smiler Junior remembered of his childhood at Waituhi in the 1920s:

> One of the main occupations was tending the kūmara plantation. ... In those days people were always so *careful* handling kūmara and other garden crops. I remember helping the old man [his grandfather] put the kūmara one by one into a flax basket, so carefully, that they wouldn't get bruised. If they got bruised they could go rotten in the kūmara pit. Then I would help him carry the kit to the kūmara pit – all the time he'd be saying in Māori, 'Careful, *careful*, e Hā!'. . . .
>
> . . . Always so much *care*. The reason? Because Māori lived from season to season and those kūmara had to last a year, between one harvest time and the next, so that there was sufficient food to keep everyone alive.'[109]

The same structure could be used to store potatoes, and the concept was adopted by some Pākehā for this purpose.[110]

European explorers brought a range of new plants to Aotearoa. In 1769, for example, Jean-François de Surville gave wheat, peas and rice to Ngāti Kahu at Tokerau Doubtless Bay, though it is unlikely that the seeds grew successfully as Māori were root-crop producers and de Surville could only give instructions for cultivation from seed through a 'pantomime of gestures'.[111] Other introductions were successful, however, and by 1810 potatoes were being grown in quantity right across the country, from the Bay of Islands to the shores of Te Ara a Kiwa Foveaux Strait. Turnips and cabbage were also widespread; cultivated in some places but also proliferating in wild forms.[112]

As trading opportunities expanded, Māori gardeners began cultivating a wider range of introduced plants. Vegetables such as cabbages, pumpkins, marrow, onions, parsnips, carrots, cucumbers, radishes and watermelons were grown throughout the motu and sold to European settlers and visitors, although none on such an extensive scale as the potato.[113] For their own consumption most hapū favoured those foods that could be cooked by existing methods: potatoes, turnips, cabbage, pumpkin, marrows and maize.[114] These supplemented existing food sources but did not supplant them, and food such as aruhe, kūmara and taro were still prevalent.[115] The kō, a wooden digging stick, was the main tool used in gardening in all areas[116] until the introduction of metal hoes, spades and mattocks – which, like the kō, were used by groups working in unison in one field.[117]

By the 1840s hapū in Te Ika-a-Māui had been able to observe missionaries growing, milling and using wheat, and they had sufficient capital to invest in ploughs and water-powered mills.[118] Governor George Grey actively encouraged this investment and gifted carts, horses and ploughs to rangatira, believing that if Māori were engaged in agriculture their property would 'be too valuable to permit them to engage in war'.[119] This commercial farming was carried out communally, and by 1855 iwi in Thames and the Waikato were cultivating sufficient produce to supply Auckland with more than 80,000 bushels of wheat and 30,000 bushels of maize.[120]

The staff of life

In *First Catch Your Weka: A Story of New Zealand Cooking*, David Veart describes bread as a source of comfort and sustenance to the settlers, as well as a statement of cultural identity:[121] 'Initially it was bread that differentiated the colonists from Maori, and getting the first loaf in the oven seems to have been an important cultural marker in the quest for civilisation.'[122] 'Pioneer' tales commonly describe the baking of the first loaf of bread in a camp oven or a colonial oven, and the trouble that went into making and keeping yeast.

In fact, Māori started making and adapting bread recipes very quickly, and recipes for rēwena were published in Māori-language newspapers as early as 1848.[123] The recipe published in *Maori Messenger: Te Karere Maori* began with instructions for making potato yeast, similar to those published in Pākehā texts but with the hops omitted.

> Scrape a good mealy potatoe till it is all in powder, then mix this pulp with some flour and sugar; put one spoonful of sugar and four of flour, mix these with some lukewarm water, pour the whole into a bottle, cork it up and put the bottle to the side of the fire, let it stand twenty-four hours before it is used.

> Tenei ano te tikanga mo te hanga Rewena. – Me waru he riwai, hei te riwai pai, hei te riwai mata; a, muri iho, me whakaranu te neho, me tetahi paraoa me tetahi huka ano hoki; kia kotahi pune (spoonfull) huka, kia wha pune (koko) paraoa. Me whakaranu enei ki te wai mahana, kia pera te mahana me to te waiu. Ringihia katoatia ki roto ki te pounamu, me puru ki te puru pakeha, a kia tata te tu o tana pounamu ki te taha o te ahi – kia kotahi ra, kia kotahi po, e tu ai. Heoi ano ka mutu.[124]

Hilary and John Mitchell, in their history of Nelson and Marlborough, give examples of Māori teaching European settlers how to make rēwena, as for example when Māori women taught Hannah Godsiff how to bake bread at Titirangi in the 1860s.

> This is how it was done:– The oven was made in a bank. Stones on the floor of it. To heat these ovens a small fire was started in the centre, then enough wood put in to heat the oven. This burned down to red hot coals which were spread evenly over the floor of the oven until all burnt away to white ashes. Next the ashes were scraped out.... The hole in the top of the bank which served as a chimney was blocked with wood or stones or the like and also the one in the front that the bread was put in through. To test the heat of the oven before the loaf was put in was carried out by sprinkling a little flour on the bottom of the oven. If it turned nicely brown the oven was just right.[125]

The women are teaching her how to bake bread using a process probably derived from hāngī technology – an example of the blending of old techniques and new ingredients in nineteenth-century cooking.[126]

From this peak, Māori food production declined rapidly in the late 1850s, as land became exhausted, 'unwholesome seeds' contaminated wheat and flour, and the Australian food import market collapsed.[127] Other significant factors were what Alan Grey describes as the 'discouragements and devastation of war', which deprived iwi in the central North Island of their best agricultural lands and shattered the economies of many tribes.[128] The Waitangi Tribunal's *Ngāti Awa Raupatu Report*, for example, traces the impact of land confiscations on Ngāti Awa hapū: it notes that after the raupatu – the indiscriminate government confiscation of land in the wake of the New Zealand Wars – they lost their best cultivatable land, trading vessels and mill, and were forced to relocate to flood-prone blocks close to the military settlement at Whakatāne.[129] While there were signs of recovery in the 1870s, Māori communities lacked the access to development finance, infrastructure and training opportunities that would have allowed them to make the move from arable agriculture to more profitable pastoralism.[130]

Large-scale commercial cropping did not return to pre-war levels, but Māori communities continued to cultivate gardens for local use, and to fulfil their customary obligations. Ngāti Hineuru witnesses for *The Mohaka ki Ahuriri Report* recall that by the early twentieth century potatoes were their staple crop – mostly a very hardy type called parakaraka.[131] Claimants from Te Tau Ihu told the Waitangi Tribunal of the importance of their gardens, particularly as other food supplies such as tāwhara (fruit of the kiekie) and karaka berries became scarce. Paul Morgan, who grew up on a small farm at Motueka in the 1920s and 1930s, reported in evidence on behalf of Ngāti Rārua that 'you could live out of your garden and there was still strong mahinga kai in terms of puha, watercress and seafood. Aside from basics like flour, tea and sugar, our families survived [with] very little need of the grocery store.'[132] Te Maata Gilbert recalls in testimony on behalf of Ngāti Tama that he was taught strict tikanga for gardening by his grandfather, such as always returning the first of the crops to Papatūānuku.[133] Gardening knowledge was passed down from generation to generation and crops were carefully tended by the whole community, as a successful garden was a matter of both pride and necessity.

Rēwena and Rabbit Stew

This photograph by Charles Peet Dawes, taken probably in the early twentieth century, shows whare nestled in beside a stand of trees, with a garden in front. Auckland Libraries Heritage Collections, 1572-1407.

Settlers also drew on centuries-old gardening traditions, and they too faced challenges in adapting their practices to suit local conditions. The first missionaries at the Oihi mission near Rangihoua pā planted a kitchen garden in 1815, but soon found that the location on a clay hillside was unsuitable for gardening.[134] The missionaries at Kerikeri had more success with seeds and plants they brought from New South Wales in 1819, and by 1822 they had nearly 3000 square metres set aside for vegetables and fruits.[135] Their kitchen garden boasted a remarkable variety of plants, including peas, hops, turnips, carrots, radishes, cabbages, potatoes, lettuce, red beets, broccoli, endive, asparagus, cress, onions, celery, melons, berries, citrus fruits, pumpkins, cucumbers, apples, pears, and a range of herbs.[136] The gardens at Paihia, probably established using seeds and plants from Kerikeri, flourished under the ministrations of Richard Davis, a tenant farmer from Dorset who set out to make the missionaries more self-sufficient.[137] In 1831 Davis moved to Waimate to manage the mission farm, and four years later, when visiting there, Charles Darwin described it most favourably as 'a fragment of old England'.[138]

From 1840 settlers took up the task of introducing and fostering the growth of imported plant species.[139] Horticultural societies were established in most major towns within a few years of Pākehā settlement, with the aim of spreading knowledge and fostering enthusiasm for gardening of all sorts. Some immigrants brought seeds and plants with them in their cabin luggage; others wrote home begging for packages of seeds, or took advantage of newly established nurseries.[140] The temperate climate and rich soils meant they could grow a wide range of exotic vegetables to enhance an otherwise fairly monotonous diet.[141]

Chinese goldminers in Otago and on the West Coast had vegetable gardens where they could plant seeds and bulbs imported from China and grow common vegetables such as potatoes.[142] Most of these miners came from the Pearl River Delta region of Guangdong province, where intensive farming was carried out year round on small plots of land. They adapted these techniques in New Zealand and often grew several crops a year, paying particular attention to soil quality and water supply.[143] As goldmining declined towards the end of the nineteenth century, the Cantonese population moved to towns and cities in the North Island, where many took up market gardening. By 1881 the Chinese population of New Zealand was 5004, and 850 of those were market gardeners.[144]

The number of market gardens and other commercial vegetable gardens (mainly growing potatoes, onions and vegetables for processing) increased steadily through the twentieth century, coinciding with a general decline in home vegetable growing.[145] This trend was probably more marked in urban areas than rural, and was driven to some extent by increasingly intensive subdivision. The 1956 census (the first to include statistics about vegetable gardening) reveals some variation between rural and urban areas: approximately 68 percent of rural households grew at least some of their own vegetables, compared with 57 percent of urban households.[146]

∧
A Chinese man with Presbyterian missionary and writer
Alexander Don beside a dwelling and vegetable garden
in Waikaia, c. 1900. Unknown photographer, McNeur
Collection: Photographs of Chinese goldminers who worked
in Otago and Southland goldfields, Alexander Turnbull
Library, 1/2-019146-F.

∧
Mr and Mrs Friend standing in their vegetable garden at Tahatika, Otago, in the early 1900s. Their daughter later wrote that her father was 'a wonderful man. Everything he did was neat. His vegetable garden was lovely to look at, all the rows straight and even' (Guthrie, 'Happy Days', 2010.182.9, Owaka Museum). Unknown photographer, Owaka Museum, CT82.1464e.

Many country families kept an orchard, often with an impressive variety of fruits, so bottling and making preserves were important seasonal tasks, usually performed by women – although in general the allocation of provisioning tasks was quite flexible.[147] As Nancy Grey Osterud notes in *Bonds of Community*, rural men and women 'interacted as producers and processors of family subsistence'.[148] For example, men usually butchered meat, but women often worked alongside them brining or salting it; men cleared the land for vegetable gardens and women tended the crops.[149]

Adela Stewart (née Anderson) started an orchard on a sheep farm at Katikati in June 1879; in it she planted '104 trees: apple, pear, peach, nectarine, cherry, plum, damson, apricot, greengage, fig, loquat, orange, mulberry etc', which, once established, provided '500 to 1,500lbs of jams, jellies, bottled fruits and marmalade every year'.[150] By the end of each summer, she 'was prepared for a siege and stood it'.[151] When Rita Ranginui (née Grey; Te Āti Haunui a Pāpārangi) was growing up at Pipiriki in the 1920s, it was her father who did the preserving: she remembered that he was very careful to utilise whatever resources he could produce on their land, so 'fruit had to be preserved or made jams from, and vegetables had to be preserved and made pickles from'.[152] Rita was one of seventeen children, so these economies were no doubt crucial.

Meat

European settlers came to New Zealand from a food culture marked by contrasts: the chronic malnourishment of the working poor, and the varied, lavish diet of the comfortably off.[153] At events such as the harvest home – an annual feast marking the end of the harvest – rural workers were able to experience some aspects of this 'alternative tradition of plenty', and these experiences shaped their food culture when they arrived in New Zealand.[154] They developed a tradition of eating meat at two or even three meals a day.

According to Tony Simpson, 'New Zealand became overwhelmingly a mutton-eating nation early in its colonial history and remained so well into the twentieth century'.[155] This has certainly been a popular impression, although statistical research from Massey

A collection of glass preserving jars, metal screwtop lids, and a pair of tongs used to hold the hot jars. Various makers including Dominion, Agee and Mason's, Mangawhai Museum, 16-62.

University's Department of Food Technology suggests it is something of a myth, and that consumption of beef has always been higher than mutton.[156] Regardless, there is no doubt that New Zealanders have historically eaten a good deal of mutton – a 1939 survey found the consumption of sheep meat was almost 40 kilograms per head per annum – and it features in many descriptions of rural life.[157]

Perhaps the best-known commentator on station life in New Zealand was the indomitable Lady Barker, who spent two years on a sheep run called Broomielaw (now Steventon) in the Malvern Hills in the 1860s. In 1867 she described the daily bill of fare:

> Porridge for breakfast, with new milk and cream *a discretion*; to follow – mutton chops, mutton ham, or mutton curry, or broiled mutton and mushrooms, not shabby little fragments of meat broiled, but beautiful tender steaks off a leg; tea or coffee, and bread and butter, with as many new-laid eggs as we choose to consume. Then, for dinner, at half-past one, we have soup, a joint, vegetables, and a pudding; in summer, we have fresh fruit stewed, instead of a pudding, with whipped cream. . . . We have supper about seven; but this is a moveable feast, consisting of tea again, mutton cooked in some form of entrée, eggs, bread and butter, and a cake of my manufacture.[158]

It is not surprising, in light of this menu, that Barker later wrote of her time in New Zealand that the 'first object of a housewife's ambition used to be to disguise, as much as possible, the perpetual mutton of which her bill of fare was sure to be composed'.[159] Mutton also featured prominently on the daily menu for shepherds and farm labourers. Shepherds, stationed at solitary outposts dotted around large estates, were allowed to kill an agreed number of sheep for meat to supplement their weekly rations of flour, sugar and tea.[160] The station cook catered for farm workers, and provided 'mutton and potatoes with potatoes and mutton by way of variety'.[161]

George Welch, the owner of a mixed sheep and beef farm just out of Masterton, recorded in the back of his diary that between March 1900 and March 1901 he killed twenty-nine sheep for his family of four and their casual workers, averaging almost two and a half sheep a month.[162] Jill Brewis's father, who purchased a small block of land on the outskirts of Whanganui in 1937, would kill a sheep if the family ran out of meat, and Jill remembered later that '[e]very bit of the sheep was eaten over the next week or so' – brain, sweetbreads, tongue, lambs fry, tripe and all.[163] It was perhaps this habit of eating every part of the animal, as well as the 'hard-times habit of killing inferior old ewes for ourselves and selling the better types of mutton to freezing concerns', that gave mutton meals a certain reputation for stodginess.[164] Guidebooks and newspapers offered hints for disguising mutton as other meats to vary the menu, such as a recipe in the *New Zealand Farmer, Bee and Poultry Journal* for 'Stewed Mutton Imitation of Venison'.[165]

Pork was a mainstay on Pākehā dairy farms; when salted, it kept well and could be used right through the winter. Farmers fed skim milk to their pigs – a by-product of the separating process to remove cream from whole milk.[166] Lydia Mitchell, who lived with her parents and sister on a subsistence block at Huiakama from 1893, recalled that pork 'was the poor man [sic] meat in those days. As they used to say only the squeal was wasted.'[167]

> Pig killing time 3 or 4 neighbours would come along & help kill scrape & hang up in high trees the pigs to set before cutting up. . . . At times the farmers would get up to find that stray dogs had come in the night & had eaten off the pig as much as they could reach sometimes head & shoulders stripped. What a waste of good meat. The bacon when cured would be hung up on hooks [from] the kitchen ceiling it got a fair ammount [sic] of smoke from the chimney it never seemed to go bad.[168]

Ann Easy of Ōtorohanga found the sound of the pigs squealing quite disturbing, so she kept away until it was done then she would help to scrape the pig, pouring over buckets of boiling water to loosen the hairs. Although it was relatively easy, it was still a big job, as 'everything is used. The trotter[s] are corned and boiled and the head makes delicious brawn, so scraping it clean is quite important.'[169]

Māori often ate pork, too, and cooked it in a variety of ways.[170] Common preparations were to steam a whole pig in the hāngī, roast it over an open fire, or boil chunks of meat or pork bones with vegetables.[171] The boil-up, as it was known, became a staple of Māori cuisine, as it was a flexible recipe and convenient for feeding large groups.[172] It also meant that all parts of the animal could be utilised: as Lady Mary Ann Martin noted in her 1869 Māori-language cookbook, the first cookbook to be published in New Zealand, the sides of a salted pig could be sold or traded and the leftovers used for soup.[173]

New Zealanders ate more beef than any other meat in the early 1900s, but in the late 1800s it was something of a luxury for rural folk. As Sophie Johnstone-Smith explains, '[i]n the early days beef was not eaten in great quantities where settlers were scattered, as to kill an ox was

far too extravagant, with the problem of keeping it fresh a real worry.'[174] It was only in areas where there were several families living in fairly close proximity that killing an animal for beef was economical. This may have become more common as rural communities grew and consolidated and travel became less difficult. Winifred Carson, who lived on a small mixed farm at Maruia, recalled that her father would occasionally kill a small cattle beast for meat: he would brine some and share the rest with neighbours.[175] Many small and subsistence farmers, however, seem to have relied on the butcher to supply their beef. R. D. Sharpe gives good reasons for this in his book *Country Occasions*:

> People who kill their own meat ... are apt to kill the animal which is most easily killed. You can run a few sheep into a small pen in some handy spot, catch one and cut its throat without any great effort, if you know what you are doing, but cattle and pigs are not so easy. Furthermore, they are too big. Even with the help of a deep freeze and several neighbours, any sort of cattle beast takes a great deal of eating.[176]

Before the advent of refrigerators, freezers and industrialised farming, processes for home-preserving produce such as meat and eggs had to be carefully managed. With the introduction of cabinet incubators in the 1930s, eggs were available all year round; but for those with free-range hens, egg-laying was still seasonal.[177] As a solution, various forms of egg preservatives were available commercially which provided 'fresh' eggs throughout the year. Norton's was a popular brand: the company promised that a one-shilling tin of their product would preserve 460 eggs, and that the eggs would keep fresh for three years.[178] Their 'premier preservative' was probably sodium silicate (also known as water glass), a solid compound which creates an alkaline solution when dissolved in water. The company recommended using one part preservative to twenty parts water, and keeping the eggs submerged in the liquid until needed.[179] Food historian Jill Brewis recalled that her family used Ovaline, 'a Vaseline-like ointment that was rubbed all over the eggs to exclude air. They were then stored in a stoneware jar kept in the storeroom at the back of the house.'[180] For those of a particularly frugal or self-sufficient

Pig day on the farm. Four men processing pig carcasses by pouring over boiling water and scraping off the hairs, 1920s–1940s. Sydney Smith photograph, Museum of New Zealand Te Papa Tongarewa, O.044699.

Annie and James Armstrong butchering a cattle beast on their farm, Becks, early twentieth century. Unknown photographer, Central Stories Museum and Art Gallery, Alexandra, 00.234.

bent, magazines such as the *Dairy Exporter* offered do-it-yourself alternatives such as this one from 1934, submitted by a reader:

> 1lb Borax, ½ benzene [kerosene] tin boiling water. Stir well, and leave till cold. Then add eggs. I have used duck eggs, which have been perfectly fresh, after having been in for twelve months.[181]

The same issue provided hints for keeping mutton or lamb fresh: the meat should be put in a cheesecloth bag, which was put in another cheesecloth bag filled with salt, and then hung in a tree.[182] This was only a short-term solution, however – if meat was to be kept for more than a few days it needed to be preserved by pickling, smoking or brining it.[183] Winifred Carson remarked of these strategies: 'it is a wonder we lived to tell the story, eating so much salted food – but we all kept fairly well on the whole and the doctor never entered our doorway'.[184]

>
A metal can of J. T. Norton's Premier Egg Preservative, c. 1930s, 125mm high x 225mm diameter. Photograph taken 26 April 2016 (cropped). Te Ūaka The Lyttelton Museum, 3878.1.

Food cultures

Migrants came to Aotearoa New Zealand with a diverse range of food traditions, and recreating familiar dishes in their adopted homeland was a way of staying connected to the places and people they had left behind. Nineteenth-century Scottish migrants were probably accustomed to an oatmeal-based diet, supplemented by kale, fish, potatoes and turnips. The ready availability of fresh produce, meat and wheat flour in New Zealand changed everyday eating habits within a generation, but special occasions were still marked with special dishes such as seedcakes, shortbread, haggis, neeps (swedes) and tatties.[185]

Robert Milliken was 'born of Irish stock', and his daughter Yuilleen recalls that he 'was brought up with meals of Irish origin. Irish stew for instance was dished up fairly regularly plus it was one way of using up neck and scrap pieces of mutton. All vegetables were thrown into that pot – the potatoes cooked until mushy which thickened the stew.' Irish champ was on the menu – 'mashed potatoes with small onions cooked and added, a large dollop put on each plate, the top hollowed out and lots of butter put in' – as was colcannon, a similar dish with cabbage and spices added.[186]

Johanna Wolff, a German immigrant who lived with her parents and siblings at Styx, recorded in her diary in 1888 that when her father brought home a beautiful piece of beef from the butcher, the family made rouladen – a rolled beef dish that her mother Mathilde had made frequently in Germany. Mathilde also made mettwurst, a type of raw, cured sausage, and at Christmastime Johanna and her sister Clare baked treats like prilleken, a ring-shaped pastry from Braunschweig, and stollen, a sweet bread.[187]

Rural labourers from Punjab managed to replicate some traditional dishes: they convinced local storekeepers to stock the wholemeal flour needed to make chapatis; beat pieces of corrugated iron into a makeshift tawa (grill) so they could cook the breads; and made vegetarian curry with vegetables supplied by their employers. Most preferred to work in gangs with other Punjabis, as this allowed them to prepare their own food and avoid any risk of eating beef or its derivatives.[188]

Some migrants came to New Zealand with food traditions they had encountered in other colonial settings. John Cracroft Wilson, a retired ex-East India Company civil servant, planted his Canterbury garden with 'almost all the seeds used in an Indian Curry'.[189] Networks across the British empire gave men like Cracroft opportunities to compare vastly different localities, and changed the nature of home and belonging for some. Cracroft considered himself an English gentleman, but he had been born in India and spent most of his adult life there, so the landscapes he was most familiar with were those of Mangalore and Moradabad, not Oxford or Surrey.[190]

Indian Curry

Slice Onions very small & fry with butter, when nearly done put in the Meat cut into small pieces & fry both till quite done — Mix a little Curry powder with warm water, which add just before dishing, also a little Cream & vinegar both separate —

Ingredients

Uncooked Mutton, 2 or 3 Onions, butter, Curry powder — Salt — a little Cream and vinegar —

Rice to be boiled as dry as possible and dished up by itself in a vegetable dish & the Curry as above by itself in another dish —

A K Taylor

Dairy

Dairy farming for export expanded rapidly in the late nineteenth century, particularly in the North Island where land-hungry settlers carved sections out of the bush. The area of land sown in introduced pasture species in the North Island increased by 4.2 million acres between 1886 and 1906; and in the half-century from 1880 to 1930, dairy exports increased from 0.17 percent to 42 percent of total exports.[191] As the dairy industry expanded, production shifted from farm to factory; instead of making their own dairy products for local trade, farmers transported their milk to factories where it was made into cheese and butter, largely for the British market.[192] The introduction of the first milking machines in the 1890s led to an increase in herd sizes, and from about 1900 home-separators allowed farmers to skim their own milk on-site and send just the cream to the factory – about one-tenth the volume and much easier to transport.[193] Whereas in the 1880s hand-milking eight to ten cows in an hour was considered 'really smart work', by the 1920s, with the benefit of a milking machine and walk-through bails, a single worker could milk up to forty-two cows an hour.[194]

Unlike the job of milking, which was usually shared by different family members, butter-churning was considered a woman's job, and rural women remember it as a real chore. Verna Jones, who lived on a small block of land just out of Kaikohe from 1904 to 1917, made butter with milk from their house cow. She described the process in some detail:

> After the milking was finished the milk was strained into a large tin or enamel dish and covered with butter muslin attached to a light wooden frame.... Twice a day it was skimmed and the cream kept for several days depending on the quantity, when it was tipped into a wooden churn with a frame inside attached to a handle which was turned until butter formed. It sometimes took a short time, but in hotter weather very much longer. When the cream had turned to butter the residue was poured off and then began the laborious job of washing it, a process which had to be repeated until all the water was crystal clear, indicating the buttermilk was removed, but there was more to follow. Every particle of water had to be removed or in a short time the butter would taste and smell anything but appetising.

‹

This recipe for 'Indian curry' – a mutton curry with rice – was handwritten by Alan Kerr Taylor (1832–1890), the owner of a 500-acre country estate on the slopes of Mt Albert. Taylor was born in India, where his father was a colonel in the British army; he came to New Zealand in 1848. Collection of Alberton, Heritage New Zealand Pouhere Taonga, XAH.A.50.

>

The Ideal No. 1 butter churn, made by Broadway Joinery Works in Auckland. The churn is 405mm high, 320mm wide, 335mm deep, and the handle is 170mm long. The wooden cylinder contains four metal paddles, which are turned by a metal crank. Collection of the Mataura and Districts Historical Society Incorporated, MT2012.121.

>

A wooden cheese hoop used to press curds into cheese. Made between 1900 and 1910, it is 230mm high and 350mm in diameter. Farmhouse cheesemaking was a time-consuming and complex process. The cheesemaker had to leave fresh milk to sit until the cream separated, heat it, add rennet, and leave it to coagulate. This created a curd, which they then separated from the whey, salted, and pressed into cheese (McCloy, *Dairy Nation*, 158). Unknown maker, Wyndham and Districts Museum, WY.0000.792.

We used what were called butter-pats to press out the water, the most tedious task of all.[195]

Catharine Squires (née Dewe) of Pyramid Creek, Southland, found this process to be so tedious that she noted in her diary that she sometimes needed 'God's help' just to get it finished.[196]

Cash and barter

Despite all the provisioning strategies put in place by rural New Zealanders to become largely self-sufficient, very few could survive solely on what they produced, caught or gathered. Where transport and communication networks allowed, rural people often established informal trade relationships, exchanging perishable goods such as fresh vegetables and meat with neighbours. Heeni Wharemaru provides a lovely vignette of this type of arrangement in *Through the Eye of the Needle*:

> Freddy Wardel owned the farm next to us. . . . We called [him] Uncle Freddy, but we didn't see a great deal of his wife. Uncle Freddy used to call at my home to see Dad. When he called, he nearly always had something in his hands in the way of food. Yes, they were on friendly terms, and sometimes he'd bring over a slaughtered sheep for the family. In season, Dad would oblige with a part of our harvest of potatoes, kūmara and other vegetables. They exchanged food, but without any sort of words being said. There was a lot of that among different families while I was growing up in those days. There seemed to be just caring – caring in the way of food, vegetable [sic] and meat.[197]

Sophie Johnstone-Smith notes in *Battles, Buggies and Babies*: 'Pigs not needed for sale or fattening were killed and shared with the neighbours, who did likewise when they had meat to share.'[198] She explains that, as it was almost impossible to keep meat fresh in the summer, the barter benefited everybody: it was '[c]ommunism at its best'.[199]

Informal trade was common among Māori and Pākehā farming families. Members of geographically isolated rural communities relied

on one another for practical assistance and resources. As Mary Scott (née Clarke) put it in her 1966 autobiography, '[i]t was impossible to be entirely independent. You were a community, and you expected to help one another in a time of need; there was, of course, no one else to turn to, and no Welfare State to take over.'[200] When cash was scarce, barter became an even more important provisioning strategy. Amy Yorke recalled in her account of farming during the Depression of the 1930s that, with no land of their own, she and her husband Howard had to work for others in exchange for food.

> The next most pressing need [after shelter] was work, in order that we might eat adequately, for this was becoming an obsession with us as hunger made its inroads on our energy and optimism. But, as we had been told ad nauseam, jobs were scarce as hen's teeth, especially jobs that were paid for in hard cash. So Howard had to be content with odd jobs for neighbouring farmers, such as cleaning or digging drains, splitting posts for battens, mending fences, and so on, and he received in return the odd sack of potatoes or bag of firewood. Occasionally, when the farmer had killed a sheep or a pig, we were given a few chops and these were real feast days for us.
>
> I was lucky enough to get a job tending the garden of an elderly lady with a bad back. She had a house cow which provided her with more milk than she required for her daily needs, so I received a billy of milk every day in return for keeping her garden tidy.[201]

Eventually Howard was able to get government relief work for fifteen shillings a week, which meant they could buy bread, tea, sugar, oatmeal and meat – things that could not be obtained by barter, 'and were all the more valued on that account'.[202]

Purchasing items such as flour, sugar and tea could present a major logistical challenge for those living in isolated rural areas. Mabel Whitaker noted in 'Pioneer Tales': 'In a back-country district, distances are a prime factor in the living of its people.' The distance to suppliers meant those living in the country had to buy and store provisions in prodigious quantities.[203] When Evelyn Hosken (née Vincent) took up the Simons Hill sheep run in the Mackenzie Country in 1911, she would order a year's worth of supplies at a time, amounting to six 200lb sacks of flour, twelve 56lb bags of sugar, a 50lb chest of tea, and rice, oatmeal, and salt in 25lb bags.[204] Mona Anderson (née Holland), who moved to Mount Algidus Station in 1940, had to get used to 'buying flour and sugar in hundredweights instead of pounds, and ordering dried fruits and canned things by the case instead of the tin'.[205] She, too, had to get stores in once a year; she explained that the stores were 'sent to the nearest rail-head about fifty miles away, from where the transport brought them up to the iron store across the river. There they stayed until someone could get the dray or waggon across to collect them.'[206] It was not just 'backblocks' households that purchased in bulk, however: Lily Winter, who lived on a farm at Karamea in the 1920s with her parents and eight siblings, recalled that their weekly grocery order included a 100lb bag of flour and a 70lb bag of sugar.[207]

Rural people who lived closer to town might have fresh goods delivered more regularly. Ann Easy, for instance, wrote that a horse-drawn butcher's cart would visit the family farm at Ormondville twice a week:

> The body was like a huge box with a door at the back. It was fastened at the top and when it was let down it formed a table for the butcher to work on. There was meat hanging from hooks around the side and from the roof. The heavier pieces were on the floor. He would bring forward whatever you asked for with a long hook. He carried his steel, knife, chopper and scales and perched upon the seat beside the driver was an enormous basket of sausages, a complete travelling butcher's shop.[208]

Ann later married and moved to Te Rau a Moa near Te Awamutu, where there was a butcher's shop with no attendant but with meat preserved in brine that the customer could cut and weigh, then record their purchase in an account book.[209] Other communities had travelling greengrocers, fishmongers and bakers – although, as Geoffrey Duff noted of the bread delivery at Tarras, not all households availed themselves of the service. Perhaps they preferred to bake their own bread, or perhaps 'the sight of the express drivers' [sic] dog reclining on the unwrapped loaves in the body of the vehicles was too much for the more fastidious'.[210]

Grocers were important figures in the communities they serviced: they provided the scattered households not only with essential foodstuffs but also with gossip and news, and they were often remembered very fondly. Rhoda McWhannell of East Taieri recals that she fell in love with the family's grocer as a child:

> His store was a fascinating place, which kept everything under the sun. A supermarket would be a featureless establishment beside the wealth of merchandise in that one small store. Mother's order was always brought and delivered at the kitchen door by Ernie Pleugh. He was a wiry little fellow who drove a big van, and his round covered many a long mile of rough country roads.[211]

Later, when their maid Cassie got engaged to Ernie, Rhoda made a special visit to the store to tell the owner she was extremely put out, as she had wanted to marry Ernie herself.

Gwen Mackenzie recalls that the local grocer would drive up once a week to their farm at Cairnsmore to take the family's grocery order, and her mother would always have scones and fruitcake ready to offer him with the customary cup of tea. Gwen suspected that this ritual was repeated in every household in the valley: 'He was probably like many parsons of the day – it was polite to have a cup of tea with every lady one calls on. It took a strong bladder.'[212] These grocers probably saw more of the New Zealand countryside than almost anyone else, and provided a crucial service for rural households.

Not all grocers were such benign figures, however, and some exploited the isolation of the communities they served to demand high prices. Itinerant rural labourers were much more likely to get into debt, as they had to purchase a greater proportion of their provisions and were not assured of a steady income. Māori became increasingly reliant on this work as their opportunities to participate in other agricultural industries diminished. Occupations such as shearing, which had a fixed season, allowed for customary food-gathering practices to continue as a supplement to store-bought goods, but for those engaged in year-round

Interior of D. A. Jolly & Sons shop, Cromwell. Unknown photographer, Collection of the Cromwell Museum.

A travelling butcher's shop on the North Island Main Trunk Line. Tibbutt photograph, originally published in the *Auckland Weekly News*, 8 February 1906, p. 10, Auckland Libraries Heritage Collections, AWNS-19060208-10-3.

A TRAVELLING BUTCHER'S SHOP ON THE NORTH ISLAND MAIN TRUNK LINE.

Tibbutt, Photo.

work such as gumdigging or roadwork there were fewer opportunities to produce, hunt or gather their own food, meaning they were dependent on the local storekeeper for provisions.

In the case of the gumdiggers of Northland, this insecure lifestyle caused whole communities to become 'ensnared in an unwholesome system of debt peonage'.[213] As the Waitangi Tribunal's *Muriwhenua Land Report* notes, gum traders usually operated the only stores on the fields, and were able to charge prices far higher than market rates. The teacher at Te Kao School noted in 1888 that:

> To the Natives the gumfields have been a curse. They have disregarded the raising of crops, as in the former years, with the exception of potatoes and kumeras. With all of their earnings upon the gumfields, they are deeply in debt, and they and their families for the most part are badly clad. All over the gumfields the Natives are in a species of bondage to the storekeepers and it is to the latter's advantage to keep them so. Gum is at present at a very low price – but such is not the case with provisions which are thirty percent higher than can be purchased anywhere else.[214]

One witness told a royal commission in 1898: 'Storekeepers do not intend that a digger shall leave the field with a shilling in his possession. If your bill at the store is not a big one he will not buy your gum, leaving it on your hands on purpose to punish you for not having dealt more largely with him.'[215] Workers were thus locked into a situation of 'precarious dependency', and later, when the bottom fell out of the market, they became trapped in poverty.[216]

In various Waitangi Tribunal proceedings since the 1990s, the crown has claimed that 'land ownership is not an economic panacea'[217] and that landlessness is not tantamount to poverty.[218] Economic alternatives were available to Māori, the crown has argued, and thus a causal link between inequality and land loss is not easily attained.[219] However, as the Tribunal found for the Hauraki claim: an 'advantage of holding on to land as an asset was that, whatever the difficulties of utilising it at any point in time, it was a form of stored wealth to be tapped when needed. This alone made it more than a simple economic equivalent to, say, labouring or road-working.'[220]

Economic alternatives to farming, such as mining or sawmilling, also failed to provide the secure subsistence that came from land ownership: when the resource was gone, the money went with it, and then the workers had no fixed assets to fall back on. Having land gave people economic options; and by implementing policies that privileged Pākehā smallholders and adversely affected Māori ownership and management of land, the crown denied Māori chances to prosper in the colonial economy.[221]

By the turn of the twentieth century the basic structures of rural New Zealand had been laid down, both physically and figuratively. The land had been divided into an orderly grid of small farms, most owned and worked by single families in cooperation with others in the community. On their smallholdings, rural households implemented a variety of provisioning strategies that allowed them to be largely self-sufficient. While there is much to admire about this industriousness and innovation, the fact remains that these smallholdings with their chicken coops, gardens and orchards were built at the expense of Māori economic power. Māori communities adopted new subsistence techniques and adapted centuries-old ones; but, as Matiu Rei reported in his evidence for Ngāti Toa, the provisioning practices that survived into the twentieth century were 'fragments or residual expressions of rangatiratanga' reflecting the 'oppression of subsistence' and not the full and undisturbed possession of lands and fisheries.[222] Nevertheless, mātauranga Māori was retained and passed down through food gathering, and the skills and knowledge inherent in these processes are still taught and celebrated within hapū and whānau. As Simon Kaan and Ron Bull wrote in 2013, 'in gathering the food, we gather the stories that give us nourishment'.[223]

4
Women's work?

Gender roles in rural Aotearoa

They talk about a woman's sphere
As if it had a limit
There's not a place in earth or heaven
There's not a task to mankind given
There's not a blessing or a woe
There's not a whisper, yes or no,
There's not a life
There's not a birth
There's not a thing on this great earth
That has a feather's weight of worth
Without a woman in it.

— 'A Woman's Sphere', unknown contributor to *Home and Country*, 1930

In this poem, written in 1930, a contributor to *Home and Country* magazine pushes against a narrow view of a 'woman's sphere'.[1] Middle-class, Christian understandings of public and private spheres dictated that a woman's role was to care for house and home while the male breadwinner went out and distinguished himself in the world of work. Although gendered labour divisions were never practised as rigorously as they were preached, a social convention developed in which the kitchen was associated primarily with women, and used only for food preparation. It became women's domain, in which they could reign supreme or, depending on your viewpoint, from which they could not escape.

Some of the middle-class assumptions shaping the idea of the kitchen as 'women's domain' were not accurate in rural settings, however. The kitchen could serve both public and private functions; it was not used solely by women; nor was the work of women confined to that space. In their autobiographical writing, interviews and contributions to rural magazines, women expressed a range of viewpoints on domestic work, shaped by dominant cultural values, emotional norms, attachment to the land and 'the country', and fluctuations of the agricultural economy. The kitchen was the setting for a wide range of experiences, and rural women negotiated their roles and responsibilities in diverse ways.

Gender and cooking in te ao Māori

If we are what we eat, reasons historian Michael Symons, the people who made our meals made us.[2] He encourages us to think carefully about the people who have cooked our food, and he points out that while there are innumerable books *for* cooks, in the form of recipe books and manuals, there are precious few *about* them. Histories of food often take it as a given that women are responsible for cooking, and instead focus on changes in diet and food preparation. But although the majority of domestic cooks across time have been women, there have also been variations across classes and cultures that deserve further attention.[3]

In pre-contact Māori society, the responsibility for cooking and other forms of labour was dictated by rank as well as gender.[4] There were three main groupings or ranks in Māori society: chiefs (rangatira); commoners (known by many names, including tūtūā, marahea and ware); and slaves (again known by many names, such as pononga, taurekareka, mōkai and hunga).[5] According to Mākereti Papakura, 'cooking was done by women and pononga (slaves), but mainly by the women, who waruwaru (scraped) the kumara and prepared the other vegetable food, and very often prepared the hangi.'[6] Those of chiefly rank were vulnerable to having their tapu contaminated or diminished by contact with prepared food, which is noa, so cooking was the work of slaves or commoners. It was most often female captives who prepared and cooked food, but male slaves are also known to have performed this work.[7]

Recent research exploring the connection between tapu and gender suggests that all Māori labour before European settlement was determined by the nature of tapu involved in a task, and that while there may have been a tendency towards gender division in the performance of some tasks, this was not the overarching determinant.[8] There was a general association between women and food preparation, but there were also distinctions. Female rangatira, for example, possessed the tapu of rank and were therefore exempt from carrying food or cooking meals. If they kept slaves they may have overseen their work, as Dubouzet noted in Otago in 1840:

> I found about a dozen Zealanders of both sexes gathered there: they were said to be slaves. The women were busy preparing the potatoes, fish and shellfish for a meal; others were making a few cloaks and baskets with native flax. They all took orders from the chief's wife who sat outside and directed the work with the harshness of a true matron.[9]

Everyone in the community worked, regardless of rank or gender, but tasks were assigned based on who was safest and sufficiently skilled enough to perform them.[10]

Wāhine Māori have the ability to whakanoa – to remove tapu or make normal – a power that is essential to the wellbeing of all Māori. As Rangimarie Rose Pere explains it:

> The influence and power of noa is very significant to the physical well-being of people by freeing them from any quality or condition that make them subject to spiritual and/or ceremonial restriction and influences. The concept of noa is usually associated with warm, benevolent, life-giving, constructive influences including ceremonial purification.[11]

Linda Tuhiwai Smith writes about whakanoa in similar terms: she suggests that '[t]he power to make things noa contains within it the power over day-to-day life, over food and over commerce.'[12]

These caring, life-giving properties were lost on early male ethnographers and anthropologists such as Elsdon Best, who took the ability to whakanoa to mean that women were perpetually noa and had no mana.[13] They cast this as a destructive force: Best wrote that 'the very fact of a woman passing over a tapu spot would pollute or destroy its sanctity, for such is the effect of that sex.'[14] Māori researchers exploring mana wāhine reject these Western interpretations of women's roles; they argue instead that before colonisation mana wāhine and mana tāne were complementary, and that while men and women had distinct tasks, they were not necessarily hierarchical.[15] Certainly, rank and power did exist in pre-contact Māori society, but social dynamics were likely dictated by whakapapa rather than gender.[16] For this reason – and many others –

> Māori men tending a hāngī pit, Gisborne, 1919. James McDonald photograph, Alexander Turnbull Library, PAColl-0477-17.

'the roles of men and women in traditional Māori society can be understood only in the context of the Māori world view'.[17]

As discussed in chapter 2, traditionally the most common method for cooking large quantities of food was the hāngī, and in the nineteenth century in many instances it was women who put down the hāngī. Mākereti wrote that women often prepared the hāngī at Whakarewarewa; and Te Rangi Hīroa noted that in his village in Taranaki, women usually commanded the cooking fires.[18] Richard Taylor, a CMS missionary who settled in the Far North and Whanganui, describes the process for putting down a hāngī in his 1855 *Te Ika a Maui*; and he notes that the cook is generally a woman (sometimes two or more) who deftly removes the hot stones, clears the embers, lines the oven, lays the food, and covers the hole with mats and earth.[19] In *Where the White Man Treads* (1905) William Baucke gives a detailed description of cooking in an earth oven, and notes that:

> It has taken longer time to write than a smart wahine, experienced in every detail, would have taken to do it. Fine judgement, quick action, and having everything to hand, are necessary to be an accomplished haangi-builder. Your eyes are of little use, because the rising, hissing steam is all over. When the haangi is ready to be opened (in from one to two hours) two women – one on each side – will take hold of the overlapping edges of the topmost mat and lift it, earth and all, off carefully; the remaining covers are also dexterously flicked aside, and when the steam has drifted away – there you are![20]

While these sources indicate that in the nineteenth century it was often women who laid the hāngī, in the twentieth century it became more commonly associated with men. In a discussion of traditional uses of fire, a kuia from Onepū suggested that 'according to tradition, the hangī was only dug on the marae and the customary practice of making, laying and upheaving the hangī was handled only by men'.[21] Patricia Tauroa (Ngāti Kahu, Ngā Puhi) explained in evidence for the Mana Wāhine Kaupapa Inquiry by the Waitangi Tribunal that in her experience most food preparation is shared by all members of the community, but 'the only activity that was deemed to be "men's work", was the preparation of the hāngi pit, putting the hāngi down, the actual care of the hāngi, and the

uncovering when food was cooked'.²² It is not clear precisely when putting down and cooking the hāngī became a job to be performed by men, but when Anne Salmond carried out her study of ceremonial gatherings in the 1970s she found that: 'Broadly speaking, men cook the main course while women prepare the food and cook the dessert.'²³

    Cooking, like most forms of labour in traditional Māori society, was a communal activity. In the eighteenth century whānau were independent economic and work units, while hapū – groups of closely related whānau – were the primary political units.²⁴ Clusters of hapū formed into communities under the authority of a rangatira, but these communities changed throughout the year as groups or individuals travelled to other mahinga kai to harvest and process various products.²⁵

Use rights for resources such as bird-trapping trees, berry trees, rat runs and fishing spots generally passed from individual to individual, rather than hapū to hapū, and whānau cultivated gardens and gathered food for their own use. Larger-scale economic activities such as annual fishing expeditions or the cultivation of crops for planned battles, constructions or feasts required cooperation at the level of the hapū or community.[26] Work such as gardening, preparing food, looking after children or building a pā was shared, and 'mutual help was a fundamental expression of blood kinship'.[27] Collective labour continued to underpin the Māori economy through the nineteenth century, directed either by kaumātua or rangatira, depending on the task and the workforce involved.[28]

Within the whānau, older women took responsibility for children while younger women performed heavier work.[29] As Kuni Jenkins explains, '[t]he home unit was part of the whole kainga. Grandmothers, aunts and other females and male elders were responsible for rearing the children of the kainga. The natural parents were not the sole caregivers.'[30] Annie Mikaere adds that this form of social organisation gave women greater flexibility than in a nuclear family, as with so many caregivers in the community women were able to take on a variety of roles, including leadership positions.[31]

In 1994 a group of Māori women lodged the Mana Wāhine claim with the Waitangi Tribunal, in which they argued that the crown's denial of mana wāhine had serious adverse consequences for the social, economic, cultural and spiritual wellbeing of wāhine Māori.[32] When the hearings finally began in 2021, witnesses gave evidence of the mana of women in te ao Māori, the balance of wāhine and tāne, and wāhine rangatiratanga.[33] Before colonisation, they argued, Māori women's lives were not ordered by the 'homemaker' model: 'Women were child bearers, lovers, writers of waiata, holders of whakapapa, te whare tapere performers, means of procreation and ensuring tribal continuity, but never the individual "mother of children" as defined today'.[34] In some iwi, female rangatira possessed the tapu of rank, and a number of Māori women were visionaries or mediums.[35]

The rich and varied lives of Māori women were invisible to the European observers who came to study them; as Jenkins puts it, '[w]hat the colonizer found was a land of noble savages narrating . . .

stories of the wonder of women'. But rather than tell those stories, they instead imposed their own understandings of the place of women and, in doing so, diminished the mana of wāhine Māori.[36] Operating within their own cultural and gender frameworks, ethnographers tended to either ignore Māori women or cast them as wanton, immoral or undisciplined.[37] As a result Māori women in the present have had to reconstruct the lives of their female forebears, and this has been fundamental to the fight for recognition of mana wāhine.[38]

Colonial officials did not recognise the political authority of wāhine Māori, and from the outset the crown chose to exclude women from political and economic discussions and decisions. The fact that only a small number of women signed te Tiriti o Waitangi was, according to Mikaere, less a reflection of Māori gender relations than 'an indication of the influence of Christianity and the fact that those seeking signatories largely ignored the possibility of women signing'.[39] While European males sought to trade and negotiate only with Māori men and assumed that Māori women's proper role was in the domestic sphere, wāhine continued to exercise their leadership by fighting in the New Zealand Wars, bringing cases to the Native Land Court, and petitioning the crown on land issues.[40] They fought to retain their sense of self despite the expectations placed on them by colonial frameworks – as demonstrated by Wetekia Ruruku Elkington (Ngāti Koata and Te Āti Awa), who married John Elkington in the 1890s:

> Just before she got married, an uncle of John Arthur gave him the advice that 'you've got to let her know right from the start who's the boss'. So the first morning after they were married John Arthur kicked Wetekia out of bed and told her to go and get him breakfast. Wetekia got up, put her clothes on, walked down to the beach, and swam home. John Arthur waited for her to come back: after two weeks he went down to see when she was coming home and her father told him, 'You can't treat her like that, she's ariki.'[41]

One way in which colonial authorities attempted to impose their own gender roles and hierarchies on Māori was through church and native schools, which placed a heavy emphasis on teaching girls domestic skills such as needlework, dressmaking and cookery.⁴² The school curriculum was designed to prepare girls for their future roles as wives and mothers within the structure of the nuclear family, and thus played an assimilatory role.⁴³

Māori collectivism came under attack as land confiscation, individualisation of land title and urban migration forced whānau to break into nuclear family units, and 'as the whānau unit became progressively smaller, the responsibilities of individual women grew'.⁴⁴ Māori women were increasingly expected to take primary responsibility for the care of children. As Arapera Blank (Ngāti Porou, Ngāti Kahungunu, Rongowhakaata, Te Aitanga-a-Māhaki) wrote in 1974, this imposed a heavy burden: 'It was one thing to survive as a member of a group in which three or more generations of an extended family nurtured the strong and the weak, as was the custom; it is another and more exacting task to manage as a small unit of father, mother, and children'.⁴⁵ Te Onehou Phillis (née Manuera; Ngāti Awa) of Te Teko explained how the family unit operated for her parents, Te Pareake and Eruera:

> While our father was developing his skills to cope with the demands of his hapū and community, our mother was also developing her own skills to cope with the demands of her own family – our health, wellbeing and comfort. In that, she had every help from Dad, who was always on the look-out for labour-saving devices that would improve our way of life. On the home front, before the modern electric stove came into our home, Dad lit the coal range every morning, making sure there was plenty of wood on hand. He cooked our porridge for breakfast, supplemented with the left-over 'boil-ups' from the previous evening meal.⁴⁶

Te Onehou and her siblings also had plenty of work to do to support Te Pareake: 'our mother was a very hard worker and expected us to be equally hard working, so there never seemed to be any let-up from the chores'.⁴⁷

Te Kui (Merimeri Penfold; Ngāti Kurī, Te Aupōuri) recalls that during her childhood in the 1920s and 1930s she was expected to help her mother cook for their large family, performing odd jobs in the kitchen as well as helping with childcare.

> My siblings, who numbered twelve, followed me in quick succession. Caring for such numbers was demanding for my mother, more so because each year brought a new addition to her flock.
>
> Under such circumstances I grew up very quickly. I became my mother's daily chief help at a very early age. I fetched and carried, cradling or feeding the baby, watching or adding wood to the fire, removing and replacing flax floor-mats when tidying the house, and gathering the washing from the fence line.[48]

Maree Millar (née Leef; Ngā Puhi, Te Arawa) grew up in Whirinaki in a family of seventeen. All of the children – male and female – were taught to cook and sew, but also to put up fences and use tools. Maree could cook a three-course meal by the time she was nine – 'no problem there' – and everyone shared in whatever work needed to be done.[49]

Cooking and other domestic work within the home were increasingly seen as a mother's responsibility, although as demonstrated by these examples, husbands and especially children had to help. In the context of the nuclear family, food preparation was transformed from a shared form of productive labour to a woman's duty, and the family kitchen correspondingly transformed, in theory if not necessarily in reality, into a gendered space.[50]

Gender and cooking in te ao Pākehā

In the early decades of the twentieth century the domestic work of Pākehā women was subjected to close official scrutiny, as their role as mothers and homemakers was seen as crucial to the survival and purity of the race. New ideas about preventative health, and concern for the future of the race and empire, elevated the status of motherhood to 'a matter of national importance'.[51] Institutions such as the Plunket Society, the Department of Public Health, the Women's Institute and the Home Science Extension Service reached out to rural women and preached to them the importance of their work in safeguarding the family's health and happiness, while at the same time introducing a set of domestic standards grounded in home science. Women were now expected not only to cook, but to cook balanced, nutritious meals in a safe, germ-free environment, thereby protecting the health of their families and, by extension, the future of the nation.⁵² More than that, because servants were scarce and men's work was elsewhere, women were expected to do it all on their own, adopting principles from science and industry to make their work as efficient as possible.

The idea of the kitchen as a gender-specific space is relatively modern, derived from middle-class ideals that became social norms in Britain and British colonies towards the end of the nineteenth century.⁵³ Sara Pennell points out in *The Birth of the English Kitchen* that the early modern kitchen was not a space that excluded male labour; in fact, male cooks ran most aristocratic kitchens. In addition, in smaller working-class homes, room specialisation was not often possible, and any notion of the space 'as functionally and exclusively female or feminized falter[ed] before the varied roll-call of servants, lodgers, children and visitors' it might contain.⁵⁴ Even in the mid-nineteenth century, the era of domesticity triumphant, the middle-class kitchen was a somewhat ambivalent space in terms of ideal Victorian womanhood. It was unclear whether the woman of the house should demonstrate her knowledge and power in the kitchen by managing servants and supplies, or 'submit to subjugation' as a hands-on housewife.⁵⁵ Pennell and others have shown that the idea of the kitchen as a gendered space, until the late nineteenth century at least, was time-, place- and class-specific. The same was true in New Zealand, where gender roles in relation to food preparation and cooking also depended on the cultural and social situation.

The rural Pākehā population in the nineteenth century was overwhelmingly male; in 1864, at the height of the ratio imbalance, there were 163 men to every 100 women.⁵⁶ As Charlotte Macdonald notes, it was therefore more common for colonial men to share a table with other men than one 'where a woman presided over teapot and breadboard'.⁵⁷ Samuel Butler, a renowned novelist who was also a runholder in Canterbury from 1860 to 1864, advised prospective pastoralists that they would likely need to hire a few good bushhands as well as a bullock driver and shepherd, but that between them they would need to manage the cooking as best they could.

> [You] must be content to wash up yourself, taking your full part in the culinary processes, or you will soon find disaffection in the camp;

but if you can afford to have a cook, have one by all means. . . .
The difficulty is that good boys are hard to get, and a man that is
worth anything at all will hardly take to cooking as a profession.
Hence it comes to pass that the cooks are generally indolent and
dirty fellows, who don't like hard work. Your college education, if
you have had one, will doubtless have made you familiar with the
art of making bread; you will now proceed to discover the mysteries
of boiling potatoes. The uses of dripping will begin to dawn
upon you, and you will soon become expert in the manufacture
of tallow candles. . . .
. . . Your natural poetry of palate will teach you the proper
treatment of the onion, and you will ere long be able to handle that
inestimable vegetable with the breadth yet delicacy which it requires.
Many other things you will learn, which for your sake as well as my
own I will not enumerate here.[58]

William Mills had a similar period of bachelorising while setting up his 550-acre property between the Rangitīkei and Pōrewa rivers in the mid-1880s. He wrote to his parents that he had taken on 'an old 43rd [Regiment] man' to help him on the farm, and that he 'is really a very good cook'.[59] Some men carried on using their cooking skills after they married: Lydia Mitchell described her father Frederick Myers as a 'great cook'; he had done a lot of cooking while camping out on roading contracts, and she recalled the lovely cakes and puddings he would make for the family at Christmastime.[60]

    A small number of households employed domestic servants to perform some or all of the work in the kitchen. The exact figures are difficult to determine, but in 1881 approximately eleven in every 100 households (rural and urban) employed servants.[61] The rural households that did employ help varied considerably: some large stations employed a dozen or more servants (see pages 44–46), but most middle-class households that employed help had only one or two 'general' servants who performed a wide range of tasks.[62] This was a historically specific phenomenon quite distinct from the 'upstairs/downstairs' structure of large houses, where servants and their employers lived together in close proximity but with markedly different levels of comfort.[63]

The supply of domestic servants never came close to meeting the demand, and as a consequence some settlers had to learn how to cook, clean and perform a host of other domestic duties they had previously considered beneath them.[64] Some revelled in the freedom this brought, and welcomed the chance to learn practical skills. Mrs William, for example, wrote in her 1883 guide for emigrating women, *Facts: Or, The Experiences of a Recent Colonist in New Zealand*: 'you can make a small fixed income go further by personal labour of a pleasing and healthy kind in the colonies than in England, where the narrow-mindedness of society in general considers, for sooth, that you lose caste by sharing in the household work; where, indeed, nothing is more unpardonable than to acknowledge that you do so!!'[65] She advised young women to take advantage of the informality of the colonial setting and to be empowered by their expanded domestic role: 'Never despise little things, nor think any work derogatory. Knowledge is power, and there are many domestic duties to learn, highly serviceable to you in any future capacity, either as wife or mother.'[66]

Not all settlers were quite so enthused about their domestic duties, however, and some found, in particular, that learning how to cook was not as straightforward as Mrs William would have them believe. Sarah Courage recounts in her 1896 autobiography *Lights and Shadows of Colonial Life* the difficulties of running a station house when she and her husband Fred had no practical cooking skills and unreliable domestic staff. Early in their tenure they discovered that their cook, known as 'Mrs Bacchus', had a drinking habit, and quickly sent her on her way.

> We were in an unpleasant predicament, to say the least.
> 'What is to be done now?' said Fred. 'What indeed?' I replied, while Jane [the nursemaid] looked on in blank amazement; for in addition to the cooking for ourselves which had to be done, there was bread to be made for two shepherds, two carpenters, ourselves and the groom. 'Who was to make it?' was the question.
> Now I had never made bread in my life; neither had Jane; and I knew very little of cooking either, so stood forth a confessed ignoramus.[67]

A group of men sitting around a table at a bush camp, 1920s. Harold Marsh photograph, W. H. Marsh Collection, Albertland Heritage Museum Inc., 2004.2.97.831.

A bachelor's home in the Far North. Unknown photographer, originally published in the *Auckland Weekly News*, 30 October 1902, p. 11, Auckland Libraries Heritage Collections, AWNS-19021030-11-1.

Sarah had a cookery book to help her, but noted that it was 'often disappointing, being vague at times and misleading at others, so many necessary details being left out'.[68] Similarly Lady Barker, although she was a good deal older than Sarah and had been married for years, found that she was still 'perfectly ignorant' of practical housework: 'Here it is necessary to know *how* everything should be done; it is not sufficient to give an order, you must also be in a position to explain how it is to be caried [sic] out.'[69] She also found cookbooks unhelpful – 'but a broken reed to lean on in a real emergency'.[70]

Some arrivals found that prosperity in the new world could be hard won, and servants were an expense they could no longer afford. Agnes Emma Hall (née Dryden) and her husband George suffered heavy losses on their station near Ashburton in 1862, 'in consequence of which the strictest economy [was] necessary'. Agnes's sister-in-law Rose wrote to a family member: 'They have to be without a servant and poor Agnes has washing and cooking and everything to do' – although later in the year Agnes was able to hire a man to do the cooking while she did all the housework.[71] Even with someone to work in the kitchen and help lift the heavy boiler on washing day, Agnes never had a moment to spare, and she wrote: 'Somehow or other I manage very well generally but I assure you it is heavy work sometimes'.[72] Later, when Agnes began to give her daughter lessons in domestic work, she wrote that 'that is knowledge every woman requires and the sooner it is learnt the better; for though I should not like to see our dear girl having to do servants' work, I should like her to know how to do *everything*, so as never to be at the mercy of her servants. . . . I do *not like* being without a servant, yet it is very pleasant to feel that if deprived of one you are not quite helpless.'[73]

The number of domestic servants declined even further in the late 1800s, and the average household had to make do without help.[74] Macdonald notes that while they were making a virtue of necessity, this was also a point of pride for many, and a strong tradition of independent householding developed 'in which the household's ability to sustain itself was highly valued'.[75] Mary Scott, who devotes an entire chapter in her autobiography to her adventures as an amateur cook, notes that: 'Whatever your job, it is always the same – a matter of getting used to it. So, of course, with housework and the problems of backblocks catering. I was very much at sea at first but I settled into it before too long.'[76] For Joan Millar, 'getting used to it' meant learning to make jam, preserves and pickles, in addition to the usual cooking; looking back, she reflected that 'now the young women have so many appliances to do all their work, they don't really know what hard work is'.[77] The physical strength, adaptability and hardiness that were a source of pride for the 'good, keen man'[78] were matched by the resourcefulness and resilience of the useful woman. She, too, had to learn to rough it, and mastering the art of backblocks cooking was a sign of success.

Alice and Bryan, possibly domestic servants, doing the washing at Clayton Station, c. 1890. James Dundas Hamilton photograph, Clayton Station Collection, South Canterbury Museum, 2011/028.507.

Domestic service in the country

There was a brief resurgence in the number of women in domestic service during the Great Depression of the late 1920s and early 1930s when other jobs were scarce. Mary Findlay (née Wilkinson), a 'daughter of the Depression', was forced to enter domestic service as a young woman, and she took up a position on a dairy farm in Central Otago. She worked for Stan and Mabel Cameron, who managed the farm for a salary, and they all lived and ate together. Mary vividly recalled her first impression of the kitchen:

> It was dominated by an enormous range, which stood in the centre of the room. Nearby was a vast table set for dinner, and on the back wall was a sideboard, fit mate for Westminster Abbey....
>
> ... Mrs Cameron had said 'a lot of hard work'. This kitchen suggested there was truth in the remarks.

After some time at the farm Mary was asked about the differences between working in town and working in the country. She explained to Stan that:

> 'It's different. I mean there's meals and dishes and cleaning up. That's the same, but everything else is different.'
>
> 'You mean the country life?'
>
> 'Well yes, I suppose that makes the differences, but I was thinking more of the change of emphasis.'
>
> 'What do you mean by "change of emphasis"? That's a bit highsounding to me.'
>
> 'Sorry. I think I meant that here some work is regarded as more important than it is in town, and vice versa.'
>
> 'Go on.'
>
> 'Take meals. You eat much more because you do hard work and have longer hours, but you don't spend so much time at the table.'
>
> There was general laughter, after which May enquired, 'You don't mean we eat like pigs?'
>
> I was trying to clarify my thoughts.
>
> 'No. I don't mean you eat fast, just that you don't fuss. No, that's not quite right either. The food here is much better than you get in town and it's just as well cooked and nicely served, at least I hope you think it is when it's my effort. But you eat in the kitchen, without all the elaborate serving dishes and decoration that I've had to cope with – all of which takes time and makes more washing up.'

She went on to explain that the work was made harder by the lack of conveniences, with a long way to walk between the water tank and stove, lamps to clean and fill, and a stove that needed endless stoking.[78]

Grace Marsh doing the washing at Wharehine, assisted by Bessie Marsh, 1913. Harold Marsh photograph, W. H. Marsh Collection, Albertland Heritage Museum Inc., 2004.2.96.40.

The labour-intensive work required to cook many meals a day, clean the house and wash the clothes, all without electricity, meant that in the absence of servants, children had to help. Most girls learnt how to keep house as children and, by the time they married, were already carrying out much of that work.[80] Lily Winter, the oldest daughter of a dairy-farming family in Karamea, recalls being taught how to make bread when she was only ten or eleven.[81] When she was fifteen, her mother was hospitalised for almost eleven months and Lily took over all of the housekeeping duties for her father and eight siblings.[82] In large families such as these, children were required to perform a variety of domestic tasks which increased in number as they grew older; they learnt the rudiments of cooking by watching their mothers and gradually taking over from them. Although some young women resented the (usually unpaid) contribution they were expected to make to the household, others derived satisfaction from mastering practical skills and the sense of shared enterprise that developed between them and their parents.

Rēwena and Rabbit Stew

The last straw

In *Life at the Oaks*, Elsie Fitz-William (née Rendell) provides some insight into the burden of having a large family and the huge amount of heavy work that went into keeping everybody fed and clothed. She recalls her mother's 'household-cleaning marathons', where all the tables and benches were scrubbed with sandsoap, the silver polished, the stove cleaned and brushed with blacklead, the washing scrubbed and wrung, starched and ironed.

> With all this daily work to do and supervise it is as well our mother was so even-tempered. That is why my memory has stored away the one outburst I saw. It came one evening and was so unlike her that it really scared me.
>
> My seventeen-year-old half-brother was studying at night-school and one day he was sitting at the kitchen-table with his book in front of him. He mumbled something under his breath. I did not hear what he said but Mother did and it must have been something very insulting because it made her lose her temper. She was standing beside the stove holding a large jug full of cold water ready to fill the boiler on the stove; instead, with one swift movement, she turned and threw the water over Alf.
>
> 'Oh, my book! Look what you've done to my book!' wailed Alf. It did not bother him one iota that he was soaking wet.
>
> For a moment Mother stared at him, then turned and walked out of the room. I supposed her day had been especially busy and Alf's remark was the last straw.

But I realise now that she was then forty-five, her youngest child was eight, the first family were grown-up and off her hands, so she should have been able to expect an easier life: instead, she was pregnant again; and facing the thought of another baby, with all that it entailed.[83]

Elsie's father James already had six children, ranging in age from three to fifteen years, when he married Anne Lepper in 1890, and together they had another five. Anne's days consisted of endless heavy work, so it is perhaps little wonder that the thought of another child was, according to Elsie, an 'almost frightening prospect'.[84]

Husbands could also be pressed into service in the kitchen. Florence Kendall (née Rose) explains how she and her husband got by in the early years of their marriage in the 1930s:

> We endeavoured not to spend money unless absolutely necessary, so we made our own butter from top milk off the cans and we made our own bread. We would come in at night, mostly about 9.00pm, to have some dinner which I had prepared before milking and left on the old coal range to cook....
>
> It seemed to take ages to churn the butter and at the same time one of us would be churning, the other was mixing the bread.[85]

Pauline Perry wrote to her mother in 1928 that while she was busy cooking her husband Len acted as 'kitchen maid'. 'I'm sure he doesn't enjoy it and it is rather too bad when he works so hard outside to be roped in for these chores just because it rains, but he is always willing to oblige.' On another occasion, the pair prepared a meal for guests together, with Len cleaning the chickens while Pauline read Mrs Beeton's instructions aloud to him.[86] When 'Dual Purpose Dad' wrote to *The Exporter and Farm Home Journal* in June 1928 reproaching female readers for their harsh depictions of rural men, many readers responded that, yes, their husbands did what they could.[87] By the beginning of the twentieth century the general expectation was that women would be primarily responsible for cooking but, as we have seen, the actual arrangements for cooking were diverse. In practice, food preparation was hard, heavy and time-consuming work, and it often required labour from a number of people across a number of spaces to get a meal to the table.

At home on the land

In te ao Māori, women as individuals traditionally had use rights over land, which could be passed to them by either of their parents.[88] The rights to land did not pass to a woman's husband when they married, so she could hand them on to her children. Throughout the nineteenth century Māori women continued to own and manage land.

Maata Te Taiawatea Rangitūkehu (Tūhourangi and Ngāti Awa) and Airini Tōnore (Airini Donnelly, née Karauia; Ngāti Kahungunu), for example, managed large properties in Whakatāne and Hawke's Bay, respectively.[89] The workings of the Native Land Court and Native Lands Act 1865 progressively undermined Māori women's land tenure, however, encouraging a transition into individual (usually male) ownership, rather than individual or community guardianship.[90] This changed the nature of Māori women's economic relationship with the land. Whereas in the nineteenth century women had performed agricultural labour in communal units on Māori land, increasingly 'they became part of a rural proletariat which depended on Pakeha (and Chinese) land owners or entrepreneurs to provide work'.[91]

Within three decades of the introduction of the Native Land Court in 1862, more than four million hectares of Māori land had been acquired by settlers.[92] Furthermore, by 1920, almost 3 million acres of land under Māori title had been leased, leaving only 1 million acres of usable land – barely enough to sustain the population.[93] Women as well as men worked tirelessly to redress the injustices of the Land Court system and protect what was left of their land, although the most pressing need was to take care of their families and communities. To this end, a number of Māori women took up paid employment, and many others worked on their farms or on communal projects.[94] Hei Ariki Algie, for example, worked as a fleece-o for her father's shearing gang, and after her marriage in 1944 she helped to run it.[95]

> I had to cook for them, and then I had to do Dad's books. When they needed a fleeoor, I got in the shed and do the shed work. I'd be away four days and come back. My children were very young then, so I took them with me. I had a very understanding husband. He knew I was out there to get money for us. He used to call in sometimes, on his way back from the Coast, and stay and give me a hand to wash the dishes. Then he would come home.[96]

Although Hei's work took her away from her husband and their home, it was more common for women to stay on the land and tend to the gardens and stock while their husbands took seasonal work elsewhere. In Maraea

Tippins' (née Bailey; Ngāti Rāhiri, Ngāti Mutunga, Te Āti Awa) family, for example, her father worked at the freezing works while her mother stayed with the children and farmed.

> Dad was working at Borthwicks before he married Mum and he carried on working there. Mum was the farmer. Her parents had some land at Hāwera; they were farming there. They decided that Dad should continue going to the freezing works, and Mum would be the manager. She was one of those people who preferred outside work rather than housework. We had a grandmother with us and she looked after us because Mum was busy all the time.[97]

Heeni Wharemaru's parents, meanwhile, worked together on the farm, and 'were partners in everything they did'.[98]

These women worked on the land in order to sustain their families and communities, adding their labour to extensive kinship-based networks. Female farmers were more visible in te ao Māori than in Pākehā communities: in the first four competitions for the Ahuwhenua Trophy, established in 1933 to encourage excellence in Māori farming, two of the sixteen top-four places were awarded to individual women. The first female winner was Mrs Tetai Hall of Te Teko, in 1940.[99] And in a prominent example, Whina Cooper (Te Rarawa) founded and became the first president of the Panguru branch of the Farmers' Union in the late 1920s.[100]

While it seems to have been relatively common and acceptable in Māori communities for women to work on the land, female farmers were not always respected in their dealings with Pākehā. Grace Hoet explained in evidence to the Mana Wāhine inquiry that when her grandmother Waina Hoete Ahipene (born 1921) was growing up at Winiata, men and women had an equal role to play in the advancement of the hapū, but outside of the papakāinga, the rules changed.

> The accountant, the lawyer, the stock and station agent, all those on the business side of the town, spoke to the man not the wife. For the wife to be heard she had to break into the conversation. When the businesses closed at the end of the day it was only the men who

> Māori women in a shearing shed at Rangatira Station, 1893. W. F. Crawford photograph, Tairāwhiti Museum, 5171.

> The Taylor family – Dorothy (with cat), 'Dad', Phyllis and 'Mum' – milking cows at Huntingdon, c. 1922. Unknown photographer, Ashburton Museum & Historical Society Inc. Collection, 04.2003.0108f.

were allowed in a certain place. Pakeha had this misconception that a women's place was at home. When in reality they were out sharing [sic] sheep, calving cows, and delivering mokopuna, collecting firewood as well as trapping and hunting manu all to feed the hapu.[101]

Pākehā rural women also performed a diverse range of tasks in support of the wellbeing of the family, and while some believed that a woman's proper sphere was in the home, attending to the welfare of the family, others found that caring for their families and communities encompassed work both inside and outside of the house. In 1934, the Invercargill branch of the WDFU held a friendly debate on the topic of whether or not women should milk cows. The winning side, represented by Mrs T. Smith, had this to say:

> One of the greatest things in this changing world of ours is unity or co-operation, working together. Is there a greater case for such co-operation than a woman helping her husband, or father, as the case may be, with the milking on the farm? If she is a woman she will want to help him; as, after all, helping is a woman's main function. She would not like it if she did not do so. She feels too important to be left out of too much.[102]

As suggested by the very subject of the debate, and by Smith's response, there is no doubt that many rural women in the early twentieth century did farm work at least occasionally, and indeed for some it was routine. A report on the health conditions and environments of rural school children, published in 1928, noted that in remote farming areas a 'large percentage' of mothers worked 'out-of-doors', and even in 'thriving' farming communities 30 percent of mothers worked on the farm.[103] Similarly, a survey of the living standards of dairy-farming families, conducted in the late 1930s, found that 38 percent of the wives did work on the farm, averaging nearly thirty-two hours each a week.[104] Eliza Dick (née Murray), who married and moved to Highcliff on the Otago Peninsula in 1927, ran the family farm while her husband worked on roads for the council. Eliza, who had a family to raise as well as cows to milk and a property to run, would combine her domestic and farm work

by darning stockings while she watched the cows grazing.[105] Ann Easy, meanwhile, was solely responsible for milking the family's small herd of cows because her husband 'had a rooted objection to them', although she notes in her autobiography that the first milk cheque she presented to him quickly changed his opinion of dairying.[106] The skill and dexterity rural women demonstrated in stoking a coal range or putting down a hāngī was matched by their ability to milk a cow or herd a flock of sheep.

As Mrs Smith noted in the debate on milking, many women who worked on the farm felt themselves to be part of an economic unit, and did whatever work was deemed necessary to advance the family's prospects. Unity and cooperation were needed to bring to fruition the hopes and aspirations that their life on the land seemed to promise. Kathryn Hunter and Pamela Riney-Kehrberg, writing about rural women in Australia, New Zealand and the United States, identify this as a 'culture of usefulness', in which activities that were considered unfeminine could be explained and excused in terms of duty to the family and farm.[107] Similarly, Claire Toynbee suggests in *Her Work and His*: 'Because New Zealand was settled late, it appears that the colonial helpmeet, the "really useful" woman, was still an important image of rural femininity to those who were themselves members of family farms.'[108]

In Pākehā farming families, gendered labour roles tended to have more fluid boundaries than they might have had in urban areas; indeed, Toynbee notes: 'There was no suggestion in these families that farming work was not suitable for women.'[109] However, while the boundaries between women's and men's work were not always adhered to, they were still very much in evidence. Myrtle Richards of Nelson, for example, noted in her oral history that she could milk a cow better than her husband, but 'he thought it was man's work to do'. After he suffered a hernia she 'wanted him to stay inside and get the breakfast and do the dishes while [she] went out and milked the cow but that was women's work inside'.[110] The opposing side of the debate in Invercargill, meanwhile, professed that '[m]ilking cows [was] not the right and proper occupation for women', and that 'woman's proper sphere [was] in the home, attending to the welfare of the family, preparing meals, and attending to household duties generally'.[111] Even those women who did work outdoors sometimes felt that they were doing men's work, as, for example, when a contributor to the

A young woman feeding pigs and chickens, location unknown, sometime in the 1930s. John Dobree Pascoe photograph, Alexander Turnbull Library, PA1-o-412-045-11.

Dairy Exporter explained that working wives bore a greater burden than their working husbands because 'it is man's work being done by a woman, in addition to her woman's work'.[112] Thus, as Hunter and Riney-Kehrberg found, women had to negotiate the 'tension between the values and needs of rural communities and the growing power of domestic ideology'.[113]

Reflections on domestic work

Women's spheres of work and influence could and did extend well beyond the kitchen. Still, most women in rural New Zealand spent a great deal of time and energy preparing, preserving and cooking food. Charlotte Macdonald and Frances Porter suggest in the introduction to '*My Hand Will Write What My Heart Dictates*' that we should think of women's texts in the nineteenth century in terms of women's 'unsettlement': Māori displaced by war, disease and dispossession; settlers by migration and separation from friends and family.[114] In this context, Pākehā women wrote about their individual efforts to settle and domesticate a new and unfamiliar homeplace, emphasising the self-reliance that colonial domesticity required, the repetitiveness and heaviness of the work, and the relative informality of social relations.[115]

Their accounts dominate the historical record of nineteenth-century domestic work, for while anthropological texts shed some light on Māori women's experiences of cooking, personal reflections are relatively scarce. This is perhaps because the sources of women's writing from the nineteenth century that are publicly available are primarily government records or archives collected by colonial officials, which tend to emphasise issues of land and Māori engagement with colonial governments.[116] Māori women often wrote as part of tribal groupings, and while their texts reveal individual opinions on a range of issues, they do not often include detailed descriptions of their daily lives. Private individual archives held by whānau may reveal more detail about domestic affairs, but decisions about when and how those details are shared rightly rest with the kaitiaki of those taonga.[117]

Biographies and autobiographies of Māori women published in the twentieth century provide more insight into ways of cooking and food production and give a sense of how this work fit or clashed with their individual and collective identities. Helene Connor, who has examined the life story of Betty Wark (Ngā Puhi) and considered the nature of Māori biography, suggests that 'Māori constructions and narratives of selfhood privileged the collective over the individual'.[118] Maintaining their collective identities was a form of resistance to colonisation and Western ethnocentrism, and was reinforced through auto/biographical writing that represented both the individual and the group.[119] We see this in descriptions of cooking and food preparation, which stress the importance of kai to the maintenance of community.

In the biography of Reremoana Hakiwai (Rongowhakaata, Ngāti Porou), for instance, the importance of food is manifest throughout the text, although there is just one brief description of how she learnt to cook: 'We had little education and each day was filled with the life about the pa learning from one's elders, learning to cook and provide food. The Maori is a great eater and his kai is important to him.'[120] Much more attention is given to preparations for community feasts, such as the visit of Tūkāroto Matutaera Pōtatau Te Wherowhero Tāwhiao (the Māori king) to Te Tapairu marae, and Reremoana's marriage to Mare Nepe Apatū in 1913.[121]

Reremoana Koopu recalled, in her reminiscences of her life at Ōtūwhare in the early twentieth century:

> We seemed to be quite happy then, as long as the work is finished, and done, and the kai cooked, and that's all that matters. As long as they can cook their kai for the visitors, and the men have the big fire going outside, and the women folks do the hāngi. They cook the kūmaras, potatoes, kamokamos, anything like that in the hāngi. We had our kitchen right on the main road – and everybody passing through, people going on to Opotiki on horseback, going on the beach, passing our kitchen: 'Hey, come on, have something to eat!' You know what Maoris are, 'Oh, haere mai, get the kai in!'[122]

Manaakitanga is one of the core values of Māori culture and a fundamental principle governing the sharing of kai (see chapter 5). It is maintained by women and men alike – and it is key to understanding Māori women's experiences of, and reflections on, cooking and food preparation.

With whānau living increasingly in nuclear family units, the burden of caring for and feeding everyone in the unit fell heavily on mothers, and this could lead to a sense of isolation. Daisy Waitere (née Hikiera; Taranaki) married in 1941, and went on to have fifteen children (three of whom did not survive). Her husband Colin noted in an interview in 1991 that 'we got married and her young life was left behind. She lived for many, many years as an individual to her family' and, because she was so busy, 'lost track of Māoritanga'. Daisy agreed; she noted that with a large family to raise she didn't have much time for anything else.[123]

Heni Brown spent the first years of her marriage living in Te Ngāwari wharenui and cooking in an old kāuta. Her great-grandmother felt sorry that Heni and her husband Ned didn't have a house, so after about three years she bought them a new house at Mangatā pā. Heni, however, 'rather liked the meeting-house, because everybody come in and have a talk to you – have a kōrero around. It was like a unity, everybody comes and talk to you, and make friends with you, and I really loved that life.'[124] At Mangatū, although Ned's parents were good to them and Ned was, in Heni's words, 'a good provider, a good husband', he would go out shearing or fencing for three weeks at a time while Heni stayed home and looked after the children. Thus, she recalled, 'I had a good life with him, but my own life, no! I had a hard life.'[125] Mira Szaszy (Ngāti Kurī, Te Aupōuri, Te Rarawa), president of the Māori Women's Welfare League, wrote in 1973 that with the introduction of Western domestic arts 'the Maori woman . . . became the modern lady of the house, or drudge, mother to her children as well as being all things to the community. In this new situation men went out to work and the women were left at home, inevitably awaiting the opportunity for change.'[126]

Increasingly a woman's place was considered to be in the home, caring for her family; but, as Szaszy notes, wider whānau ties were not severed. Wāhine Māori had ongoing responsibilities to the community and, in turn, 'the community [took] a greater load off the shoulders of the Maori mother' than the support Pākehā women had from their community.[127] Vera Morgan (née Warmington; Ngā Puhi) grew up with her mother and two siblings on a farm in the Hokianga in the 1920s and 1930s. Her father was a bushman who, in her early childhood, would come home only infrequently, and later not at all. Vera writes of her mother and grandmother that: 'Mum loved us and she was very caring in terms of seeing that we had our clean clothes, lunches and things like that, and for a country cook she was a very good cook, but she always had strict boundaries for us. Nana [who lived nearby] was the one who gave us the spiritual side, the karakia side.' Although the family had a tough life and everyone, including the children, had to work very hard to survive, they had support from their grandmother and from others in the community:

> Our life in the village was not so much about going to the marae, but about working together to grow all our own food. There were plantations of kūmara, potatoes, corn, pumpkin, onions. We had to prepare all that to last twelve months. It was all work that had to be done seasonally. We called it mahi apū. The people got together and shifted from place to place to help each other.[128]

Because of these communal efforts, and her mother's survival skills and tenacity, Vera suggests that, in retrospect, her family were poor moneywise but very lucky.[129]

Vera's early life wasn't centred on the marae, but for other Māori women that was where the continued strength of community and kinship ties were most evident. The wharekai was a collective space, as Te Onehou Phillis explained of her early years at Te Teko:

> I began to see the huge amount of work that mum put in to the hui that were held at Kōkōhīnau. Days before an expected event, she would be making preparations of her own: picking pūhā; bagging up potatoes and kūmara; making jams and pickles if the fruit and vegetables were at hand, although her larder always contained dozens and dozens of preserves; baking rēwena; and ordering me to bake cakes to add to her stores. Then, once at the marae, she would get the meeting house ready by cleaning up and preparing the beds. She would be joined by Para Emery and Keita Moses, with others coming to help out in the wharekai. Everyone had their own tasks to do and pitched in to ensure that the marae was tidy and ready before the visitors arrived.[130]

The work performed in the kitchen was vital to the success of any marae occasion, as the manaakitanga offered to guests was a reflection of the mana of the hosts.[131] Kitchen work also served as an apprenticeship for other, more formal roles on the marae, such as participating in the rituals of encounter on the marae ātea.[132] There was pride in gradually being able to take on different responsibilities in support of the hui, as Heni Sunderland recalled of her young adulthood in Muriwai: 'When I grew up and was old enough to have a responsibility at the marae, we were given a crash course before we were allowed to help serve in the dining-room. We were quite privileged to be one of the waitresses in the dining-hall.'[133]

A good deal of the food consumed in rural Māori communities was grown, gathered or caught on the land, taken from rivers, wetlands or the ocean, preserved in earthen pits, gourds or pōhā, and cooked over wood fires or in the earth. As such, day-to-day tasks reinforced physical attachments to land which also contributed to a secure sense of identity and connection to home place.[134] Witarina Harris (née Mitchell; Ngāti Whakaue), who grew up in Ōhinemutu in the early 1900s, writes: 'The steam holes over the ngāwhā were our hāngi for cooking (at home we only had an open fireplace). We mostly cooked at the ngāwhā. That's why, when I got married, I didn't know how to cook on a stove.' The family bought flour, some bread, butter, sugar, tinned meat and Highlander condensed milk, but otherwise ate almost exclusively food they produced themselves or received from relatives. Pork was home-killed and put in the ngāwhā to loosen the hairs before butchering; they grew kamokamo, potatoes and pumpkin in the garden, gathered watercress from the creek and freshwater pipi and kōura from the lake. Dried pāua came from relatives down the coast, family who lived by the sea brought karengo, and their father arrived with pikopiko from the bush whenever he came back from surveying. Kūmara didn't grow well at Ōhinemutu, apparently because it was too cold, but there was one spot on Mokoia Island where it would grow. Each of these processes required an understanding of and interaction with the natural environment; knowing what grew where, how to harvest it, how to harness the power of steam, fire and earth to cook it, and how to produce enough that it could be shared with whānau.[135] This intimacy with the land and its natural resources not only ensured the sustenance of the group, it also allowed people to gain status in the community and nurture their relationships with whānau and whenua.[136]

While gathering, cooking and sharing food could strengthen Māori women's connections to people and place, their writings on domestic work also reveal some of the painful accommodations they were forced to make on account of colonisation. Mihipeka Edwards lived with her grandparents at Manakau in the 1920s, and went to the local school where she was expected to dress and behave like the Pākehā students. On her first day at school Mihipeka's kuia gave her rēwena bread with pork fat and slices of pork, as well as a piece of eel, but when she saw the Pākehā students getting out their nice thin sandwiches and cake wrapped in white napkins, Mihipeka felt ashamed.[137] Her kui enlisted the help of a Pākehā neighbour to teach her to make the new foods she knew Mihipeka liked. At one particularly memorable meal the family had roast pork 'cooked like Pakeha kai', followed by pudding and custard, and Mihi enjoyed it so much that she ate until she could hardly walk. Then, she reports, her kui said '"Mihi, I also know how to make cake, so you will have a nice lunch when you go back to school next week. I also have some nice napkins to wrap your lunch in. My friend showed me how to make them."' In that moment Mihi recognises: 'She has always understood my feelings. I go over, put my arms around her, hold her silently for a while, tears running down my face.'[138] Mihipeka was being taught in a Pākehā environment that devalued her culture and language, and it must have been extremely painful for both her and her grandmother to feel they had to adapt to new domestic norms.

Pākehā women's writing reveals quite different cultural values and modes of self-identification than that of Māori women. Domestic work features prominently in Pākehā women's magazines and autobiographies through the twentieth century, although the regularity and monotony of cooking, which according to Kathryn Hunter and Lynette Squire renders it almost invisible in letters and diaries, is downplayed in favour of humorous or illuminating anecdotes.[139]

Women writing for publication knew that people would read their work, and their comments reflect certain tropes and conventions that would be familiar and acceptable to their audiences. Nancy Grey Osterud explains in her analysis of rural women's oral histories that 'in telling their life stories, people are always aware of normative ideas and common discourses that circulate in the culture and compose their narratives with positive and/or negative reference to prevailing ideologies'.[140] While we need to interpret life stories with care, these sources can nevertheless offer valuable insights into women's experiences and capture an array of voices and perspectives.

The archetypes and cultural images evident in Pākehā women's writing share many characteristics with those of other pioneering or frontier societies across the Anglophone world. Canadian scholar Leigh Matthews found that the quality of 'cheerfulness' that was so necessary for the successful helpmate evolved into a cultural myth that permeated prairie women's settlement texts and dominated their self-representation.[141] The same is true of New Zealand women's contributions to magazines such as the *Dairy Exporter*, which had extensive women's sections and provided a forum for women across the country to discuss issues of relevance. A contributor with the pen name 'Alys' exemplified the cheery outlook of the helpmate when she wrote in 1927:

> I think farmers' wives are mostly optimistic, and much need we have to be too. My dear man, after working against hardships and misfortunes for the last twenty years, is just at the age when things are beginning to look hardly worth while – our family of six sturdy youngsters growing up, and our mortgage so slowly being lifted. Mum's part is to help and cheer him up. . . . My habit of looking on the bright side has helped us in many a gloomy place, but sometimes my eyes fill with tears as I look at his greying head and wrinkling face, and wonder 'Has it been worth while?' Has it? A thousand times 'Yes.'[142]

Other contributors wrote about how important it was to manage your own attitude to life. In 1939 'Daphne' wrote that she had once felt a failure and as if her special talents were being wasted, but that if you 'make up your mind to like your work, be interested in it and really, silly as it sounds, you do get to like it and work much better and more happily'.[143]

Although contributors to the *Dairy Exporter* did tend to write with optimism and cheerfulness, this was not exclusively the case; the women's pages could be a place for serious and honest conversations. Popular media in the interwar period has commonly been viewed as a platform for conservative and conventional domestic ideologies, but in fact forums such as women's pages could be contested arenas where a variety of opinions were aired.[144] In October 1926, for instance, 'P. J.' wrote that she felt contributions to the magazine 'mostly seem to echo the "sorry for ourselves" idea of the country woman', but in the months that followed, other women wrote in to contradict her.[145] 'Swede Turnip' found the contributors to be 'a jolly band of women simply setting forth facts as they have found (and faced) them. . . . If a correspondent is a little worried over things, and it helps her to write of her difficulties, why not?'[146] 'Cake walk' meanwhile, anticipated the censure of 'cheerful ladies' when she wrote of the monotony and exhaustion of baking:

> I bake twice a week, scones, buns, pies and a fruit cake and a sponge, and when the kitchen's like an oven and the flies buzz and I'm tired and hot and bothered I thank my stars that's over for a day or two, and rise next morning quite light-hearted. But only two days and all over again the hated performance. O, yes, you cheerful ladies, I know I'm lucky to have heaps of food to bake and healthy, hearty appetites to satisfy – I do really thank heaven every day for that – but when you've slammed 100 cakes every year for ten years in the same oven, and 500 pies, and 1000 small goods – and, oh, help, I can't bear to think of how many raisin pies and roasts – you really begin to think that 'Paradise' . . . would be a wee house somewhere with a bun shop round the corner.[147]

The responses to her letter were mostly positive, with other women admitting that they did not necessarily feel light and cheerful while sweating over cakes and pies, either.

A recent study of New Zealand farm women's engagement with the feminist movement throughout the twentieth century found that by the 1980s women were more willing to admit that the 'grin and bear it' philosophy, although still very much in evidence, was used to disguise a high level of anxiety.[148] There are similar clues in women's writing from earlier in the century that cheerfulness was not universally felt, and that it was often performed for the benefit of others. Take, for example, this poem, submitted to the *Dairy Exporter* in 1931 by 'Ginger':

> Peace, comfort, and a quiet mind
> Are rare, if possible, to find,
> But to pretend they're yours is kind
> To someone else
>
> The sun still shines and though you doubt
> Its power to put the clouds to rout
> It's helpful just to point it out
> To someone else
>
> Of course at best it's only bluff,
> But though you know that well enough
> There's just a chance it seems good stuff
> To someone else
>
> And after all this much is real
> That in response to your appeal
> The someone smiles, and then you feel
> Cheered up yourself.[149]

Cheerfulness was part of a culture of emotions rural women internalised, signalling to others through their good cheer that they could solve their own problems and manage their own wellbeing.[150]

Another common refrain women used when describing their work in the kitchen was that it was their contribution to the family partnership. The idea that a husband and wife were partners in the pioneering enterprise, each with their own skills and duties, was central to the vision of the true helpmate. This was particularly evident when family members worked together on the farm, but rural women did not necessarily have to be working beside their husbands in order to feel that they were working with them. In the January 1926 edition of the *New Zealand Dairy Produce Exporter*, Anne Rennie encouraged rural women to think of their work in the home as equal to men's work outdoors; she noted that both forms of labour contribute to 'the common living'.

> How best to reduce the housewife's tasks, to organise them systematically by the use of adequate equipment, managerial devices, and by co-operation with other members of the household – this knowledge is just as necessary in housekeeping as in any other business enterprise. Thus the value of the housekeeping product is revealed, and shows the housewife's career as productive in nature and as economically independent as that of her husband.
> Both are seen working in partnership, each contributing approximately an equal share, and each paid an equal real wage, the individual share of the common living secured.[151]

Although Rennie was a home economics and domestic science teacher she was not, according to the editor of the journal, a 'high-flown theorist who [would] suggest impossibilities', and indeed it does seem that a number of rural women viewed their domestic work in Rennie's terms.[152] As one of the respondents in Margaret Sing's study of dairy-farming women in the Tatuanui community put it, '[f]armers and their wives were very much of a "unit", and it wouldn't have occurred to my mother to see her contribution quite apart from my father's.'[153] Despite Rennie's confident assurances that this productive work made them equal partners, however, it does seem that domestic labour went largely unacknowledged day-to-day, and women sometimes had to gently remind their husbands that they, too, worked day and night for the good of the farm. For those who worked tirelessly without help or acknowledgement, life could be, as 'Truthful Trixie' put it in 1927, 'just one damned thing after another'.[154]

While women's writing in magazines and memoirs revealed a range of viewpoints, few could be described as reluctant farmers; indeed, most expressed deep and resounding commitment to rural life. Many women wrote of the beauty and tranquillity of their life on the land, which, although not directly related to their domestic work, nevertheless shaped how they perceived those experiences – such as in this 1926 letter:

> I wonder which of us (town or country women) really has the most to be thankful for? Sometimes when I am doing the washing and carrying bucket after bucket of water till every bone aches, I think of the tubs and hot water taps, and electric coppers, and every

Isabel Witheford embroidering outdoors, Albertland district, c. 1910. Harold Marsh photograph, W. H. Marsh Collection, Albertland Heritage Museum Inc., 2004.2.97.1220.

device of our city sisters, who start washing as soon as it pleases them to get up, and don't have to milk cows, cook breakfast, wash separators, etc., before ever they can begin upon it. But, somehow, when I hang the clothes out, knowing they will remain the same snowy white, and not turn to grey, the clean, sweet breeze from the blue hills blows every trace of envy away, and the daisies and young grass under my feet, I would not exchange for all the asphalted back yards in Wellington.[155]

Jan Maybury found in her more contemporary study of rurality and gender that even in the late twentieth century, rural women were 'forcefully' committed to the rural ideal and made certain sacrifices in order to sustain the lifestyle they so valued. After conducting twenty-one interviews with non-farming rural people, Maybury concluded that women respondents' options were 'primarily constrained by individual household strategies that centre around sustaining a rural lifestyle rather than structural realities reified in ideological beliefs about gender and domestic responsibilities'.[156]

Still, there were dissatisfactions that emerged in Pākehā women's work and in their writing, especially later in the twentieth century, as rural women became increasingly aware of alternative futures. A 'sustained challenge' to the model of femininity that had defined women in the nineteenth and early twentieth centuries came from the 'new woman' of the interwar period, and rural society was not insulated from those modernising influences.[157] The 'new woman' had much greater access to higher education than her mother or grandmother had had, and her expectations had changed: she expected to have a period of independence before marriage, when she could take paid employment; she expected to be able to purchase some of the trappings of modernity; and she expected to have roles and interests outside of the family and home.[158]

Young rural women shared this modern outlook with their urban counterparts, although they found it more difficult to achieve economic and personal independence. Joan Millar moved to Greenhills with her parents in 1929 at the age of fifteen, and because her mother was unwell, she was required to stay at home and help with domestic chores.

She received no wages but, according to her reminiscences, she felt no resentment about her situation; she noted that her parents 'were good to [her] in their own way'.[159] It was only later, when she realised that certain freedoms were never going to be available to her, that she chafed at the duties she had to perform.

> I was thinking that as my sister had had three years secondary school, she would leave at the years end and come home and let me go out to work. Evidently, this never **occurred** to her, as one night in December, she came home and proudly announced that she had a job in H & J Smiths' a big shop in Invercargill. I was really flabbergasted, but nobody else seemed to think it strange. I was really taken for granted.[160]

Even Mary Scott, a firm advocate of rural life, mentioned the lack of options available to young women in her popular collection of rural stories, *Barbara and the New Zealand Back-Blocks*. In 'Traps', she writes of an isolated farm where the father, mother and thirteen-year-old daughter milk thirty-two cows by hand. A visitor arriving at the house asks after the girl, Nora, and is told that she has left school because it is too far away. The visitor responds, 'So she's at home now and likes that better, I expect?' but is told that 'No. She frets all the time. She didn't want to leave. She made a rare fuss and tried to run away. But there was nowhere to run to. . . . She's needed here, her dad says; you see, she can milk ten cows easy.'[161] Catching the girl's eye, the visitor sees 'anger, bitterness [and] revolt. Her spirit was chafing, her mind was starved, her heart hot and rebellious.'[162] While it is undoubtedly a dramatic account drawing on aspects of the common victim trope, still, this story depicts what was a reality for a number of young rural women. By the end of the 1920s being 'modern' was considered an essential element of a young woman's life, although '[t]his sympathy with and expression of the modern . . . contrasted sharply with the material realities of farm women's daily lives'.[163]

Older rural women were also increasingly aware of new opportunities. Marilyn Irvin Holt, in her study of home economics in the United States, found that as rural households became materially better off there was also an evolution in rural women's roles: 'when the means of production change, so do the workers'.[164] Not every rural home had modern conveniences, but 'their existence suggested alternatives' and 'influenced attitudes about what was important'. Women began to view their work in a different light, and '[s]entiment for the traditional way of doing things held little allure if the new [ways] eased their lives'.[165] The amenities and appliances that were advertised to women in magazines and newspapers and demonstrated at meetings of the WI and WDFU suggested that their work could be made easier, their burden made lighter. Structurally the nature of their role would not necessarily change, but these 'electric servants' could give women more time for leisure activities and intellectual pursuits. When these were withheld from them, seemingly unfairly, it could be a source of considerable dissatisfaction. In 1932, for instance, a woman named 'Marie' wrote to the *Dairy Exporter* in defence of 'growling' wives who, in the majority of cases, were:

> overworked, harassed women being kept going at high pressure till the nervous system is un-strung. Too often the 'growler' is cook, washerwoman, dressmaker, general charwoman, nurse, wife and mother rolled into one. Well might she be forgiven for wishing aloud that the same Providence that provides up-to-date farm implements and costly stock would peep into her domain and see the conspicuous absence of anything in the line of modern conveniences![166]

And 'Meryl B' wrote in August 1939:

> Recently, I stayed with an old friend who has married a man who has a good job in the city. Every morning at 8.15 he left for work, returning about 5.30. There was a washing machine, vacuum cleaner, electric stove and refrigerator in the house, the vegetable garden was looked after by hubby in the weekend; he was a handy man, and, as he worked only 40 hours a week, had time enough to do or make all sorts of odd things about the house.... On a farm, without those conveniences, we have to cope with large meals at all hours, farm hands, a big garden, and a host of other things. For the most part

our husbands sit back and expect to be waited on; a meal should be ready as soon as they put in an appearance, the children must not annoy them, and so on. In the really big things of life I am ready to find the country men heroes – I do not even doubt that they are just as fond of their wives – but in every day life? Yes, they do work hard, but in the main the inventions of our age do more to lighten their burden than ours.[167]

A lack of modern conveniences could become a source of considerable resentment – although not all rural women placed the blame for this on rural men. In their responses to 'Meryl B's contribution, published in the following month, her fellow readers offered sympathy but were quick to defend their husbands. 'Fifty-Fifty' summarised the general feeling when she wrote: 'Some men are certainly thoughtless, while others are downright selfish, but it makes no difference to these whether their surroundings be city or rural.'[168] As other women were quick to point out, the lack of conveniences in their homes was often due simply to a lack of money, in which case their husbands often went without as well.

The heart of the home

In a 1939 article in the *New Zealand Journal of Agriculture*, the Association for Country Education asks:

Did you know – you busy mothers who cook for your husband and family – that you spend about 70 per cent. of your day in the kitchen? Yes – between two-thirds and three-quarters of your time is spent working in the kitchen preparing food and cleaning and clearing away after meals. Let that fact sink in, and then ask yourself whether your conditions of work are as near the ideal as they should be.

The article suggests ways of making the kitchen a more efficient workplace, such as planning the work steps needed to complete particular tasks, grouping together equipment for particular processes,

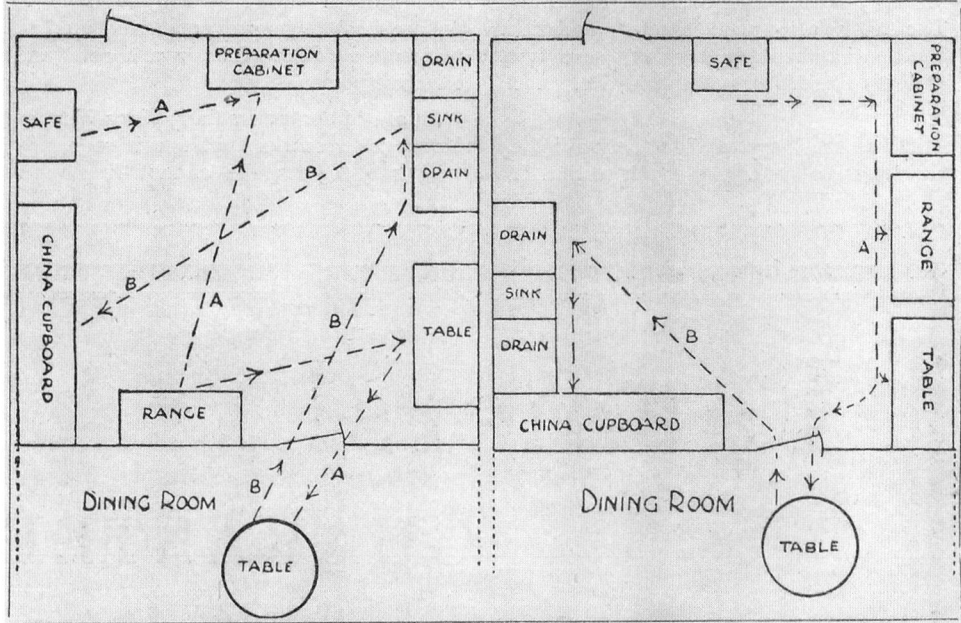

Left: Diagram showing badly arranged equipment, which makes a confused intersecting chain of steps in either preparing or clearing away a meal. Right: Proper arrangement of equipment, which makes a simple chain of steps. (A, preparing; B, clearing.)

The ideal design for reducing fatigue in the kitchen. 'Reducing Fatigue in the Kitchen', *New Zealand Journal of Agriculture*, 20 May 1939, p. 460, National Library of New Zealand.

and organising the kitchen bench along the lines of the mechanic's workbench, with everything in its place.[169] A kitchen modelled on the workshop ideal had no room for a dining table, no space for children to play or bathe, no comfortable sofa, no reading nook. It was a place for the work of the housewife alone, a space in which efficiency was the overriding principle.

As the article and image above demonstrate, home scientists advocated a utilitarian approach to housekeeping based on concrete strategies for household management and scientifically sanctioned health and hygiene measures.[170] In reality, kitchens in most rural Pākehā and Māori homes were both practical and homely spaces, and this proposed kitchen design bears little resemblance to the various chaotic and cosy places described in memoirs and reminiscences. Kitchens were places for cooking and eating, but also for telling stories, imparting wisdom, sharing fun times, offering consolation, and a hundred other purposes. As Rangimarie Rose Pere noted in 1982:

> some marae complexes retain an open fireplace in their kitchen, where people continue to congregate and talk while keeping a watchful eye on the cooking of food in big pots and camp ovens. Many of the issues discussed around the hearth reflect a way of life handed down the generations. A wood fire reminds one of the elders of fantastic story-telling and legends of different types of wood, of laughter, or various foods and related activities.[171]

Processes carried out in and around the kitchen generated sights, smells and feelings that evoked a sense of home and security.[172] Cooking and eating are always sensory experiences, but to be in a space dominated by an open fire or a coal range was to experience it viscerally – to be immediately aware that here were food and warmth. Pere wrote of her childhood experiences at Ōhiwa and Waikaremoana that 'the fires in and around the kainga always seemed to burn day and night, and gave . . . a feeling of warmth and life, a strong sense of security'.[173] For those who worked outdoors it would have been a relief to come home to the comfort of a blazing fire, a well stocked larder and the sights and smells of a meal cooking – all signs of the success of the family's shared enterprise.

Writer Maurice Gee, who grew up in Henderson, West Auckland, in the 1930s and 1940s, describes the kitchen in his childhood home, and the nearby creek, as the two poles he moved between as a boy. Those two places formed his moral and emotional universe, highlighting contrasts between familiarity and mystery, safety and danger, dark and light, good and evil. The creek was full of adventure and possibility, while the kitchen was 'the safe place [where] harm could never come'. Even when he was in his eighties, hearing the word 'kitchen' could still evoke powerful images for Gee of his mother at the stove stirring stew, his father's socks hanging on a drying rack, a worn mat and wooden table on brown lino, a Philco radio on the mantelpiece.[174]

Helene Connor grew up in East Auckland but has very fond memories of her grandparents' dairy farm at Motunui. She remembers the kitchen well:

> There was a long dining table with a form seat positioned next to the wall where us mokopuna sat. Poppa had a large wooden chair at one end of the table and all the 'grown-ups' sat in chairs nestled around the dining table. Nannie tended to sit at a chair strategically placed close to the coal range which was positioned in the middle of the room in a bricked recess. A coal shuttle and a basket for wood and pine cones sat on the hearth in front, and above the coal range there was a metal rack where pots and pans could be stored. The coal range was the heart of the whānau and everything happened there. My mother, Tui, recalled the babies were bathed in front of the coal range. The endless meals were cooked there and it provided warmth and comfort for the whole family.[175]

In these examples, Gee and Connor look back on kitchens they remember from childhood, and to some extent the romance and nostalgia they attach to those spaces may be because they didn't have to work in them all day: they could retreat to the kitchen after a day of work, school or play and enjoy the food and warmth conjured by the labour of others. For those doing the cooking and washing up, the kitchen was a place of heavy and time-consuming work, but while some rural women viewed it exclusively in these terms, others managed to make the kitchen their own. Gee recalls that he would sometimes creep down to the kitchen late at night and find his mother Lyndahl 'sitting with her feet in the oven to get the last warmth from the stove, writing a poem or story in an exercise book'. He speculates that 'hundreds of New Zealand women behaved like that, after their husbands and children had gone to bed'.[176]

In a 2014 article on power and gender dynamics in domestic spaces, Angela Meah examines the meanings women assigned to their work in the kitchen, and suggests that while women may have viewed the kitchen as a place of oppression, they have also seen it as a place of empowerment.[177] Women can and have appropriated their kitchens for a range of purposes; and although the kitchen and the stove can be seen as symbols of oppression, they can also symbolise pleasure and fulfilment. This dichotomy emerges in a series of essays by contributors on the topic of 'A cure for the blues', published in the *New Zealand Journal of Agriculture* in 1944. 'Star' of Rangitīkei felt that 'a big percentage of farm

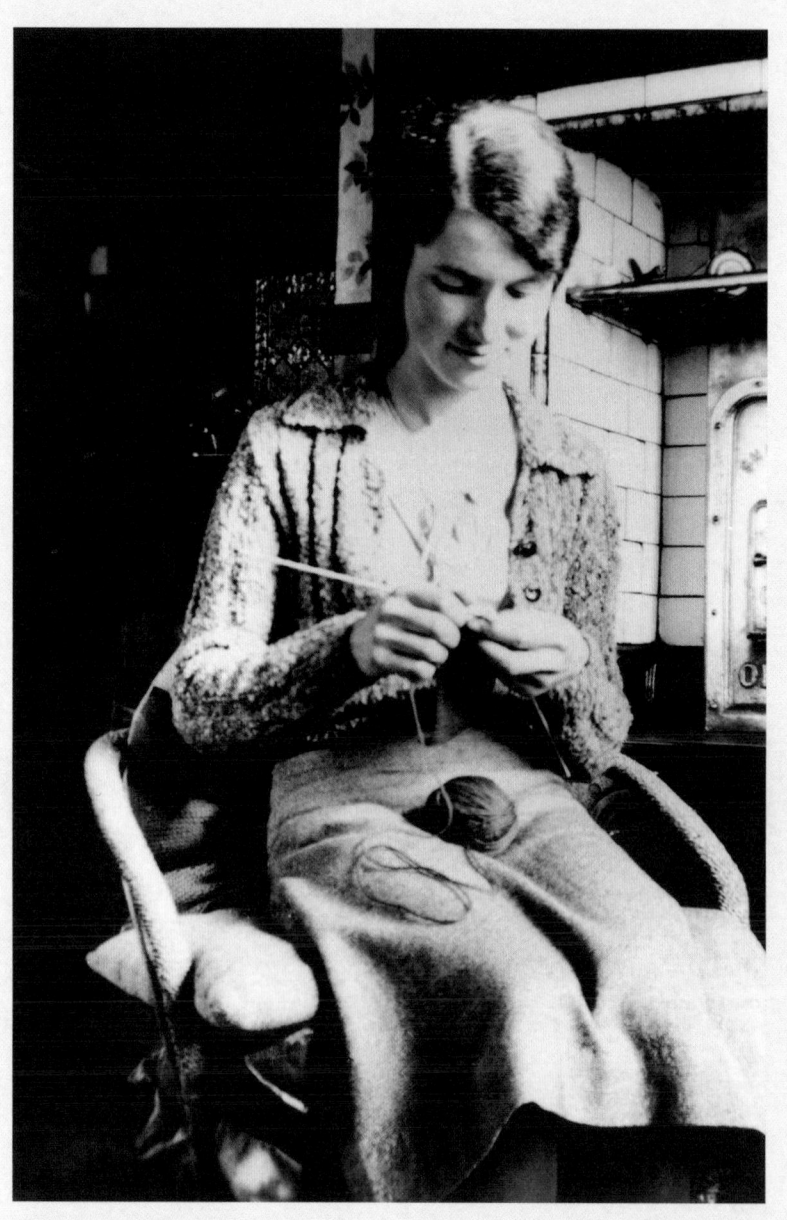

‹ PAGES 222–23
Two photographs from rural Auckland in the 1930s. One shows Gwen Kelly busy knitting in front of the range in the kitchen of her home at 25 Massey Road, Manurewa, June 1938. The other shows Muriel Bettany at work in the kitchen of her two-room 'whare' in Riddell Road, Glendowie. Kitchens could be places of work, rest and recreation, as well as serving many other purposes. Gwen Kelly knitting, Manurewa, 1938. Valma Kelly photograph, Auckland Libraries Heritage Collections, Footprints 02657. Muriel Bettany in the kitchen, Glendowie, 1931. Arnold C. Bettany photograph, Auckland Libraries Heritage Collections, Footprints 04038.

wives suffer from too much kitchen' and should try to get outdoors, whereas two other writers said that their cure was to get into the kitchen and do some cooking or baking. 'S. J. M.' liked to experiment with new recipes – she found that the sense of achievement cured her blues; and 'Lady Jane' would cheer herself up by putting on a colourful apron and making treats to share with her neighbours or family.[178]

In the late nineteenth and early twentieth centuries, social mores derived from the ideals of the middle classes decreed that men and women had separate spheres and that a woman's place was in the home. So powerful were these ideals that they created a hegemonic idea of the kitchen as a gender-specific space, but as we have seen, this was not necessarily the case in rural settings. Different households, families and communities had different ways of assigning cooking tasks, and depending on the time and place, men, women, children, servants, neighbours or friends might take up these duties. Furthermore, women in rural New Zealand carried out a wide range of tasks both inside and outside of the home, pushing at the boundaries of their 'sphere' in order to be useful to their families. The model of the 'mother homemaker' toiling away on her own in the kitchen was not relevant or desirable to many Māori women, and rural Pākehā women also experienced tensions between domestic ideology and the reality of their lives. Women's observations on domestic work and on the kitchen reflect their individual and collective identities, dominant cultural images, emotional norms, connection to the land, commitment to the country, and fluctuations of the agricultural economy, ultimately revealing a very wide range of experiences and viewpoints. To quote the poet I introduced at the beginning of the chapter, while they might have talked about the women's sphere as if it had a limit, in reality those limits were not always firmly fixed.

5

Hākari, feasts and picnics:

Manaakitanga and rural hospitality

'On the whole we were a happy little community. Differences, even quarrels, there were; but it only needed one of the belligerents to get into some difficulty, however trivial, to make his erstwhile enemy rush to his assistance.

Not that all forbearance or forgiveness was always a manifestation of the Christian spirit. Often good neighbourliness was simply good policy, a mutual need saw to it that the rents in the fabric of friendship were soon patched up and pride pocketed as soon as compatible with honour. The settlers couldn't afford to let offences rankle for they were so dependent one on the other. . . .

Adversity is the best adhesive plaster for drawing together the torn edges of the body social. Pretty generally it was the women who were the peacemakers. There would be a wordy battle royal going on between two men but their wives would still 'visit', even at the risk of a row in their own homes, and violent quarrels could scarcely be kept up under such circumstances.'[1]

Jean Boswell grew up in Mangawhare on the outskirts of Dargaville in the 1890s, living with her parents and eleven siblings on the edge of the bush. In the quote above, taken from her autobiography, *Dim Horizons*, she recalls the hardships of the family's first years in the settlement where, for the most part, they lived on pigeons, pork and potatoes, and her father and brothers went gumdigging every Sunday so they would have something to trade for gunpowder and shot.[2] There were only ten other families in the community, and, as the extract above suggests, they relied on each other for resources and labour, bound together by their 'mutual need'.

The vision of rural Pākehā New Zealand that Boswell paints – of small, isolated communities pulling together to help each other in times of trouble – has endured in the popular imagination; and, perhaps for this reason, has been roundly debated by historians and social scientists. Somerset describes in *Littledene* the strong bonds of association and 'a vigorous community spirit' within the settlement at Oxford.[3] Miles Fairburn later argued that these characteristics had been misapplied to nineteenth-century communities: until at least the 1880s settler society was too transient to allow solid attachments to form between neighbours, and social isolation was acute.[4] His biting reassessment of colonial life inspired equally fervent responses, most notably from Rollo Arnold and Caroline Daley, who argued that Fairburn's statistical analysis missed the informal but well understood rules underlying community cooperation, and ignored the social worlds of women.[5] The kitchen can provide a window into these social worlds, and food rituals reveal aspects of community life – or lack of it – in rural Pākehā society.

In te ao Māori, manaakitanga is one of the key values underpinning tikanga, and there are expected standards of behaviour for hospitality and the care of others in every social setting.[6] Hazel Petrie argues that food was the fundamental measure of wealth in pre-contact Māori society, as it represented economic power, reputation and social status.[7] Elaborate feasts were staged to demonstrate the wealth of the hosts and uphold the mana of their visitors, reaching unprecedented size in the nineteenth century and continuing in the twentieth century on a slightly smaller scale. Manaakitanga was also an important guiding principle in everyday situations, where it was less about the material goods offered than the spirit in which hospitality was extended. According to Rangimarie Rose Pere, '[t]he luxury and splendour of a mansion is of no consequence if the people who own it cannot emanate warmth, respect, kindness and sincerity to anyone who may enter and cross its threshold. On the other hand, one may enter a most humble abode and be wholly impressed by the welcome and the warmth of the host group.'[8]

This chapter explores the role of culinary diplomacy in the making of community, and analyses the social dynamics revealed by the breaking of bread. The concept of culinary diplomacy – the idea that food and cuisine can be used as a form of crosscultural communication and can improve interactions and cooperation within and between communities – is an ancient one, discussed in Plato's *Politics* and figuring in the Bible as a way of constituting community.[9] In the social sciences the term is often applied to contemporary international relations, but it can also be used as a framework to explore modes of communication and cooperation within nonpolitical communities.

While rural hospitality (both Māori and Pākehā) is sometimes romanticised – used as evidence for an inexact but long-held popular view of rural society as uniquely egalitarian – the impulse to share a meal with neighbours could in fact be quite pragmatic. It was often necessary to call on neighbours for support, so civility – if not sincere cordiality – was the wise and necessary course. Sharing food was one way of fostering cooperation and mutuality, mending tears in the social fabric, enhancing the prestige of the food provider, and bolstering the health of the whole community. In this chapter we see how the factors considered so far – the spaces, technologies, ingredients and work processes necessary to prepare meals – can all come together to create settings for social interactions. Rural New Zealanders understood that the way in which they provided hospitality could clearly communicate where they considered themselves and others to be on the social ladder, the values they considered important, and the community obligations they chose to uphold. The kitchen was a place where they made those important social statements.[10]

Manaakitanga and rural hospitality

Raukura Erana Gillies (Ngāti Wheke, Ngāti Irakehu, Ngāti Hinekura, Ngāti Kurī, Ngāi Tahu) lived at Rāpaki in the early 1900s with her parents Teone Taare Tikao and Matahana Toko Horomona. Herries Beattie described the family home as 'a European house to the outward eye, but run on the traditional lines of Maori hospitality', and a recent biography adds to this picture:

> The family had milking cows and a large orchard. As a child and adolescent, Raukura was present when her father hosted kaumātua, tohuka and iwi leaders. These hui provided the training ground for

Raukura to refine her manaakitanga – she became renowned for her generosity, hospitality and care for others.[11]

The idea of hospitality comes up often in Māori and Pākehā accounts of rural life, and although the Māori concept of manaakitanga is often taken to mean hospitality, the concept has many interpretations and applications and can be best understood within the wider frame of Māori culture.[12] Suzanne Duncan and Poia Rewi explain in their introduction to tikanga Māori that Māori conceive of the world 'as a large genealogy made up of links, networks and bonds', recognising that human existence depends on other people and on the environment. These things must be protected and treasured, and therefore principles of love and care, such as whanaungatanga, manaakitanga and aroha, are governing principles of Māori society.[13] Manaakitanga – defined by Hirini Moko Mead as 'nurturing relationships, looking after people, and being very careful about how others are treated' – is an expected standard of behaviour that applies in any situation, no matter the circumstances.[14] It underpins all tikanga, and continues to be one of the most fundamental principles governing the sharing of kai.[15]

Tūhoe tohunga Hohepa Kereopa explained in an interview with Paul Moon that, when you're talking about kai, you must also understand the concept of manaaki.

> We were told to Manaaki. If we saw anybody, we would always call out to them. And when people talk about karanga, they think of the marae, but for us, the karanga was always practised here. When you saw someone going past on the road, you'd karanga them, and offer them a cup of tea. And when they accepted your offer, you would race around trying to figure out how you were going to get a cup of tea. And our people have always said, even if it's just a cup of water, the most important thing is that you offer it.[16]

The most conspicuous displays of hospitality in the Māori world were at hui, but everyday displays of manaakitanga were equally important. Indeed, for individuals such as Rita Ranginui, who grew up in Pipiriki in the 1920s, one of the guiding principles of life was to 'see that all the cupboards were full of different kai, and to see that everything was clean [for] the manuhiri'.[17]

The importance of manaakitanga was impressed on Māori children by kuia and other kaumātua. Hārata Solomon (Ngāti Toa, Ngāti Raukawa, Te Āti Awa) of Waikanae learnt from her grandmother Ria Te Uira, who was 'well known as an excellent hostess'.[18] As soon as she spotted visitors walking up the drive, Ria would have the kettle on and put a batch of scones in the oven. Amiria Stirling's mother-in-law Mihi 'couldn't bear to see people going past her home [at Raukōkore], they had to call in. Even if you were going by yourself on horseback, she'd stand on the verandah and wave you in to have a cup of tea.'[19]

Te Onehou Phillis grew up in Te Teko, and during events on the marae it was her job to set the tables, serve guests and clear up at the end of the meal.

> There was a protocol with regard to hospitality. We were told that we were never to begin clearing up, not even to whip away an empty plate, until the visitors had vacated the dining room. The reason, apart from simple discourtesy, was that it suggested that we wanted to get rid of them.[20]

Dorothy (Naki) Savage (Ngāti Kahungunu) of Te Ore Ore felt quite hard done by growing up in the 1920s, because her Nanny Rose would make her help with the work of entertaining visitors even if it disrupted her own social activities. On one particular occasion she made a faux pas that she still remembered vividly some fifty years later:

> [O]ne day, now this is something that I think is very good to record, these people, I'm getting fed up by this time, after all these dishes, and having to replenish the dishes on the table, and these people are still talking and eating, and I'm in a hurry to go to the pictures or go somewhere, and I had to stay there so, they hadn't finished and I started clearing the table away. Next minute I get a hit . . . 'Well, what was that for?' And then she [Nanny Rose] spoke to me in Māori. 'If you've had enough to eat, worry about other people. Those people haven't finished eating. You are rude to clear the table.'[21]

Nineteenth-century European observers were often overwhelmed by the generosity of their Māori hosts: as Anglican priest James West Stack found during his travels around Banks Peninsula in the 1860s, 'profusion was the measure of Maori hospitality, and consumption the measure of its appreciation'.[22] Stack was fully aware of the importance of paying due respect to his hosts, and when he and his wife Eliza set out to visit Māori communities on Banks Peninsula they agreed that whatever happened, neither of them would mention it if they disliked anything they received. 'They were to be our hosts, and we their guests, and the least we could do was to show them that we appreciated their kindly hospitality.'[23] Surveyor John Turnbull Thomson, travelling around Otago in the 1860s, found himself stranded by the weather at the home of Reko and his family, and noted that 'the most pleasant part of it, no doubt, was the sincere hospitality evinced by our sable host. A day's acquaintanceship had warmed into friendship, and he bestowed no little pains in providing his best.'[24] Thomson characterises his relationship with Reko as one of friendship, although historian Tony Ballantyne notes that these encounters between colonial authorities and high-ranking Māori could also be strategic and were often designed to encourage cooperation and allow officials to gather valuable information about local landscapes and social practices. This information was in turn used to shape colonial policy and practice.[25]

In 1845 the Society for Promoting Christian Knowledge suggested that the hospitality shown by Māori communities was something Pākehā 'should do well to imitate'.[26] Providing hospitality to guests became a matter of pride for many Pākehā rural people, an aspect of a rural way of life mythology that emphasised kindness and community spirit.[27] In 1965 the popular radio show *Open Country* featured a story by Te Awamutu woman Pamela Harrington, titled 'You Too Might Make a Farmer's Wife', which exemplified this ethos. Pamela had been raised in the city, and when she moved to the farm she was surprised to find that rural women were judged by an entirely different set of standards from those that were applied to their urban counterparts: standards promoted and policed by an 'old brigade' of experienced farmers' wives. She recalled:

I'd been a farmer's wife for years before I became aware of the judgement of the much older, longer-standing wives of farmers to describe the district's brides. You either 'fit in perfectly' and take everything in your stride, I've discovered, or you're 'just lovely, but,' and here's the rub, 'a city girl at heart'. . . . If you're aiming for top marks you must cope with the unexpected without any visible evidence of the sudden enormous reorganisation, either mental or physical, that you've had to do. . . .

[Y]our reaction to unexpected visitors will be noted. I beg of you, if mealtime is drawing near and they aren't making a move don't sit it out. Even if they have made a few noises about going give in smilingly early in the piece and insist that they stay. This is in the very best tradition of the farmer's wife . . . And strange though it may seem after a while it becomes automatic and you enjoy the challenge and, let's hope, the company.[28]

This expectation of open hospitality could have been influenced by Māori expressions of manaakitanga, although other influences may have played a part. The authors of the 1967 book *At Home in New Zealand*, for example, write that 'of the things the whalers brought to New Zealand only the most durable have survived – a few big iron trypots, and a tradition of generous hospitality'.[29] And Eileen Soper contends, in *The Otago of Our Mothers*, that hospitality is 'a national characteristic of the Scots' which, in New Zealand, had 'every scope for expression'.[30]

Perhaps the most likely explanation, however, is that geographic and social isolation simply made neighbourliness a prudent and wise social nicety. As Mary Murphy argues in relation to rural areas of the United States and Canada, hospitality was a key ingredient of settler society, 'binding people to each other through webs of reciprocity'.[31] Whether in Alberta or Taranaki, settlers had to secure the needs of their own families while also being attentive to the needs of the community, balancing generosity and self-sufficiency in daily acts of culinary diplomacy.[32] Frederick Mieville, who lived in Southland in the 1850s, found he had little choice but to extend hospitality to visitors who had nowhere else to go, just as the visitors had little choice but to avail themselves of the charity of others. The establishment of accommodation houses did not keep pace with the extension of European settlement, and it was not uncommon for travellers from afar to arrive at their destination with no food or shelter.[33] Although it could be a 'great tax' to feed and lodge everyone, Mieville wrote that he always did his best for them in case he should ever find himself in the same plight.[34] This expectation of hospitality set a standard for welcoming visitors that continued in many rural areas, '[l]ong after the more urgent necessity had ceased to exist'.[35] As Helen Simpson put it in 1940: 'The habit of "turning up" unannounced, even in places where every facility exists by which due warning may be given, the New Zealander has never entirely outgrown.'[36]

In rural settings and communities, then, providing hospitality and helping others became the social norm, and there was an underlying expectation that, when called on, the recipient would reciprocate. Hospitality and manaakitanga were displayed in both everyday and ceremonial settings, such as in the cookhouse, at picnics and at hui. As the examples below demonstrate, this did not mean that there were no social hierarchies in operation. It would have been unusual to turn someone away if they needed a meal, but the way in which they were received and treated revealed a great deal about their place on the social ladder.

The limits of hospitality

Rural hospitality did inevitably have limits, and letters included in the women's section of the *Dairy Exporter* reveal that the ritual of visiting at times reflected stratification in the community. It was rare for visitors to be turned away if they needed food or help, but failure to pay a visit to someone's house could be considered a snub and an indication that the person considered themselves to be of a higher social class. As 'Enid' wrote in 1939:

> In our district, if a woman and her husband take a job as [a] married couple on a farm, very few farmers' wives will visit her, but if a farm is bought, the new people will immediately receive plenty of callers. A young couple came to work on a farm near here; being good workers, they were there for some years. In fact, only leaving because the farm was sold. During those years only one farmer's wife called on that little woman, but how pleased she was to have that one friend. When the place was sold it was a different tale; the neighbours called in a very short time (the new people have money).[37]

When letters such as this were published there was usually a fast response from other readers, to the effect that rural women were simply too busy to pay visits and that there was never any insult intended. Indeed, in this instance, a contributor named 'J. M.' responded to Enid by asserting that in *her* district there was no such snobbery, and that:

> as long as newcomers are decent people it makes not one scrap of difference whether they own their own farms, are working for wages, or sharemilking; and neither it should. ... [W]ithout wishing to hurt anyone's feelings might I suggest to lonely newcomers that instead of remaining grimly and virtuosly [sic] at home waiting for the neighbours to call and often becoming grieved and indignant when they fail to appear, that they inquire from the grocer or butcher if there is a branch of the W.I. or W.D., and see if it is possible to attend. If there is a concert or school picnic, make a point of being there.[38]

As 'J. M.' suggests, social occasions such as picnics and dances were events in which the whole community could participate, and thus they acted to de-emphasise the importance of people's occupational and social standing. Experiences such as Enid's, however, suggest that stratification was still evident in rural communities. As Elvin Hatch found in his 1992 study of social status in rural Canterbury, the 'egalitarian emphasis in the community [did] not preclude the manifestation of hierarchy',[39] but in comparison to the rigid stratification of rural English society, these manifestations were far more subtle.

The rural workforce

This section considers the place of wage earners in rural households and communities by examining mealtime rituals and exploring the unspoken social statements made by station owners, small farmers and itinerant workers across the dinner table. Economist Horace Belshaw wrote in 1933 that 'in spite of the great importance of farming industries in New Zealand, there is in that country no hereditary class of farm labourers, and hired labour in agriculture is probably of less importance than in most other young countries'.[40] Subsequent historians reinforced this claim: in their view the rise of the family farm, and the opportunities for social mobility offered by easy access to land, diminished the significance of the rural labour force and limited the emergence of a rural working class.[41] John Martin, in his 1990 book *The Forgotten Worker*, offered a counterargument to this: he demonstrated that rural labourers were vital to the agricultural economy not only in the nineteenth century but also into the twentieth, and that rural workers had far more limited opportunities for land ownership and upward mobility than the notion of New Zealand as a workingman's paradise might have implied.

As part of his study, Hatch examined various hierarchies that contributed to a person's status in rural New Zealand – including wealth, farming ability, occupational standing, and refinement. These hierarchies are expressed and maintained through what he calls distancing forms: social rituals that overtly display social distance.[42] One such ritual is eating; and shared meals can often be self-conscious displays of wealth and refinement. Hatch distinguishes between one-table households, where everyone eats together regardless of employment status, and two-table households, where workers eat separately from the boss. The former dignifies labour and recognises work as a means of achievement and a measure for judging the worth and standing of others; whereas the latter reinforces social distance between those of different occupational standings, and creates a clear demarcation between the 'rough' and the 'refined'.[43]

Most nineteenth-century stations and estates operated as two-table households, with the owner and their family eating in the big house while the workers ate in a separate cookhouse. To some extent this was a practical necessity, as both arable and pastoral farming were carried out on a large scale and were extremely labour-intensive. Established sheep runs usually had a dozen or so permanent staff, and large pastoral estates might employ anywhere from a dozen to forty full-time workers. The 1891 census recorded 20,500 permanent rural workers in New Zealand, and just as many again took up seasonal employment during the busy summer season.[44]

Given the number of employees on large estates and stations, it made sense for workers to take their meals in a separate cookhouse dedicated to that purpose. The distinction between the cookhouse and the big house was not just a matter of practicality, however; it also served a social function. In *A Southern Gentry*, historian Stevan Eldred-Grigg suggests that runholders in New Zealand were 'almost feverish' in their attempts to reconstruct old world status rituals and social distinctions, using their wealth to bind the majority of the workforce into positions of dependence while establishing for themselves lives of grace and leisure.[45] While Eldred-Grigg has been criticised for generalising too freely, there were certainly runholders who fancied themselves members of a landed gentry and enforced rigid social hierarchies. Sarah Courage, for example, moved to Waipara Station with her husband Frank in the 1860s, and the couple chose not to eat with their servants.[46] In fact, Sarah was genuinely baffled when she discovered, during a visit to her neighbour Mrs Iscariot's house, that others in their position did.

> When we sat down to tea there was a vacant chair between Mrs Colton and myself; and it was allotted, I heard, to one of Mrs Iscariot's farm hands – her 'factotum,' as she called him – of whom I knew nothing more than he was spoken of as Piggot....
> I was not anxious to make the creature's acquaintance, though he did enjoy such a commanding position at Sunnylands, and avoided him as much as possible during the evening; but before it was over one of the Iscariot boys told me he was 'great fun, though he was a little brusque'. All the same, I felt as the other guests did that his proper place was in the kitchen, and it was beneath Mrs Iscariot, as a gentlewoman, to be so familiar with such a boor; but there is no accounting for tastes.[47]

According to Sarah's description, the farmhand's lack of refinement put him well below the other guests in terms of social standing, and she felt that this social distance should be made more explicit by having the man eat in the kitchen.

On some stations, there was an equally regulated social hierarchy operating in the cookhouse. At Brancepeth, for example, senior staff such as the station clerk, head shepherd and station manager ate in the saloon – a dining room separate from the rest of the cookhouse – and distanced themselves spatially and socially from the rest of the staff.[48] Even then there were differences in the perceived levels of refinement among the senior staff, as Miller, the station clerk, found the head shepherd's table manners extremely objectionable. In the main cookhouse, meanwhile, the permanent hands did not like to eat with swaggers, so insisted on being fed first, and the shepherds demanded their own special meal schedules.[49] Māori guests and workers slotted into the hierarchy in accordance with their social standing. Senior visitors such as Hori Te Huki were received in the big house, other guests dined with Miller in the saloon, while Māori farm workers ate in the cookhouse with everyone else.[50]

While runholders still enjoyed considerable social power in the early twentieth century – especially in places like Canterbury with a long history of pastoralism – it was increasingly common for rural households to operate on the one-table model where everyone ate together.[51] Brooking suggests that New Zealand's rural society was most fluid in the last decades of the nineteenth century, and that there was no clear distinction between part-time farmers, small farmers and small pastoralists.[52] This hierarchy became more fixed in the early twentieth century as land values increased and small farmers began to reap the benefits of refrigeration. Part-time farmers became full-time, and no longer needed to take on off-farm work to supplement their incomes; while full-time labourers began to feel that they had little chance of ever becoming farmers in their own right.[53] Although the distinctions between landholders and labourers became more permanent, the emphasis on egalitarianism and equality in the community endured, and was expressed through social rituals that emphasised the work and values they shared, rather than the differences between them.[54]

The one-table arrangement expressed a fundamentally different social hierarchy. In general, households that opted for this arrangement valued work as a means of achievement and a measure for judging the worth and standing of others. Although the boss could still hire and fire the men working for him, the one-table arrangement lessened the social distance between employer and employees: 'they called him by his first name, labored alongside him in the paddocks, and ate with him at the dinner table'.[55] J. S. Mackay's description of Longlands Station in the 1920s is a good example of this social hierarchy at work:

> The family home was at 'Plashwood', Oamaru, but during the busy season he [the owner, Joseph Preston] made frequent though short visits to Longlands. He engaged actively in the work of the station, and when mounted on a horse was as good as the best, mustering or droving....
>
> [During shearing season] all hands from J. P. to the newest cowboy, fed at the cookshop.... On one occasion during this period J. P. showed his displeasure when given preferential treatment in the matter of food by sweeping his plate and full pannikin of tea to the floor and angrily demanded that he be given the same as the men.[56]

The men must certainly have been aware that Preston occupied a higher social position than they did, but in this setting, in a space associated with work and with a community of men, Preston chose not to acknowledge the distance between them.

Rēwena and Rabbit Stew

SHEARERS' HUT AT NIGHT TIME.

Colonial 'mateship'

While the cookhouse could be a hierarchical and occasionally tense place, it was also a place in which many of the elements of pioneer 'mateship' could be freely expressed.[57] Pākehā men developed their own community and culture, arising out of the hardships of the colonial frontier, with a distinct code of behaviour. These pioneer men took pride in their ability to 'rough it', developing a unique vocabulary (which was said to both mystify and appal newcomers with its coarseness) and a set of social rituals that demonstrated their contempt for formalities.[58] Although the pub was the primary space in which these rituals were enacted, the cookhouse served a similar function. This description of the cookhouse at Molesworth Station recalls the busy shearing period when extra men were employed:

The station was changed. It was thronged with men – big men and little men, strong men and weak men; clean men and dirty men. . . .

Our meal hours depended upon the work to be done, but sometimes we fed with the shearers. There were about seventy of us, all told, and the cooks were hard-worked. Each man, on entering the cookshop, grabbed the necessary tools, while the cook dished his food. It was then carried to the table and eaten. The din was terrific, and our language much to the point. The unavoidable smell of wool and grease and hot men made meals a trial for some of us.[59]

When women entered this space they had to adapt to the established set of behaviours. J. S. Mackay, a musterer at Longlands Station in the 1920s, noted that their cook, a Scotswoman named Mrs Beverley, 'fed the men well and was unruffled at the prospect of extra work caused by the musterers, whose company and rough good humour she certainly enjoyed'.[60]

<
Shearers' hut at night time, 1885. Unknown artist (initials H. M. R.), originally published in the *Illustrated New Zealand News*, 19 January 1885, Alexander Turnbull Library, PUBL-0110-1885-002.

∨
The kitchen, Piha. Interior of the cookhouse at the Piha Mill timber camp, 1915–16. Albert Percy Godber photograph, Collection of albums, prints and negatives, Alexander Turnbull Library, APG-0353-1/2-G.

Hatch found that by the 1920s, most small farms in Canterbury adhered to a one-table arrangement, and anecdotal evidence suggests that this was becoming an expected, if not universal convention in other parts of rural New Zealand.[61] Jim Boswell, who worked on a dairy farm on the Hauraki Plains in the 1920s, actually left his job because of the two-table arrangement.

> Apart from the boss there was another chap, Donny, a Fijian, He was getting a bit more pay than I was as he'd been there longer.
> We both lived on the farm, not in the house, but in some quarters there. It was an early start to get 90 cows milked. When we had finished the morning milk, the boss's wife would give us our breakfast out in the kitchen. We would be given some fruit and a sandwich. The boss would come in and he would have porridge with cream, and eggs with all the trimmings, in the dining room. Donny and I decided that we couldn't put up with this sort of discrimination. ... we both left the farm and took off for the bush.[62]

In a society that emphasised equality and cooperation, such overt displays of social hierarchy were increasingly considered unacceptable.

In practice, however, the social levelling implied by the ritual of labourers and employers eating together was probably more symbolic than real. As 'Sea Bird' wrote to the *Dairy Exporter* in 1935, 'although [an employee] has meals with us, and other privileges, his leisure time is his own; and he must vacate the room on finishing his meal'.[63] This woman felt it necessary to dignify the work of farm labourers by eating with them, but she freely acknowledged that 'class distinctions do exist, and to preserve a just distinction between employer and employee is the farmer's duty'.[64]

Furthermore, workers did not necessarily adhere to the social niceties that would have marked them as respectable members of the community. This anecdote comes from historian James Watson's article 'The Significance of Mr. Richard Buckley's Exploding Trousers', although it is actually a reminiscence shared by his colleague Basil Poff, describing his childhood in Canterbury in the 1940s. The Poff family had a farm worker named Bob Halfyard, who always ate with them at the main dining table.

> Bob was an extremely good teamster.... However, [his] table manners were somewhat mixed. True, he said 'excuse me, Missus' before reaching over the table to help himself to the bread, but the effect was more than spoiled by the sleeve of his old coat trailing through the butter and his neighbors' food. He admired the cruet set, with its little glass containers, but failed to appreciate that in the best families Worcester sauce is not swigged straight from the bottle. The lady of the household suffered agonies as she sought to balance the need to bring her children up with good manners while not offending a good worker. Eventually the tractor, replacing Bob, came to the rescue.[65]

The tractor may have saved this family from their crisis of respectability, but farm vehicles did not become common on small farms until after the Second World War. In the meantime, workers were needed, and the expectation was that farmers would dignify their labour by sharing a meal. To borrow a phrase from Brooking, a 'relatively egalitarian social order' prevailed, but this 'had to be won, consolidated and nurtured'.[66]

There were other social bonds and community expectations that were tested during the peak summer season. On large properties, the responsibility for feeding workers rested with the hired cook, but on smaller farms, the women of the household were expected to do the cooking. In *Five on a Farm*, Rosemary Smyth describes the extra work her mother did during the busy summer season, providing food not only for workers on their own farm just out of Oamaru, but also for the men on their neighbour's farm.

> Mum would cook mountains of scones, biscuits and cakes for the shearers and harvesters. It must have been a mammoth task on the temperamental coal range which roared or sulked, depending on the wind. Mum also mixed up gallons of barley water and billy tea; the tea tasted so good when we were hot and thirsty. We would have to bring the 'smoko' baskets, fighting about the left-overs.
>
> Our mother [also] cooked for our bachelor neighbour, Jimmy Walker, when he had the shearers or crutchers, but Jimmy always made delicious apple pies in advance for the meal, and we loved these.[67]

Gwen Wingate Mackenzie, who lived on an 1180-acre property near Palmerston North from 1926, recalled that the shearing season was a particularly busy time for her mother: each day began very early so that the men could be working by six a.m.

> Ten o'clock was 'smoko time.' Hot tea in billies, and heaps of freshly baked scones and biscuits would be taken down to the shed. No sooner was smoko done than Mother had to organise the men's midday dinner. She roasted mutton or beef each day, rich with good dripping and plenty of baked vegetables. The men would scrub up in order to look respectable for the kitchen table laden with hot food. There was always a big steamed or baked pudding to follow with plenty of fresh cream and custard.[68]

Gwen notes that her mother did not mind this extra work, however: 'It was her share in the partnership of running a farm.'[69]

Women often called on neighbours to provide an extra set of hands at busy times such as this. Florence Beck (née Spencer) had a friend who would come and assist with the millhands' dinners, bringing any baking she had with her; and Pauline Perry of Pōkuru, near Te Awamutu, had her neighbours Mrs Wheeler and Mrs Cummins make sandwiches for the haymakers while she made blackberry tarts, sausage rolls and cakes.[70] In large families where the mother could not leave her own work, younger members went to assist. Emily Ross (née Elliott) looked after her young neighbour George Mills while his mother cooked for the harvesters, and Mary Cranstoun of Edendale noted in her diaries (for 1905–07 and 1925–26) that she and her younger sisters would travel to their neighbours' and help with the cooking – and presumably the favour would be returned.[71] 'There was a co-operative spirit among neighbours', as Hamilton farmer Alicia Chitty put it, and this was manifest in the cooperative efforts undertaken by both men and women during seasonal peaks.[72]

Dinnertime at Manuka Point Station, 1943. From right: owner Laurie Walker, farm worker Ted Porter, station cook Grace Porter (Ted's wife), and their daughter Shirley. John Dobree Pascoe photograph, Alexander Turnbull Library, 1/4-045899-F.

Māori and Pākehā: Lonely in one another's company?

It is difficult to gauge the extent to which Pākehā networks of sociability and hospitality intersected with Māori ones; to know whether Pākehā women popped in for tea with their Māori neighbours or were invited to events at the local marae. Anthropologist Felix Keesing wrote in 1928 that 'both Pakeha and Maori must always be "wary, and often a little lonely, in one another's company"', although this sense of caution was probably more pronounced in some places than in others.[73] In 1930s Waikanae, for example, Hārata Solomon lived in a very closeknit community and frequently had Pākehā visitors, some of whom became 'like members of the family'.[74] Such stories of easy social relations are fairly scarce, however, and Hārata's experiences may in part have been influenced by her family's relative affluence.[75]

Barbara Brookes and Margaret Tennant suggest that until the mid-twentieth century contact between Māori and Pākehā women was limited (more limited, probably, than between Māori and Pākehā men, who would on occasion have cause to work together), and that when they did interact, 'sisterhood was far less evident than cultural misunderstanding'.[76] There were some interconnections, for example through membership of national women's organisations such as the Women's Institute, or local groups such as Te Ropu o te Ora Women's Health League in Rotorua. Members of these organisations 'had womanhood in common, and shared broad commitments to the health and welfare of families', so worked in close cooperation to further their aims.[77] Te Ropu o te Ora was primarily a Māori women's organisation, founded with the support of Te Arawa elders, but some Pākehā women were also members. Alice Fitness was appointed branch secretary in Reporoa in 1938, and although the Māori women were initially shy in her company, 'she'd stoke up the coal range, soup would be cooking, food on the table and that was that'.[78] Not all groups fostered such openness, however, and according to J. C. Sturm (Taranaki, Te Whakatōhea), some Māori members of the Women's Division and Women's Institute felt 'too diffident or self-conscious to confess the inadequacies of their homes to a group of Pakeha women'.[79] The Māori Women's Welfare League was later founded to address this concern, held together 'simply by the feeling, well, here we are, all in the same boat, what can we do about it?'[80]

In general, it seems that while there were points of contact between Māori and Pākehā in rural communities – particularly around seasonal work such as shearing and harvesting – and genuine friendships and loving relationships were not rare, in most cases they lived separately, divided by an agricultural economy which prioritised Pākehā small farmers and ignored Māori interests.[81] Joan Metge found, in her study of a rural community in Northland in the 1950s, that the relationships between Pākehā farming families and tangata whenua were 'amicable but not intimate': Pākehā farmers 'were separated from their Maori neighbours by their cultural

Hākari, feasts and picnics

Members of the Rangataua Women's Institute, including Miss Burleigh (standing second from left), Mrs Morris (standing third from right), and Pararie (kneeling, holding a child), November 1934. Unknown photographer, Tauranga City Libraries, Photo 06-216, Pae Korokī.

background, their relative wealth and their whole way of life. In every case their holdings were larger than the largest Maori farms and much more fully developed.'[82] There were connections, as the children of the district all went to the same school, Pākehā farmers attended Māori gatherings, and the whole community cooperated on common causes such as roading and school facilities. Despite this, Metge concluded that 'in the circumstances of their day-to-day living and in their social organisation, the Maoris could be legitimately regarded as a separate entity'.[83]

Hākari – feasts

Hākari are rituals of great significance in te ao Māori: they serve many social purposes beyond the satisfaction of physical hunger.[84] Traditionally hākari were staged to mark major life events or the completion of communal activities, and the stakes for hosting a feast were high, as Te Rangi Hīroa notes:

> Inasmuch as the welcome by speech on the *marae* had to be followed by a welcome with food, the *marae* could not maintain its prestige unless it was supported by storehouses plentifully stocked with food. Thus the storehouses formed a third element in the complex [along with the wharenui and the marae ātea] which administered to the social needs of the tribe, maintaining and increasing its reputation with outside people. In addition to household stores it was necessary to have a reserve supply to assist in the extra demands made by tribal gatherings and, above all, by the entertainment of visitors. The home people could live upon scanty rations in times of scarcity, but visitors had to receive the best or shame enveloped the community.[85]

Feasts were crucial to the maintenance of mana: they enhanced the hosts' reputation for hospitality and provided an opportunity for social and political contacts to be made, and for obligations to be repaid.[86] The sharing of food after a pōwhiri, tangihanga or other event where levels of tapu were raised was also the final act of whakanoa, reducing the tapu on everyone and allowing them to return to the common world.[87]

Raymond Firth, who wrote extensively about hākari in his 1929 study of Māori economic systems, divided these feasts into four categories: hākari held to mark life events such as births, naming ceremonies, marriages and hahunga; phases of the maramataka such as harvests or the rising of Matariki or Puanga (depending on the iwi or hapū); political gatherings for summoning allies, making peace, exchanging goods or hosting important visitors; and community activities such as building a house or launching a waka.[88] Elsdon Best recorded that Māori feasts could be divided into those that came under the mana of Tū, the war god, and those that pertained to Rongo, the god of peace.[89]

Some feasts were initiated by individuals or whānau, but the most significant occasions involved the whole community.[90] Each community had different strategies in place for provisioning and cooking these feasts. In *The Old-Time Maori*, Mākereti Papakura scoffs at the idea that 'Maori made himself poor by giving a feast'. She describes in detail the communal effort that went in to collecting food for a hui.[91]

> Take as an example an important gathering to discuss affairs of state, given, we will say, at Te Wairoa where Te Keepa Te Rangipuawhe, a chief, lived with his hapu Tuhourangi. Although the hui would be spoken of as being arranged by the chief Te Rangipuawhe, the food collected to feed the various members of the hapu attending was not supplied only by the people of Tuhourangi who lived at Te Wairoa. All the hapu of Tuhourangi, and they were many, when they heard that there would be a hui, began at once to collect food to help to feed the multitude. A hapu living near the sea began getting fish and preparing them a year or more beforehand, and clans living near a forest collected birds and berries and fruits. Extra cultivations of kumara, taro, and hue would be planted, and aruhe would be collected in quantities. These foods would be brought to Te Wairoa as they were ready, and stored, and greater quantities were brought by the many hapu when they arrived a week or two before the meeting.[92]

This food was cooked in a large kāuta or in a wharau attached to the principal house of the village, and distributed to guests by the head man of the cooking party.[93]

Large intertribal or inter-hapū feasts involved staggering amounts of food, particularly in the nineteenth century when new foodstuffs, processing technologies and trade opportunities allowed for surplus food production on an unprecedented scale.[94] Food was set in stacks, placed on whata (see page 31), or displayed on specially built hākari stages – huge conical or pyramid-shaped structures that could be up to 30 metres tall.[95] The 1849 feast given by Waimate chiefs for Ruhi, who was

← PAGES 250–51
Feast at the Bay of Islands, September 1849. This enormous wooden hākari stage was erected to hold food for a feast at Kororāreka in August and September 1849. The feast was initiated by Ngā Puhi rangatira Tāmati Wāka Nene to promote peace in the wake of the Northern War. Captain Richard Oliver, purchased 1995 with New Zealand Lottery Grant Board funds, Museum of New Zealand Te Papa Tongarewa, 1995-0003-1.

also Ngā Puhi, apparently featured one of the largest hākari stages ever constructed. It was described in great detail in local newspapers:

> For six months, throughout the whole of the district inhabited by Na Manu and the other chiefs, the preparations for the feast have been the one object of paramount importance, and nothing has been spared or left undone that could in any degree add to its extent or hospitality. The 'Potehe,' or Temple of Food, (on which the food for the feast is stored,) erected at Kororarika [sic], is one of the largest ever put up. It is of an oblong form, measuring 211 feet in length, and 18 feet in width at the base, and is at the top about 8 feet wide . . . the total height of the turret in the centre [is] from 115 to 130 feet, from which 8 other turrets, ranging from 70 to 80 feet run the length of the erection. On these turrets are erected, at elevations of from 10 to 12 feet above each other, from the ground to their tops, the platforms on which the food is laid out, which consists of potatoes [,]cooked pigs, dried sharks, pumpkins, kumeras, &c.[96]

Lavish hākari continued throughout the nineteenth century, although not all were quite on this scale. Maria Amina Maning recalled that at the hahunga for Arama Karaka Pī, chief of the Māhurehure hapu of Ngā Puhi, held in 1870, the food for distribution sat in a long line that looked from a distance like a low wall: 'Such endless kits of potatoes & kumaras piled up one upon another – bags of flour, rice, sugar, boxes of tea – melons everything, esteemed among them as edible.'[97] Maning recognised that to those unaccustomed to the ritual it might seem an ill-considered use of resources, and she gave this caustic characterisation of an interfering missionary: '"Just like them!" sneers Mr. Missionary "incorrigibly improvident & extravagant, they will be starving presently, mark my words!"' As Maning explains, however, this demonstration of lavish hospitality honoured the chief, and signified to those assembled the great mana of their leader. As such, the self-denial and labour required to gather the provisions were part of the ritual.[98]

The first meal of any gathering was cooked by the hosts for their guests, but not all the food at hākari was intended to be eaten right away. Part of the ceremony was to distribute food to invited guests to take back home, and the portions assigned corresponded with the number and rank of the people in each group.[99] Richard Taylor described a ceremony he observed during his time in the Far North and Whanganui:

> When the guests arrive they are received with a loud welcome, and afterwards a person, who acts as the master of the ceremonies, having a rod in his hand, marches slowly along the line of food, which is generally placed in the *marae,* or chief court of the pa, and then names the tribe for which each division is intended, striking it with his rod. This being done, the chief of that party receiving the food, sub-divides it amongst his followers. The food is then carried off to their respective homes.[100]

Te Rangi Hīroa recalled being one of the 'stay-at-homes' and receiving a string of dried clams from relatives who had been away at a hui. When the attendees arrived home the first question asked was '"He aha nga kai o te hui?" ("What were the foods at the gathering?") [and] reputations rose or fell upon the reply.'[101]

By the twentieth century grandiose displays of food on this scale were no longer expected, but key elements of traditional hākari were upheld, such as the communal effort to prepare for the event and the generosity displayed in food and gifts to guests.[102] In his 1907 diary, for example, Wairarapa farmer Irāia Te Whāiti described a hākari held to celebrate the completion of a tattooing ceremony: he noted that there were speeches, the gifting of cloaks and money, and then everyone enjoyed 'all sorts of Maori and Pakeha food'.[103] Maaka Jones (née Delamere; Te Whānau a Apanui, Ngāi Tahu, Te Aitanga-a-Māhaki, Ngāti Porou) of Whitianga, who grew up in the Ringatū faith, recalled that on the first of November each year the tapu was lifted from the growing crops and the nearby river opened for fishing. This marked the beginning of the harvest, and was celebrated with a hākari.[104]

In the nineteenth century, rangatira would direct the work in preparation for a feast, but in the twentieth century everyone pitched in to get the work done.[105] Vera Morgan of Waimā, Hokianga, explained that in the garden, 'every family had to have an extra row of everything – of kūmara, of rīwai, of kānga, of poukena – for the hui'.

Food for Maori Feast, Hokianga

Boiling puddings at a Maori Feast.
C. Dawes. Photo.

These photographs by Charles Peet Dawes show preparations for the opening of the wharenui at Tauteihiihi marae, Hokianga, 1910s. In one, women sit among sacks of kūmara preparing them for the feast; in another, a man stands beside large pigs hanging from a wooden pole; and in the third, Jessie Dawes (right) and her son Earle stand with another woman beside a huge pot being used to boil puddings. Charles Peet Dawes photographs, Auckland Libraries Heritage Collections, 1572-1291; 1572-1285; 1572-1286, reproduced with permission of Rewi Tolich, chairperson of Tauteihiihi marae.

> Some would have fowls and stock to kill.
> So everybody had something to contribute. It was pre-prepared. Every year you knew what you had to do. They planned ahead for the events that they sort of knew would happen (except ngā mate). You'd know if there was to be a wedding, or someone was going to be twenty-one. Those things were prepared for by everybody. Then when the time came you wouldn't have to go around saying 'Oh give us a couple of pounds,' you know? It was already prepared for.[106]

Dorothy Savage of Te Ore Ore noted in her oral history, recorded in 1983, that '[now] there's not one garden around this pā, and yet once upon a time, they used to feed all them they had at the meeting house. Everybody used to grow things so that when anybody came they've got food. Because they had no money in those days, so that was their contribution.'[107] Amiria Stirling remembered that in the 1920s her inlaws Mihi Kōtukutuku and Duncan Stirling were often called on to contribute food for hui, and they always did.

> He had a lot of pigs and cows on the farm, but if the people wanted some meat for the tangi, they went to his wife.
> 'E Mihi, we want some meat for the marae.'
> 'Oh yes, yes.'
> It was all O.K. to her. She'd just tell the old man to kill some meat, and because it was the Maori way, he had to do it.[108]

When it came time to cook the food, each community had their own system depending on the facilities available. Hei Ariki Algie remembers the feasts at Rūātoki in the 1920s:

> They never had a meeting house, or a kāuta. All their little houses – you see them coming out with whatever they have cooked, for the meal. Not like us [at Manutuke]: you have one kāuta and you cook everything in that kāuta. No, they were coming from all round, their little homes, each one bringing something for the table. You might have the potatoes, and I'll have some meat, and someone else will have meat – and whatever.[109]

^
Group of people having an outdoor meal at a hui on an unidentified marae, c. 1920s. Possibly Henry Norford Whitehead photograph, Alexander Turnbull Library, 1/1-004478-G.

At Hongoeka, Patricia Grace (Ngāti Raukawa, Ngāti Toa, Te Āti Awa) recalls that during her childhood in the 1930s and 1940s they had no meeting house so, if there was a tangihanga, they would set up a marquee as a dining area. They cooked the food outdoors on open fires using large iron pots, and heated water in kerosene tins.[110]

Whatever the arrangement, providing food for visitors was the host community's responsibility. It could be considered an insult if visitors offered to contribute to hākari, because it suggested that the hosts could not provide adequately for their guests. When Amiria was to marry Eruera Stirling, for example, her people at Taumata o mihi sent a telegram saying that they were bringing food for the wedding.

> Mihi started to fight about it.
> 'Oh! There's that Ngati Porou people again. They think I've got nothing here, and they want to bring everything. No! I've got *tons* to eat, plenty kai, plenty of everything. All they've got to do is come themselves.'[111]

The hosts were also honour-bound to provide their guests with food and comfortable lodgings, and their ability to do so reflected on the prestige of the marae.[112]

> A temporary shelter erected for a feast, 1914, possibly at Tauteihiihi, Hokianga. Charles Peet Dawes photograph, Auckland Libraries Heritage Collections, 1572-0954, reproduced with permission of Rewi Tolich, chairperson of Tauteihiihi marae.

Wharekai

Having reached its zenith in the late nineteenth century, the construction of whare whakairo (carved meeting houses) declined sharply in the early twentieth century, and by the end of the First World War customary Māori art and architecture were in serious decline.[113] In 1926 influential politician Apirana Ngata established the School of Maori Arts and Crafts, hoping to foster tribal unity and revitalise the whare whakairo as a symbol of the strength of Māori culture. In the decades that followed the school was responsible for over forty building projects, and was instrumental in modernising the 'traditional' wharenui and adapting it to new social practices.[114]

Before the 1930s, most of the food for large gatherings was cooked in a hāngī, and communal meals were eaten outside or in tents.[115] Although many marae had whareumu or kāuta, either permanent or erected for the occasion, large cooking and dining structures like those found on most marae today were rare.[116] One of the innovations Ngata promoted was the construction of permanent dining halls and Pākehā-style kitchens adjacent to the whare whakairo: this provided a venue for communal gatherings and tapu-free marae occasions.[117] The new architectural form was popular not only on the East Coast but far beyond, and was used as a community hall as well as a dining room. Often there was a stage at one end where cultural performances were held and, later, rock-and-roll concerts and dances.[118]

∨
Te Poho o Rāwiri wharenui with the wharekai Te Poho o Hine i Tuhia o te Rangi alongside in Kaitī, Tairāwhiti Gisborne. The church on the hill overlooking the marae is Toko Toru Tapu, a historically important Māori church that is associated with the marae. Photographer unknown, Tairāwhiti Museum, 34531, acknowledging Te Poho o Rawiri marae.

Picnics

Picnics were a popular social occasion for Pāhekā communities.[119] Gathering together and sharing a meal that everyone had contributed to was a great way to build and maintain social connections,[120] especially in rural areas where the population was relatively small. Well documented in writing and photographs, they were a demonstration of the principles of hospitality and egalitarianism that applied in other rural settings.

Local newspapers published detailed descriptions of community picnics, which, when supported by photographs such as those on pages 263 and 264, give a vivid sense of these events. For example, in January 1884 the *Mataura Ensign* featured this report on the annual picnic at Otaria, Southland:

> The first part of the day looked anything but promising, but about ten o'clock it cleared up, although the wind was rather cold. On the ground steam was soon got up, when Messrs Stewart and Smail produced an excellent cup of tea. The ladies spread out their stores of substantials and fancies upon the green sward, the gipsy fashion adding zest to the enjoyment. After every person had been well satisfied with tea, sandwiches and the usual fancy bread accompaniments, games of all sorts were improvised – men's races, boys' and girls' races, vaulting, tilting at the ring, and a married woman's race. . . . [E]verything was carried out without a single hitch occuring to mar the good feeling and enjoyment which prevailed amongst all classes of the community.[121]

In February 1892 the same newspaper printed a full description of the picnic at nearby Kelso, noting that it was 'pronounced by all a thorough success'.

> All and sundry were invited to accept of the kind hospitality of the good ladies, and it is needless to say a very large number, especially the juvenile portion of the community, responded to the kind invitation. The threatening nature of yesterday's weather was enough to dampen the ardor of the committee in their endeavor

> to make each successive year eclipse the last, but it certainly did not do so, judging by the completeness of all the arrangements, the splendidly brewed tea, and quantity and perfect quality of the many dainty eatables.[122]

The newspaper accounts of these events made mention of the inclusion of 'all and sundry' as evidence of the strength of community spirit. Descriptions and photographs of picnics seemed to suggest that here was a group of people with shared ideas and aspirations getting together to enjoy a meal and light entertainment before returning to their daily lives.

These community gatherings continued to be an important ritual in rural areas into the twentieth century, and many remember the annual picnic as a real highlight in the social calendar. Winifred Carson of Maruia recalled that she and her family attended two picnics each year in the 1920s: one to their neighbour Mr Bailey's to gather plums for jam; the other a school picnic attended by students and their parents. The fathers were responsible for organising the games and races, and the mothers and children prepared and brought the food.[123] Not everyone found the annual picnic to be quite such a highlight but, as Elvira Begg (née Green) discovered when she married and moved to a farm in Wyndham in 1939, attendance was still expected.

> When your neighbour invited you over the telephone to the school break-up, which took the form of an outdoor picnic, you did not do as I did and reply 'Oh no thank-you I wouldn't know anybody.' You went because everyone went, and that was where you got to know people.[124]

In communities where organised recreational events were still relatively rare, particularly for those with families, picnics fulfilled an important function. They provided a convivial setting where newcomers could meet their neighbours, established social bonds could be renewed, news and gossip exchanged, and experiences shared and discussed.

As Sarah Courage said of the New Year's picnic held near Waipara Station each year, 'the eating part formed the pith and kernel' of these events.[125] Consequently, a large amount of preparation and labour was

The Rāwene school picnic at Pākanae, c. 1900.
Charles Peet Dawes photograph, Auckland Libraries
Heritage Collections, 1142-D179.

˅
Picnic at Marcrofts, Wharehine, c. 1910. Harold Marsh photograph, W. H. Marsh collection, Albertland Heritage Museum Inc., 2004.2.00.19.

necessary to make them a success, and very often this work fell to the rural woman, who was '[e]ven more devoted in the service of any good cause than her husband . . . always ready to provide one more supper or afternoon tea for any sort of gathering'.[126] Almost every dance, concert, ball or other occasion required the ladies to 'bring a plate', and some took great pride in offering dishes of 'dainty appointment and generous provision'.[127] As a new arrival remarked in 1883, 'New Zealand ladies can turn out a table, heavily laden with a variety of cakes and sweets, quite astonishing to behold'.[128] As well as adding greatly to the festivity of these occasions, contributions of food were 'an easy and graceful way of doing good', as the sweets and baked treats could be auctioned off to raise funds for community projects.[129]

Indoor gatherings and events were usually held in the local hall. These halls 'were the social heart of the New Zealand country community. . . . Within their chambers, meetings ebbed and flowed with hot debate, social clubs interacted and the romantic heart of the community fluttered.'[130] Sara Newman recalls of her childhood in the Nelson region in the 1930s that Christmas parties were held in the local hall and were run with military precision by the women of the district.

> [W]ith the children lined up on forms, the women on chairs around the sides of the hall and the men lurking by the door, out of the line of fire if possible, it was pinnies off and everyone settled down to some serious eating. When most of the food was gone and the squashed cream cakes scraped off the wooden floor, the women retired to the kitchen to rearrange leftovers for afternoon tea, wash up and pack cutlery and china which had been carefully labelled with sticking plaster and indelible pencil. It was a logistical exercise that would have challenged the army, but By Joves they got it right.[131]

R. D. Sharpe suggests in *Country Occasions* that this 'tradition of service', whereby women were primarily responsible for facilitating community events, 'may have arisen when such were the only occasions on which a country housewife met a group of friends'.[132] This is backed up by Daisy Schepens' description of a Northland farming family in the 1920s:

> Once a month all the men of the district would attend the Kaihu cattle and sheep sale. This meant a fifty mile ride, leaving at 7 a.m. and returning at 10 or 11 p.m. These were long, lonely days for the women folk and after Marcel had left in the morning, Floss would indulge in a good howl, cursing her luck at being a woman.[133]

Rural men had opportunities to interact on a fairly regular basis, brought together at various times by their shared work routines. Women, however, tended to work in isolation, and had far less opportunity to move around. They therefore had to create their own opportunities for social interaction, and work hard to see them succeed. That they chose to do so indicates considerable engagement in the wider community – and the community was stronger for their efforts.

It is difficult to know to what extent Māori were included in these supposedly all-inclusive community gatherings. It may have been that although they were formally invited they were informally discouraged from attending by subtle social cues. There is evidence, though, that community feasts did sometimes include both Māori and Pākehā, and that everyone enjoyed the genial atmosphere. The Matarawa picnic of 1883 was described as a 'merry gathering of friends and neighbors, both European and Natives, from all parts of the Valley . . . between 400 and 500 being present'.[134] And settlers in Waimamaku, south of the Hokianga, marked the Christmas of 1889 with a picnic hosted by their Māori neighbours:

> We determined that we would not allow the merry season to pass unrecognised, but would hold a picnic. Our Maori neighbours soon got to know, and promptly came with a cordial invitation to spend it with them. . . .
>
> At 5.30 a.m. on Boxing-Day, Rupini Hoani came along from the Maori settlement with a horse and trap, to convey small articles – including babies, if necessary – to the locality chosen, his pleasant grass paddock. . . .
>
> . . . Arrived on the ground we found the Native women already busy with match-box lids and mussel shells peeling riwai – potatoes – by the hundred-weight. Hung up to a tree was the

> carcase of a goodly bullock slaughtered for the guests. Cooked in the 'hangi' (Maori oven), both meat and potatoes were perfect. New flax mats were made there and then, spread on the grass, the good things placed upon them, all scrupulously clean, grace was reverently said, and the pakeha was invited to 'fall to'.[135]

Joan Millar recalled that during her childhood in the 1930s her neighbour, Mrs Haberfield, would organise a slightly different type of picnic at the local beach:

> About three times in late autumn she would organise a big picnic, at what we called the back beach. . . . There would be a crowd of us, boys and girls, and we loved it. We would get mussells [sic] off the rocks and build a big bonfire. . . . Mr Haberfield would all this time be round the rocks cutting off the bull kelp and he and his wife would cut it into various lengths and stack it on the beach. When it came time to go home, we all were given a bundle of kelp to carry home, boys the heaviest. I can see now that they made the most of their picnic to get the kelp home, but when they returned from the Titi Islands, they always gave us a good feed of mutton birds.[136]

The picnic brought the neighbours together to enjoy a shared meal, but it also cemented a reciprocal relationship where labour was exchanged for goods – a relationship that continued long after the event.

In a 1990s study of the ideology of rural life, Claudia Bell found that rural Pākehā New Zealanders shared a firm belief in a set of common 'rural' values, including participation in nature, a strong work ethic, the prioritisation of family, and the importance of community togetherness.[137] These values, according to her interviewees, constituted a distinctive way of life that was superior to life in the city, and they held to it tightly. Their commitment to being rural people – people on the land – cut across other social variables such as gender and class, and they expressed that commitment in their daily practices.[138] This is not to say that rural communities were uniquely egalitarian, for there is plenty of evidence that class and status divisions were enforced. Still, through rituals involving food, people could draw together the edges of the body social, encourage mutual aid, and demonstrate their continued dedication to place and community.

The values of Pākehā rural society didn't necessarily align with those of Māori communities, and Māori used acts of culinary diplomacy for their own political and social ends. All rural New Zealanders used the sharing of food as a mode of communication and, accordingly, the kitchen, kāuta, cookhouse, hall and wharekai were key sites for the formation and consolidation of individual and community identity.

Conclusion

Conclusion

In the introduction to this book I suggested that the kitchen provided the perfect vantage point from which to examine aspects of everyday life, and that, when taken together, glimpses of historical kitchens offered in diaries, magazines, autobiographies and oral testimonies would provide a broad picture of rural life in New Zealand. Looking in through the kitchen window, we have witnessed quiet moments of love and friendship – intimate scenes that testify to the beauty, pain, monotony and unpredictability of daily life. We have seen how the sharing of meals provided opportunities for conversation and reflection, while the warmth and familiarity of the kitchen made it a place in which to feel 'at home'.

We have also seen the space humming with work and animated by the frenetic movement of people and goods. The kitchen was the site of vital daily tasks that required the labour of the entire household, and that drew on resource networks extending across rural New Zealand and beyond. Looking out from the kitchen, we saw traces of those networks: vegetables growing in orderly rows; cows ambling in for their daily milking; untamed bush ringing with birdsong; and rivers teeming with fish and eels. Moving in and out of the frame were grocers, butchers, neighbours, friends and whānau, arriving with resources or to lend a hand and enjoy a meal.

My goal throughout the book has been to demonstrate the diversity of rural lives, and to incorporate as wide a range of viewpoints and experiences as possible. For many Pākehā New Zealanders, the prevailing view of 'the country', both as it was in the past and in its present configuration, derives from an inherited structure of feeling that stresses naturalness, constancy, simple virtue and stability. Here I have presented a more complicated view, one that leaves room for aspects of the treasured rural myth while still subjecting it to scholarly critique. Certainly, there is evidence here of the strength of community, of mutuality and egalitarianism, of commitment to family and connection to the land, but this exists alongside evidence of conflict, contradiction and injustice.

There is nothing inherently 'natural' about rural New Zealand as we now picture it, and to bring it into being, previous generations of 'pioneers' transformed the existing environmental, political and social landscape, refashioning it to suit their land-owning aspirations with little consideration of the consequences for tangata whenua. Having achieved this transformation, rural people did work to establish cohesive communities based on relative social equality and mutual aid, but their society was never as egalitarian as the ideal of the 'working man's paradise' implied. Our seemingly stable and idyllic countryside thus has a fraught and fractured history, examined here in relation to food production and cooking.

The rural population is and always has been a diverse group, and while certain facets of rural life such as geographic isolation and reliance on the land could perhaps be considered common to all, there has been as much to divide rural people as to unite them. Rural Māori structured their communities around whānau, whakapapa and connections to land, adopting new technologies, foods and housing while upholding fundamental aspects of tikanga Māori. Te ao Māori and the Pākehā rural world intersected at times – particularly in work settings – but remained largely separate through the late nineteenth and early twentieth centuries. Rural Pākehā people, meanwhile, shared certain beliefs about the superiority of rural life and the need to avoid the social evils of the old world, but day-to-day their experiences varied greatly depending on their location, gender and class. It is impossible to capture all of those experiences in one book, but I have tried to introduce as broad a range of rural people as possible.

If the popular view of rural New Zealand has it that life in the country is stable and unhurried, the corollary of that view is that rural people are inherently conservative and rural life is unchanging. I dispute that notion, for, as the preceding chapters have illustrated, rural people have embraced change, and their responses to social and economic shifts have been contemplative and pragmatic. The kitchen has been a site of adjustment for Māori and Pākehā: a place where new ideas and technologies have been introduced and accommodated. Some changes were forced on Māori communities by discriminatory mechanisms of power within the colonial administration, but they retained agency

Conclusion

in their response to those changes. As Michael Stevens demonstrated so convincingly in his study of muttonbirding in Murihiku, tradition and modernity are not mutually exclusive, but they fit together in different ways for different groups of people.[1] Examining the shifts and repositionings that occurred within individual households and kitchens over the nineteenth and early twentieth centuries has provided valuable evidence of these negotiated modernities, giving some sense of the values that rural people held to in their evaluations of new ideas and technologies, but also demonstrating the malleability of tradition.

The kitchen sat at the centre of a web of relationships and processes that dictated the form and function of the space, and that web was slightly different in every household. All rural people had cooking and eating facilities, and most also had spaces for processing food resources and storing them, but the arrangement of those facilities and the equipment used to carry out that processing varied greatly. As demonstrated in chapter 2, a range of cooking techniques and technologies were utilised by rural people, depending on their financial situation, the permanence of their dwelling, their access to electricity, and their personal preference. Furthermore, while some families used their kitchens for both cooking and eating, and therefore required large kitchen spaces that could accommodate groups of workers and neighbours as well as the cook, in other cases food processing, cooking and eating were divided across a number of discrete spaces. In many Māori homes, for instance, cooked food was kept separate from the activities of the main house and all cooking was carried out in a separate kāuta. Cooking facilities were gradually incorporated into the dwelling, and although this caused significant disruptions to tikanga Māori, families continued to adhere to principles of tapu and manaakitanga in their daily routines, establishing their own ways of living in Pākehā housing forms.

Māori and Pākehā rural families also had different notions of ideal houses and ideal homes, and, as discussed in chapter 1, this resulted in different physical constructions and emotional conceptions of cooking spaces. For Pākehā, the notion of 'home' was closely tied to the private family house and, in this context, the kitchen was associated with notions of comfort, security and love. As it was often the only living space, and was always the warmest room in the house, the kitchen was used for reading, playing games, telling stories, practising dances, sharing intimacies and hundreds of other family rituals; it was the spatial embodiment of intimate familial relations. To enter the space was to feel that you were in a place of refuge – giving rise to the popular expression that the kitchen is the heart of the home. However, the underlying implication of this adage is that 'home' is synonymous with the private family dwelling, and for Māori this was not necessarily the case. As discussed, notions of home in te ao Māori centre on whenua and whakapapa, and encompass a much broader range of spaces than just the family house. As the nature of the whare changed, communities invested in marae, wharenui and wharekai as places to come home to; places to share kōrero and kai.

Throughout this period, most, but by no means all, cooking was done by women. Given the arduous and mundane tasks they performed in the kitchen day after day, it would be easy to assume that rural women felt trapped there – tied to the stove and relegated by their gender to a life of drudgery. Certainly, some women did feel trapped in their homes and burdened by their domestic responsibilities, but evidence from magazines, oral histories and biographies reveals a far greater range of viewpoints and experiences than the idea of the kitchen as a 'woman's sphere' might seem to imply. Rural kitchens could serve both public and private functions and were not exclusively used by women, while rural women's work could and did extend far beyond the domestic realm. Furthermore, Māori and Pākehā women attached a range of different meanings to food preparation: some found satisfaction and self-identity in food preparation and cooking, while others looked for alternative roles and futures.

Preparing meals over an open fire or in a coal range could be back-breaking work, but it was also absolutely crucial to the wellbeing of the family and the maintenance of community. Indeed, if this book has one overarching theme it is the importance of food not just as a source of sustenance but also as a focus for social interaction and a means by which to transmit culture. As Sidney W. Mintz reminds us in *Tasting Food, Tasting Freedom*, the foods we eat and the techniques we employ to prepare and cook foods have histories, as do the symbolic meanings that govern our breaking of bread.[2] Both Māori and Pākehā used food to build and maintain social relationships, revealing through the sharing of meals who they wished to associate with and how they wanted their communities to develop. The meals themselves were quickly consumed, but the connections made in the kitchens and wharekai of rural New Zealand survived long after the plates had been cleared, demonstrating the importance of informal social interaction in the making of community. The need to cook and eat food shaped rural homes, routines and relationships – and as such, to look at the kitchen is to see the hub and the heart of rural life.

Notes

Abbreviations

AJHR	*Appendices to the Journals of the House of Representatives of New Zealand*
ANZ	Archives New Zealand, Wellington
ATL	Alexander Turnbull Library, Wellington
CMS	Anglican Church Missionary Society
ENZB	Early New Zealand Books database, University of Auckland
HC	Hocken Collections, University of Otago, Dunedin
NZETC	New Zealand Electronic Text Collection database, Victoria University of Wellington
NZJH	*New Zealand Journal of History*
PP	Papers Past online database, National Library of New Zealand
Te Ara	the Encyclopedia of New Zealand

Introduction

1. Lévi-Strauss, 'The Culinary Triangle', 28.
2. Mintz, *Tasting Food*, 6.
3. Ibid., 6–7; Counihan and Van Esterik, 'Introduction', 1.
4. Counihan and Van Esterik, 'Introduction', 1.
5. Campbell, *Farming Inside Invisible Worlds*, 90. See, for example, Arnold, *New Zealand's Burning*; Cant and Kirkpatrick (eds), *Rural Canterbury*; Eldred Grigg, *A Southern Gentry*; Gardner, *The Amuri*; Hatch, *Respectable Lives*; Holland, *Home in the Howling Wilderness*; Peden, *Making Sheep Country*.
6. See work by Pita King, especially 'When the Marae Moves into the City'. Melissa Matutina Williams found in her study of migration from Panguru (a rural location in the Hokianga) to Auckland in the mid-twentieth century that, for most of those who migrated, the two locations coexisted as home places: Williams, *Panguru and the City*, 248.
7. Waterhouse, *The Vision Splendid*, 11.
8. For theoretical discussions of rurality, see Newby, 'Locality and Rurality', 209–15; Hoggart, 'Let's Do Away with Rural', 245–57; Whatmore, 'On Doing Rural Research', 605–07; Halfacree, 'Locality and Social Representation', 23–37; Woods, *Rural Geography*, 3–16; Riney-Kehrberg, 'New Directions in Rural History', 155–58.
9. Wynn, 'Scoping Yeotopia', 7.
10. Kenneth B. Cumberland quoted in Wynn, 'Scoping Yeotopia', 7.
11. Swarbrick, 'Rural Services', Te Ara, https://teara.govt.nz/en/rural-services
12. Leach, *Kitchens*, 146, 165.
13. Phillips, 'Rural Mythologies', Te Ara, https://teara.govt.nz/en/rural-mythologies; Derby, 'Māori-Pākehā Relations – Māori Urban Migration', Te Ara, https://teara.govt.nz/en/maori-pakeha-relations/page-5
14. Phillips, 'Rural Recreation', Te Ara, https://teara.govt.nz/en/rural-recreation
15. Massey, *Space, Place, and Gender*, 120.
16. See Campbell, *Farming Inside Invisible Worlds*, 84–85.
17. Ibid., 86.
18. Star, 'On the Edge of Canterbury Settlement'; see also Star, *Thomas Potts of Canterbury*.
19. West, *The Face of Nature* is one example.
20. See, for example, Stevens, 'Muttonbirds and Modernity'; Williams, 'E Pākihi Hakinga a Kai'.
21. See, for example, Ashworth, *The Bungalow in New Zealand*; Austin, 'Polynesian Architecture in New Zealand'; Brown, *Māori Architecture*; Fearnley, *Colonial Style*; Prickett, 'Houses and House Life'; Salmond, *Old New Zealand Houses*; Shaw, *New Zealand Architecture*; Stacpoole, *Colonial Architecture*; Stewart, *The New Zealand Villa*; Toomath, *Built in New Zealand*.
22. See, for example, Ferguson, *Building the New Zealand Dream*; Petersen, *New Zealanders at Home*; Schrader, *We Call It Home*; Brookes (ed.), *History, Houses, People*; Wanhalla, 'Housing Un/healthy Bodies'.

Notes

23 Leach, *Kitchens*.
24 Rolshoven, 'The Kitchen: Terra Incognita', 10.
25 Blunt and Dowling, *Home*, 2.
26 Somerset, *Littledene*, 64.
27 Belich, *Making Peoples*, 379.
28 See Walker, *Ka Whawhai Tonu Matou*; Anderson, Binney and Harris, *Tangata Whenua*.
29 Paterson, 'Ngā Reo o Ngā Niupepa', 169; Paterson, *Colonial Discourses*, 103–04.
30 Fairburn, *The Ideal Society*.
31 Hedley, 'Mutual Aid', 26–39.
32 Hatch, *Respectable Lives*.
33 McAloon, 'The Colonial Wealthy', 60; Brooking, 'Larkrise to Littledene'.
34 Arnold, 'Community in Rural Victorian New Zealand', 3–21.

1 What makes the ideal kitchen?

1 Maudlin and Herman, 'Introduction', 20.
2 See Ross, 'The Throat of Parata', 23; Mercier, 'What is Decolonisation?', 42.
3 Ross, 'The Throat of Parata', 23.
4 Petersen, *New Zealanders at Home*, 18. This idea comes from Rachel Buchanan, who argues in *The Parihaka Album* that the buildings at Parihaka spoke their own language, and through them the community was able to tell its stories of resistance. Buchanan, *The Parihaka Album*, 127–39.
5 See Blunt and Dowling, *Home*, 100.
6 Jackson, 'Where to Next?', 137–39.
7 Ross, 'The Throat of Parata', 23.
8 'Kitchen', Wikipedia entry, https://en.wikipedia.org/wiki/Kitchen (accessed 1 October 2023).
9 'Kitchen', Merriam-Webster Dictionary Online, https://www.merriam-webster.com/dictionary/kitchen (accessed 1 October 2023). My approach has been informed by Elizabeth Cromley, who explored changes in American architecture in relation to the many related spaces used for cooking and eating (such as storage spaces, smokehouses, pantries, kitchens, dining rooms and parlors). Cromley calls this the 'food axis', and although I did not adopt that terminology, I kept her broad definition in mind as I developed my own conception of the kitchen. See Cromley, *The Food Axis*, 2.
10 Sharp (ed.), *Duperrey's Visit to New Zealand in 1824*, 73–74.
11 Anderson, 'In the Foreign Gaze', 132–33.
12 Schrader, 'Māori Housing – Te Noho Whare', Te Ara, https://teara.govt.nz/en/maori-housing-te-noho-whare
13 Davidson, *Prehistory of New Zealand*, 157.
14 Anderson, 'In the Foreign Gaze', 132–33; Petersen, *New Zealanders at Home*, 15.
15 Marsden, 'God, Man and Universe: A Māori View', in T. A. C. Royal (ed.), *The Woven Universe: Selected Writings of Rev. Māori Marsden*, Estate of Rev. Māori Marsden, Ōtaki, 2003, 122, quoted in Duncan and Rewi, 'Tikanga', 39.
16 Duncan and Rewi, 'Tikanga', 41.
17 Petersen, *New Zealanders at Home*, 19; Stack and Stack, ed. Reed, *Early Maoriland Adventures of J. W. Stack*, 107.
18 Makereti, *Old-Time Maori*, 159–60.
19 Petrie *Outcasts of the Gods*, 21.
20 Petrie, 'Decoding the Colours of Rank in Māori Society', 214.
21 Ibid., 220.
22 Sharp (ed.), *Duperrey's Visit to New Zealand in 1824*, 38.
23 Prickett, 'Houses and House Life', 41.
24 Phillipps and Huria, *Māori Life and Custom*, 51.
25 Ibid., 52.
26 Savage, *Some Account of New Zealand*, 15.
27 Phillipps and Huria, *Māori Life and Custom*, 51.
28 Ibid., 52–53. See also Best, *The Maori, Volume II*, 578.
29 Dieffenbach, *Travels in New Zealand, Volume II*, 43.
30 Makereti, *Old-Time Maori*, 285.
31 Anderson, 'In the Foreign Gaze', 155; Paama-Pengelly, *Māori Art and Design*, 93.
32 Hiroa, *The Coming of the Maori*, 130. See also Paama-Pengelly, *Māori Art and Design*, 93.
33 Hiroa, *The Coming of the Maori*, 115, 130; Galbreath, 'Agricultural and Horticultural Research', Te Ara, https://teara.govt.nz/en/diagram/19623/kumara-pits
34 Makereti, *Old-Time Maori*, 159.
35 Ibid., 159–60.
36 Best, *The Maori, Volume II*, 578.
37 Ballantyne, *Entanglements of Empire*, 80.
38 Petersen, *New Zealanders at Home*, 17; Smith, *Pākehā Settlements in a Māori World*, 109.
39 Ballantyne, *Entanglements of Empire*, 80; Petersen, *New Zealanders at Home*, 17.
40 Ballantyne, *Entanglements of Empire*, 82.
41 Petersen, *New Zealanders at Home*, 17.
42 Anderson, 'Old Ways and New Means', 165; Binney, O'Malley and Ward, 'Rangatiratanga and Kāwanatanga', 243.
43 *New Zealand Spectator and Cook's Strait Guardian*, 17 February 1847, 2. PP, https://paperspast.natlib.govt.nz/newspapers/NZSCSG18470217.2.4; see also Petersen, *New Zealanders at Home*, 21.
44 *New Zealand Spectator and Cook's Strait Guardian*, 17 February 1847, 2. PP, https://paperspast.natlib.govt.nz/newspapers/NZSCSG18470217.2.4
45 For example, when visiting Te Wairoa in 1864 Lieutenant Herbert Meade called on Tūhourangi chief Te Keepa Te Rangi-pūawhe, a member of the Church of England, and 'found him living in a weatherboard house with flooring, door and windows, which together with his furniture, had all been constructed by himself'. The rest of the community at Te Wairoa lived in whare, although

as tourism in the area increased, structural elements such as corrugated iron and timber were incorporated into the construction. (Simmons, 'Te Wairoa', 56–58).
46   Wakefield, *Adventure in New Zealand, Volume I*, 330–31.
47   Ballantyne, *Webs of Empire*, 125.
48   Petersen, *New Zealanders at Home*, 20.
49   Anderson, 'Old Ways and New Means', 162, 165.
50   Ministry for Culture and Heritage, 'British & Irish Immigration: Summary', NZHistory, https://nzhistory.govt.nz/culture/immigration/home-away-from-home/summary
51   Denison and Yu Ren, *The Life of the British Home*, 250.
52   Swarbrick, *Creature Comforts*, 42.
53   Ibid., 44.
54   Courage, *Lights and Shadows*, 53.
55   Carson, *I Was Young*, 9–10.
56   Schrader, 'A Bi-cultural Townscape', 12–13; Schrader, *The Big Smoke*, 79–80.
57   Harman, '"Some Dozen *Raupo Whares*"', 43.
58   Schrader, *The Big Smoke*, 82–83; Salmond, *Old New Zealand Houses*, 32.
59   Isaacs, 'Early Building Legislation', 90–91; Schrader, *The Big Smoke*, 85–86.
60   Isaacs, 'Foundations of Control', 59; Harman, '"Some Dozen *Raupo Whares*"', 45.
61   Northcote Bade, 'Early Housing in New Zealand', 2; see also Wilkes and Wood, 'The Social Relations of Housing in Early New Zealand', 188.
62   See, for example, Ward, *A History of Domestic Space*, 156.
63   Petersen, *New Zealanders at Home*, 35; Sales, 'Early New Zealand Cottages', 99; Salmond, *Old New Zealand Houses*, 74.
64   Salmond, *Old New Zealand Houses*, 74.
65   Ibid., 75.
66   Ibid., 67.
67   Ibid.
68   Mitchell, 'Reminiscences', MS-Papers-10712, ATL.
69   Mackenzie, Diary, 1890–1, MS-0137, HC.
70   Wolff, Diary, MS-Papers-8078, ATL.
71   Toomath, *Built in New Zealand*, 5–6.
72   Miller, *Sturdy Sons*, 37–38.
73   Salmond, *Old New Zealand Houses*, 60.
74   Whitaker, 'Pioneer Tales', ARC2001-134, Puke Ariki.
75   Shaw, *New Zealand Architecture*, 38; Metson, 'The Farm Home', 359.
76   Hodgson, *The Big House*, 4–5.
77   Ibid., 12.
78   Barker, *Station Amusements*, 184–85.
79   Hodgson, *The Big House*, 19–20.
80   Ibid., 52–53.
81   Metson, 'The Farm Home', 359.
82   Carruthers, *'There Goes the Bell!!'*, 3.
83   Whereas most wharepuni had a fire in the centre defining the use of the space, in these dwellings the fireplace was at the end of the house and the door was on a side wall (Newman, 'Contact Period Houses', 23–24).
84   Martin, 'The Maori Whare After Contact', 86.
85   Ibid., 88.
86   Ibid., 72.
87   Davidson, *A Home of One's Own*, 19.
88   Wilkes and Wood, 'The Social Relations of Housing in Early New Zealand', 193.
89   Ferguson, *Building the New Zealand Dream*, 21–23.
90   Wilkes and Wood, 'The Social Relations of Housing in Early New Zealand', 198; Ferguson, *Building the New Zealand Dream*, 57.
91   Ferguson, *Building the New Zealand Dream*, 59; Schrader, 'Housing and Government', Te Ara, https://teara.govt.nz/en/housing-and-government
92   'Statement by the Hon. Sir Apirana T. Ngata, Native Minister', *AJHR*, 1931, I-II, G-10, iii; Boast, *Buying the Land*, 260–01.
93   Lange, *May the People Live*, 22–23.
94   Ibid., 139, 150.
95   Schmidt, 'Sir Maui Pomare's Clean Up of Maori Architecture', 86.
96   'Report of Dr. Pomare, Health Officer to the Maoris, to the Chief Health Officer', *AJHR*, 1902, I, H-31, 62.
97   Ibid., 63.
98   Durie, *Whaiora*, 42–43.
99   Ibid., 42.
100 'Report by Dr. Pomare on Sanitary Conditions of the Maori', *AJHR*, 1909, II, H-31, 60.
101 'Report of Dr. Pomare, Health Officer to the Maoris', *AJHR*, 1906, II, H-31, 75.
102 Lange, *May the People Live*, 152–53.
103 Hiroa, *The Coming of the Maori*, 135.
104 'Report by Dr. Pomare on Sanitary Conditions of the Maori', *AJHR*, 1909, II, H-31, 60.
105 Lange, *May the People Live*, 240; Wanhalla, 'Housing Un/healthy Bodies', 102.
106 Wanhalla, 'Housing Un/healthy Bodies', 102.
107 Dow, *Maori Health and Government Policy*, 150.
108 Division of Maori Hygiene, Annual Report of the Director-General of Health, *AJHR*, 1925, I, H-31, 49.
109 Schmidt, 'Sir Maui Pomare's Clean Up of Maori Architecture', 82; Harman, '"Some Dozen *Raupo Whares*"', 53.
110 Wanhalla, 'Housing Un/healthy Bodies', 115.
111 'Report of Dr. Pomare, Health Officer to the Maoris, to the Chief Health Officer', *AJHR*, 1902, I, H-31, 62.
112 Maudie Ruaka Reweti-Logan quoted in Takiari, *Women of the River, Part One*, 5.
113 Binney and Chaplin, *Ngā Mōrehu*, 5.
114 Brown, *Māori Architecture*, 103; Coney, *Standing in the Sunshine*, 69.
115 Smiler, 'Eldest Son', 67.
116 Warner Interview, 26 July 1995, OHInt-0633/5, ATL.

Notes

117 Wanhalla, 'Housing Un/healthy Bodies', 115; Turbott, Maori Health File, 88-059-2/09, ATL.
118 Ferguson, *Building the New Zealand Dream*, 115.
119 Boast, *Buying the Land*, 238–39, 245.
120 'Statement by the Hon. Sir Apirana T. Ngata, Native Minister', *AJHR*, 1931, I–II, G-10, xvii–xviii.
121 Wanhalla, 'Housing Un/healthy Bodies', 111.
122 Brown, *Māori Architecture*, 104–05; Turbott, 'Health and Social Welfare', 244.
123 Wanhalla, 'Housing Un/healthy Bodies', 115.
124 Krivan, 'The Department of Māori Affairs Housing Programmes', 35.
125 Ibid., 35–36.
126 Michael Joseph Savage, General Report, Native Land Development and the Provision of Houses for Maoris, including Employment Promotion, *AJHR*, 1938, I, G-10, 6.
127 Ferguson, *Building the New Zealand Dream*, 164.
128 Wanhalla, 'Housing Un/healthy Bodies', 111, 116.
129 'Homes for the Maori People', *Te Ao Hou* 3, no. 2, April 1955, 26–31.
130 Brown, *Māori Architecture*, 103.
131 Maori Conference at Putiki, Report on Conference, 1927, *AJHR*, 1928, I, G-8, 2.
132 Paterson, 'Rēweti Kōhere's Model Village', 28.
133 See Wanhalla, 'Housing Un/healthy Bodies', 117; Rosenberg, 'House Plans for Maori Families', 45.
134 Fairburn, 'Rural Myth', 8.
135 Metson, 'The Farm Home', 361.
136 Duff, 'The Development of House Styles', 15; Salmond, *Old New Zealand Houses*, 154.
137 Stewart, *The New Zealand Villa*, 49.
138 Ibid.
139 Salmond, *Old New Zealand Houses*, 185, 201.
140 Ibid., 185.
141 Ibid., 198, 201.
142 Salmond, *Old New Zealand Houses*, 200; Leach, *Kitchens*, 55.
143 Metson, 'The Farm Home', 361.
144 State Advances Corporation, Rural Housing Designs and Specifications, AELE 19203 SAC1 233/35/113/1, R20054195, ANZ.
145 Richards Interview, 9–16 January 1987, OHInt-0053/25, ATL.
146 Winter, *Memories*, P Box 920.72 MEM 2000, ATL, 23.
147 State Advances Corporation, Rural Housing Designs and Specifications, AELE 19203 SAC1 233/35/113/1, R20054195, ANZ.
148 Arbury and Cram, 'Housing on Māori Land, c.1870–2021', 127.
149 Rural Housing Bill, *Parliamentary Debates*, 1939, Vol. CCLVI, 321, 337.
150 Ibid., 325.
151 *New Zealand Official Yearbook, 1990*, Statistics New Zealand Digital Yearbook Collection, https://www3.stats.govt.nz/new_zealand_official_yearbooks/1990/nzoyb_1990.html#idsect2_1_28242
152 Fairburn, 'Rural Myth', 12; Callister and Didham, 'Workforce Composition – Workforce by Sector', Te Ara, https://teara.govt.nz/en/workforce-composition

153 Callister and Didham, 'Workforce Composition – Workforce by Sector', Te Ara, https://teara.govt.nz/en/workforce-composition; Brooking, 'Economic Transformation', 250.
154 Fairburn, 'Rural Myth', 8; Campbell, *Farming Inside Invisible Worlds*, 93.
155 Fairburn, 'Rural Myth', 12.
156 Carter, 'Most Important Industry', 27–28.
157 Jackson, 'Where to Next?', 137.
158 Boulton, Nee and Allport, 'Haukāinga', 6–8.
159 Pehi and Johnson, 'Whenua Whānau', 186.
160 Connor, 'Land, Notions of "Home" and Cultural Space', 159.
161 Boulton, Nee and Allport, 'Haukāinga', 6.
162 Connor, 'Land, Notions of "Home" and Cultural Space', 167.
163 Ibid., 168; Austin, 'Polynesian Architecture', 199.
164 Boulton, Nee and Allport, 'Haukāinga', 7.
165 Ibid., 11.
166 Moeke-Pickering, 'Maori Identity Within Whanau', n.p.
167 Boulton, Nee and Allport, 'Haukāinga', 9.
168 Makereti, *Old-Time Maori*, 285.
169 Gilabert, 'Labours of Love', 50.
170 See Davidoff and Hall, *Family Fortunes*.
171 Hareven, 'The Home and the Family', 255.
172 Davidoff and Hall, *Family Fortunes*, 74.
173 Middleton, *Pēwhairangi*, 95.
174 Olssen, 'Families and the Gendering of European New Zealand', 40.
175 Fitzgerald, 'Archives of Memory', 667–68.
176 Henry Williams, quoted in Fitzgerald, 'Archives of Memory', 668.
177 Gilabert, 'Labours of Love', 36.
178 Amiria Manutahi Stirling, quoted in Gilabert, 'Labours of Love', 33.
179 Kohere, *The Autobiography of a Maori*, 102, 105.
180 Ibid., 105.
181 R. Walker, 'The Urban Maori', in New Zealand Planning Council (ed.), *He Matapuna: A Source* (Wellington: R. Walker, 1979), 37, quoted in Moeke-Pickering, 'Maori Identity Within Whanau', n.p.
182 Beaglehole and Deaglehole, *Some Modern Maoris*, 270–71.
183 See Awatere et al, 'Tū Whare Ora – Building Capacity for Māori Driven Design in Sustainable Settlement Development'; Hoskins et al, 'Ki Te Hau Kainga'; Kake, 'Pehiāweri Marae Papakāinga'.
184 Smith, 'Rural Organisations', NZHistory, https://nzhistory.govt.nz/women-together/theme/rural-women
185 'About Ourselves', *Home and Country*, May 1, 1934, 1.
186 Campbell, *Between the Kitchen and the Creek*, 22–23.
187 Somerset, *Littledene*, 22–23, 59.
188 Ibid., 22–23.
189 Courage, *Lights and Shadows*, 157.
190 Davidoff and Hall, *Family Fortunes*, 359.
191 Flanders, *The Making of Home*, 67.
192 Ibid., 67–68; Ward, *History of Domestic Space*, 6.
193 Hareven, 'The Home and the Family', 267.
194 Petersen, *New Zealanders at Home*, 18; Flanders, *The Making of Home*, 72–73.

195 Davidoff and Hall, *Family Fortunes*, 90.
196 Coleman, *A Memoir of the Rev. Richard Davis*, 407.
197 Paterson, 'Rēweti Kōhere's Model Village', 34–35.
198 Ward, *History of Domestic Space*, 160.
199 Moeke-Pickering, 'Maori Identity Within Whanau', n.p; Taonui, 'Tribal Organisation', Te Ara, https://teara.govt.nz/en/tribal-organisation
200 Makereti, *Old-Time Maori*, 100–01.
201 Census of the Maori Population (Papers relating to), *AJHR*, 1906, II, H-26A, 20.
202 Makereti, *Old-Time Maori*, 100–01.
203 Johnstone-Smith, *Battles, Buggies and Babies*, 47.
204 McWhannell, Reminiscences, Misc-MS-0784, HC.
205 Ibid.
206 Flanders, *The Making of Home*, 102.
207 Ibid., 80.
208 Ibid., 84.
209 Pauline Perry to her parents, 4 April 1927, 'Chronicle of Leonard and Pauline Perry', MS-Papers-5504, ATL.
210 Pauline Perry to her parents, 21 February 1928, 'Chronicle of Leonard and Pauline Perry', MS-Papers-5504, ATL.
211 'Household Hints', *New Zealand Farmer, Bee and Poultry Journal* 12, no. 3, March 1892, 151.
212 Trotter and Trotter, *Margaret's Story*, 35–37.
213 Women's Division, *My Rural Home*, 27.

2 Hāngī stones and hot stoves

1 'Homes I Have Missed', *Auckland Star*, 18 June 1938, 6, Supplement. PP, https://paperspast.natlib.govt.nz/newspapers/AS19380618.2.176
2 Ibid.
3 Teal, 'Changing Kitchen Technology', 71.
4 Allen, *Home*, 230.
5 Ibid.
6 Beaton, 'A Contemporary Māori Culinary Tradition', 28, 59–60.
7 Stone and Langer, 'Te Ahi i te Ao Māori', 18.
8 Beaton, 'A Contemporary Māori Culinary Tradition', 29.
9 Ibid., 29–33.
10 Stone and Langer, 'Te Ahi i te Ao Māori', 18; Richardson, '3 Feet Under', 9.
11 Williams, 'Māori Fire Use', 178.
12 Richardson, '3 Feet Under', 12.
13 Thomson, *The Story of New Zealand*, *Volume I*, 159.
14 Beaton, 'A Contemporary Māori Culinary Tradition', 35.
15 Makereti, *Old-Time Maori*, 265.
16 Leach, 'Cooking with Pots – Again', 56.
17 Ibid., 56; Thomson, *The Story of New Zealand*, *Volume I*, 160.
18 Beaton, 'A Contemporary Māori Culinary Tradition', 60.
19 Leach, 'Cooking with Pots – Again', 66.
20 Ibid.
21 Ibid., 64.
22 Soper, *The Otago of Our Mothers*, 33–34.
23 Moore, 'The Farmhouse Kitchen', *New Zealand Journal of Agriculture* 83, no. 3, 1951, 235.
24 Thomson, *Rambles with a Philosopher*, 145; see also Johnstone-Smith, *Battles, Buggies and Babies*, 7.
25 Leach, 'Cooking with Pots – Again', 63.
26 Reremoana Koopu, quoted in Binney and Chaplin (eds), *Ngā Mōrehu*, 62.
27 David Maxwell, quoted in Harris and Lancaster, *Remember the Hokianga*, 216.
28 'Stoves and Firewood', *New Zealand Farmer, Bee and Poultry Journal* 10, no 6, June 1890, 241.
29 Drummond and Drummond, *At Home in New Zealand*, 87.
30 Mackenzie, *Pioneers of Martins Bay*, 18.
31 Carson, *I Was Young*, 21.
32 Ibid., 21–22.
33 'Stoves and Firewood', *New Zealand Farmer, Bee and Poultry Journal* 10, no. 6, June 1890, 241.
34 Drummond and Drummond, *At Home in New Zealand*, 88.
35 Moore, 'The Farmhouse Kitchen', *New Zealand Journal of Agriculture* 83, no. 5, 1951, 405.
36 Angus, *The Ironmasters*, 21.
37 Bryant, 'Reminiscences and Reflections', MS-Papers-3899, ATL.
38 Angus, *The Ironmasters*, 7.
39 Gaffney, *The Coal Range Handbook*, 4.
40 Ibid., 4–5.
41 Angus, *The Ironmasters*, 21; Burton, *Two Hundred Years*, 23; Teal, 'Changing Kitchen Technology', 75.
42 Burton, *Two Hundred Years*, 23; Teal, 'Changing Kitchen Technology', 75.
43 Angus, *The Ironmasters*, 13–21.
44 Ibid., 21.
45 'Our Industries', *Otago Witness*, 1 March 1894, 35. PP, https://paperspast.natlib.govt.nz/newspapers/otago-witness/1894/3/1
46 Angus, *The Ironmasters*, 22–23.
47 Advertisements, *Otago Daily Times*, 7 November 1879, 8. PP, https://paperspast.natlib.govt.nz/newspapers/otago-daily-times/1879/11/7
48 Angus, *The Ironmasters*, 22; Burton, *Two Hundred Years*, 23.
49 'The Exhibition', *Star* (Canterbury), 4 September 1885, 3. PP, https://paperspast.natlib.govt.nz/newspapers/star/1885/9/4
50 Advertisements, *Oamaru Mail*, 12 July 1892, 3. PP, https://paperspast.natlib.govt.nz/newspapers/OAM18920712.2.29.4
51 Advertisements, *Wanganui Herald*, 31 May 1888, 1. PP, https://paperspast.natlib.govt.nz/newspapers/wanganui-herald/1888/5/31
52 'Our Industries', *Otago Witness*, 1 March 1894, 35. PP, https://paperspast.natlib.govt.nz/newspapers/otago-witness/1894/3/1
53 Advertisements, *Otago Daily Times*, 21 July 1893, 1. PP, https://paperspast.natlib.govt.nz/newspapers/otago-daily-times/1893/7/21
54 Advertisements, *Mataura Ensign*, 26 November 1903, 1. PP, https://paperspast.natlib.govt.nz/newspapers/mataura-ensign/1903/11/26;

Notes

Advertisements, *Marlborough Express*, 2 January 1903, 1. PP, https://paperspast.natlib.govt.nz/newspapers/marlborough-express/1903/1/2; Advertisements, *Ashburton Guardian*, 2 January 1903, 1. PP, https://paperspast.natlib.govt.nz/newspapers/ashburton-guardian/1903/1/2

55 Angus, *The Ironmasters*, 43; Teal, 'Changing Kitchen Technology', 73–81. See also Cyolopedia Company Limited, *Cyclopedia of New Zealand, Volume 3*, 311; Cylopedia Company Limited, *Cyclopedia of New Zealand, Volume 4*, 321.
56 Chitty, 'Autobiographical Sketch', qMS-0446, ATL.
57 Carson, *I Was Young*, 22.
58 Department of Statistics, *New Zealand Population Census, 1945, Volume 11, Dwellings and Households*, 34. In line with the definitions given in the 1945 yearbook, I have defined the urban population as those in cities and boroughs, and the rural population as those in counties, all town districts, and extra-county islands. Statistics New Zealand, Digital Yearbook Collection, 1945, https://www3.stats.govt.nz/New_Zealand_Official_Yearbooks/1945/NZOYB_1945.html?_ga=2.134520434.2052059682.1694647436-1234002850.1693353856
59 Tintown, Makarita [sic] and Anaura Housing Surveys, Department of Maori Affairs, ACIH 16036 MA1 607/ 30/3/37, R19528234; ACIH 16036 MA1 607/ 30/3/16, R19528225; ACIH 16036 MA1 607/ 30/3/35, R19528233, ANZ.
60 Makarita [sic] Housing Survey, Department of Maori Affairs, ACIH 16036 MA1 607/ 30/3/16, R19528225, ANZ.
61 Waimiha Housing Survey, Department of Maori Affairs, ACIH 16036 MA1 608/ 30/3/65, R19528259, ANZ.
62 Yorke, *The Animals Came First*, 23.
63 Ibid., 78; Angus, *The Ironmasters*, 39.
64 Strasser, *Never Done*, 188.
65 Johnstone-Smith, *Battles, Buggies and Babies*, 89.
66 Angus, *The Ironmasters*, 39.
67 Millar, *Joan's Journey*, 10.
68 'Home on the Range', *Dairy Exporter* 14, no.7, March 1939, 75.
69 'Between Ourselves', *Dairy Exporter* 14, no. 4, December 1938, 63.
70 Teal, 'Changing Kitchen Technology', 86.
71 Angus, *The Ironmasters*, 57; Trapeznik, *Dunedin's Warehouse Precinct*, 142.
72 Veart, *First Catch Your Weka*, 135; Leach, *Kitchens*, 68–69.
73 Moffats Ltd, *Cooking by Moffat*, 4–5.
74 Leach, *Kitchens*, 68.
75 Reilly, *Connecting the Country*, 34.
76 Ibid., 52–55; Paris, *Two Per Mile*, 18–20.
77 Paris, *Two Per Mile*, 21.
78 Nevill, 'The "Electric Servant"', 61.
79 Rennie, *Power to the People*, 93–94.
80 Paris, *Two Per Mile*, 30.
81 Reilly, *Connecting the Country*, 110; Newport, 'Country Living in the 1920s', 30.
82 Paris, *Two Per Mile*, 37.
83 '"Power-Hungry" People Not "Standing Asleep"', *Northern Advocate*, 8 April 1949, 2. PP, https://paperspast.natlib.govt.nz/newspapers/NA19490408.2.4
84 'Huge Programme of Construction Ahead', *Northern Advocate*, 2 June 1949, 6. PP, https://paperspast.natlib.govt.nz/newspapers/NA19490602.2.62
85 'Shift Centre From Auckland To Kaikohe', *Northern Advocate*, 31 October 1949, 2. PP, https://paperspast.natlib.govt.nz/newspapers/NA19491031.2.6
86 'Huge Programme of Construction Ahead', *Northern Advocate*, 2 June 1949, 6. PP, https://paperspast.natlib.govt.nz/newspapers/NA19490602.2.62
87 Isaacs, Camilleri and French, 'Hot Water Over Time', n.p.
88 Williams, *Panguru and the City*, 156–57.
89 Leach, *Kitchens*, 70–71.
90 'Let's Brighten Our Homes', *Dairy Exporter* 14, no. 5, January 1939, 62.
91 Doig, *A Survey of Standards of Life*, 42.
92 O'Donnell, '"Electric Servants"', 179.
93 Leach, *Kitchens*, 35.
94 Maisie Dalbeth, quoted in Boyd, *Daughters of the Land*, 22.
95 Endt-Ferwerda, *Aunt Dorothy's Memories of Sunnydale*, 9.
96 Cowan, *More Work for Mother*, 45.
97 Ibid., 64.
98 Ibid., 98.
99 'Plain Jane: On Spring Cleaning', *New Zealand Farm and Home* 1, no. 1, March 1932, 333.
100 'A Brand New House', *Dairy Exporter* 12, no. 8, March 1937, 60.
101 'Between Ourselves', *Dairy Exporter* 12, no. 10, May 1937, 93.
102 Fairburn, 'The Rural Myth', 3–21.
103 Brooking, 'Economic Transformation', 233.
104 Fairburn, *The Ideal Society*, 128, 161–87; Ballantyne, 'On Place, Space and Mobility', 66.
105 Martin, *The Forgotten Worker*, 31, 33.
106 Ibid., 11, 14.
107 For more on plough camps see Martin, *The Forgotten Worker*, especially p. 161.
108 'Back Country Workers', *Press*, 22 August 1908, 7. PP, https://paperspast.natlib.govt.nz/newspapers/CHP19080822.2.32
109 Wilson, *My First Eighty Years*, 106.
110 Brooking, 'Economic Transformation', 236.
111 D. O. Williams in 'Agricultural Organisation in New Zealand', New Zealand Institute of Pacific Relations (1936), 185, quoted in Doig, *A Survey of Standards of Life*, 97.
112 Weaver and Munro, 'Country Living, Country Dying', 933.
113 Binney, O'Malley and Ward, 'The Land and the People', 314.
114 Ariana Rene, Brief of Evidence, quoted in Waitangi Tribunal, *Te Tau Ihu o te Waka a Maui, Volume III*, 1085.
115 Martin, *The Forgotten Worker*, 43; Hei Ariki Algie, quoted in Binney and Chaplin (eds), *Ngā Mōrehu*, 110.

116 Binney, O'Malley and Ward, 'The Land and the People', 313.
117 Martin, *The Forgotten Worker*, 151.
118 McNeill, 'Northland's Buried Treasure', n.p.
119 Koning and Oliver, 'Economic Decline', 25; Reed, *The Kauri Gumdiggers*, 51–52.
120 Binney, O'Malley and Ward, 'The Land and the People', 313.
121 Ibid.
122 Binney and O'Malley, 'The Quest for Survival', 341.
123 Wharemaru and Duffié, *Through the Eye of the Needle*, 32.
124 Waitangi Tribunal, *Muriwhenua Land Report*, 367–69.
125 Wairama Maihi te Huhu and others to Prime Minister, 6 January 1936, quoted in Waitangi Tribunal, *Muriwhenua Land Report*, 370.
126 Brooking, 'Economic Transformation', 243.
127 Shoebridge and McLean, 'Feeding Britain', NZHistory, https://nzhistory.govt.nz/war/public-service-at-war/feeding-britain; Brooking, 'Economic Transformation', 231.
128 Brooking, 'Economic Transformation', 231, 243.
129 'President's Monthly Message', *Countrywoman* 1, no. 9, January 1934, 1.
130 Wilson, *My First Eighty Years*, 205.
131 Boswell, *Dim Horizons*, 176–77.
132 Parker, 'Farm Women in the 1950s', 222.
133 Richardson, '3 Feet Under', 17, 32–33.
134 Ibid., 50.
135 Shaw and Brookes, 'Constructing Homes', 210.
136 Strasser, *Never Done*, 8.
137 Hollard, 'Reminiscences', qMS-0989, ATL.
138 Allen, *A Childhood at Cairnsmore*, 36.
139 Stephanie Tuhoro, quoted in Morrison (ed.), *Te Ropu o te Ora*, 81–82.
140 Duncan Interview, 28 July 1996, Central Stories Museum and Art Gallery, Alexandra.
141 Staples, *Cooks and Shepherds Come Away*, 154.
142 Easy, *Looking Backward*, 11.
143 Ibid.
144 Salmond, *Old New Zealand Houses*, 71–72.
145 Ibid., 143.
146 Easy, *Looking Backward*, 11.
147 Winter, *Memories*, P Box 920.72 MEM 2000, ATL, 24.
148 Sophie Kaa, quoted in Fyfe (ed.), *Matriarchs*, 44.
149 Isaacs, Camilleri and French, 'Hot Water Over Time', n.p.; White, *Springfield in the Foothills*, 30; Smyth, *Five on a Farm*, S478.5.08 S69 1979, HC, 14.
150 Beck, *These Days Were Mine*, 11.
151 Nessie Krippner, quoted in Boyd, *Daughters of the Land*, 15; Isaacs, 'Hot Water the Old-fashioned Way', 94.
152 Isaacs, Camilleri and French, 'Hot Water Over Time', n.p.
153 Editorial, *New Zealand Farm and Home* 1, no. 1, March 1932, 12.
154 Brookes, 'Nostalgia for "Innocent Homely Pleasures"', 210, 222.
155 Ibid., 221.
156 Ibid., 218, 225.
157 Worsley, *If Walls Could Talk*, 241.

158 The term 'shifts and makeshifts' comes from Kate Buckland's reminiscences. She writes of her first home at Deep Stream, Southland, which she moved to after her marriage in 1903, noting that 'I had been little in the country never in the Back blocks. I had no idea of the shifts and the makeshifts necessary there & in mining districts.' (Buckland, 'Reminiscences – Homes of Ours', MS-Papers-3892-3, ATL.)

3 Rēwena and rabbit stew

1 Connor, 'Whakapapa Back', 10.
2 Simpson, *A Distant Feast*, 63.
3 Ibid., 49–50.
4 *Labourers' Union Chronicle*, 26 June 1875, quoted in Simpson, *A Distant Feast*, 110.
5 See Williams, 'E Pākihi Hakinga a Kai'; Williams, 'Mahika Kai'.
6 Firth, *Economics of the New Zealand Maori*, 68.
7 Simpson, *A Distant Feast*, 83.
8 Weaver, *Great Land Rush*, 43, 83.
9 Campbell, *Farming Inside Invisible Worlds*, 45.
10 Brooking, '"Yeotopia" Found', 70.
11 Narotzky, 'Provisioning', 78.
12 Anderson, 'Emerging Societies, AD 1500–1800', 113; Binney, O'Malley and Ward, 'The Land and the People', 290.
13 McAloon, 'Land Ownership', Te Ara, https://teara.govt.nz/en/land-ownership
14 Keane, 'Te Māori i te Ohanga – Māori in the Economy', Te Ara, https://teara.govt.nz/en/te-maori-i-te-ohanga-maori-in-the-economy/page-4
15 Durie, 'Will the Settlers Settle?', 452.
16 Durie, 'Ancestral Laws of Māori', 8–9.
17 Weaver, *Great Land Rush*, 49, 74; Campbell, *Farming Inside Invisible Worlds*, 45.
18 Campbell, *Farming Inside Invisible Worlds*, 89–102.
19 Brooking, 'Use It or Lose It', 145–49.
20 Ibid., 147–48.
21 Ibid., 149.
22 Easton, *Not in Narrow Seas*, 189.
23 Gardner, 'A Colonial Economy', 81. See also Adams, *The Transformation of Rural Life*, 49–50; Fink, *Open Country, Iowa*, 32.
24 Te Rūnanga o Ngāi Tahu, 'Claim History', https://ngaitahu.iwi.nz/ngai-tahu/the-settlement/claim-history/; Boast, 'Te Tango Whenua – Māori Land Alienation', Te Ara, https://teara.govt.nz/en/te-tango-whenua-maori-land-alienation
25 Ministry for Culture and Heritage, 'Māori Land Loss, 1860–2000', NZHistory, https://nzhistory.govt.nz/media/interactive/maori-land-1860-2000
26 Lange, 'The Social Impact of Colonisation and Land Loss', 77. Raeburn Lange offers a number of examples in her study of land in the Rangitīkei, Manawatū and Horowhenua region, and notes that

Notes

'successful Māori farmers in this region are not difficult to locate'. On his land near Bulls, for instance, Hoeroa Marumaru had seventy to eighty cows, an electric milking shed and a cheese factory; while at Aorangi, John Mason Durie took over and extended the farm built by his parents and provided employment for unemployed Māori men during the Depression.

27 Easton, *Not in Narrow Seas*, 318; Lange, 'The Social Impact of Colonisation and Land Loss', 77–84.
28 European farming methods were taught as part of the native schools curriculum, which prioritised practical training based on Pākehā knowledge systems and aimed 'to lead the Maori boy to be a good farmer and the Maori girl to be a good farmer's wife' (Waitangi Tribunal, *The Wananga Capital Establishment Report*, 6–9).
29 Waitangi Tribunal, *Te Tau Ihu o te Waka a Maui, Volume III*, 1074–83.
30 Christopher Love, Brief of Evidence, and L. McDonald [sic], Brief of Evidence, quoted in Waitangi Tribunal, *Te Tau Ihu o te Waka a Maui, Volume III*, 1082–83.
31 Binney and Chaplin (eds), *Ngā Mōrehu*, 45, 62–63.
32 Harris, 'Persistence and Resilience', 367–72.
33 Ibid., 370; Harris, 'Maori Land Development Schemes', 125.
34 Harris, 'Persistence and Resilience', 371.
35 Harris, 'Maori Land Development Schemes', 20.
36 Campbell, *Farming Inside Invisible Worlds*, 47.
37 Leach, 'Maori Cookery Before Cook', 22–26.
38 Belich, *Making Peoples*, 68.
39 Paulin, 'Perspectives of Māori Fishing History and Techniques', 11–12.
40 James Cook, Journal Entry 5 December 1769 (for date see 'James Cook – A Journal of the Proceedings of His Majesty's Bark *Endeavour* on a Voyage Around the World', State Library of New South Wales, https://transcripts.sl.nsw.gov.au/page/james-cook-journal-proceedings-his-majestys-bark-endeavour-voyage-round-world-lieutenant-550), quoted in Paulin, 'Perspectives of Māori Fishing History and Techniques', 14.
41 Meredith, 'Te Hī Ika: Māori Fishing', 138.
42 Paulin, 'Perspectives of Māori Fishing History and Techniques', 42; Davidson, 'Explorers and Pioneers', 47–48.
43 Whaanga, 'Mātaitai: Shellfish Gathering', 144–45.
44 Best, *The Maori, Volume II*, 417–19.
45 Paulin, 'Perspectives of Māori Fishing History and Techniques', 15.
46 Ibid., 15–16, 41–42.
47 Eruera Paati, Brief of Evidence, quoted in Waitangi Tribunal, *Te Roroa Claim*, 177.
48 Kelly R. Wilson, H8, Evidence on Mahinga Kai, AG-653/177, HC.
49 Waitangi Tribunal, *Te Tau Ihu o te Waka a Maui, Volume III*, 1049.
50 Te Kui, 'The Rhythm of Life', 83.
51 See Waitangi Tribunal, *Te Tau Ihu o te Waka a Maui, Volume III*, 1046; Wharemaru and Duffié, *Through the Eye of the Needle*, 44; Binney and Chaplin (eds), *Ngā Mōrehu*, 45.
52 Burton, *Two Hundred Years*, 10, 12.
53 Edwards, *Mihipeka*, 46.
54 Ruku Arahanga, quoted in Rogers and Simpson (eds), *Te Tīmatanga Tātau Tātau*, 2.
55 Dacker, *The People of the Place*, 13.
56 Waitangi Tribunal, *The Ngai Tahu Report, Volume III*, 893.
57 Waitangi Tribunal, *The Whanganui River Report*, 62. They were, however, prey to trout fishermen, who considered them vermin and went to great lengths to try and exterminate them from target waters. See McDowall, *Ikawai*, 700–03.
58 McDowall, *Ikawai*, 169–79.
59 Rawiri Te Maire Tau, H6 – Evidence on Mahinga Kai, AG-653/176, HC.
60 Dot Davis, quoted in Takiari, *Women of the River. Part 1*, 26.
61 Park, '"Swamps which might doubtless Easily be drained"', 184; Hooker et al, H8 – Evidence on Mahinga Kai, AG-653/177, HC.
62 Wanhalla, 'Living on the Rivers' Edge', 138.
63 Charles Hursthouse, *New Zealand or Zealandia, The Britain of the South*, Edward Stanford, London, 1857, quoted in Park, '"Swamps which might doubtless Easily be drained"', 174.
64 Park, '"Swamps which might doubtless Easily be drained"', 174, 180.
65 Waitangi Tribunal, *Te Tau Ihu o te Waka a Maui, Volume III*, 1073; Dacker, *The People of the Place*, 12–13.
66 Keane, 'Te Tāhere Manu', 152–59.
67 Burton, *Two Hundred Years*, 10.
68 Mere Hutchinson (née Te Kuru) wrote: 'Mum used to put the hinu [fat] in the pot, in a great big boiler on the stove or open fire. Then, when this meat is dry, then you put it all into the hot fat – just like doing fish and chips. We leave it in the hinu and put it in a kerosene tin and leave it. Then you melt the fat if you want the tahu meat. When you eat it, it's just like roast meat.' (Rogers and Simpson (eds), *Te Tīmatanga Tātau Tātau*, 55–56.)
69 Heni Sunderland, quoted in Binney and Chaplin (eds), *Ngā Mōrehu*, 121–22.
70 Evidence of Henare R. Tau, quoted in Waitangi Tribunal, *The Ngai Tahu Report, Volume III*, 845.
71 Anderson, 'A Fragile Plenty', 47.
72 Willmshurst, 'Human Effects on the Environment', Te Ara, https://teara.govt.nz/en/human-effects-on-the-environment
73 Grey, *Aotearoa and New Zealand*, 256.
74 Wynn, 'Destruction Under the Guise of Improvement?', 129.
75 1913 Royal Commission, quoted in Waitangi Tribunal, *Te Tau Ihu o te Waka a Maui, Volume III*, 1078.
76 Alfred Elkington, Brief of Evidence, quoted in Waitangi Tribunal, *Te Tau Ihu o te Waka a Maui, Volume III*, 1079.
77 Priscilla Paul, Brief of Evidence, quoted in Waitangi Tribunal, *Te Tau Ihu o te Waka a Maui, Volume III*, 1079.
78 Husband, 'Mike Stevens: Bluffies and Kāi Tahu', *E-Tangata*, https://e-tangata.co.nz/korero/mike-stevens-bluffies-and-kai-tahu/
79 Evidence of Henare R. Tau, quoted in Waitangi Tribunal, *The Ngai Tahu Report, Volume III*, 885.
80 Emily Paniora, Brief of Evidence, quoted in Waitangi Tribunal, *Te Roroa Report*, 210–11.

81 Rawiri Te Maire Tau, H6 – Evidence on Mahinga Kai, AG-653/176, HC.
82 Dacker, *Te Mamae me te Aroha*, 105.
83 Waitangi Tribunal, *Te Tau Ihu o te Waka a Maui, Volume III*, 1048.
84 Ropata Stephens, Brief of Evidence, quoted in Waitangi Tribunal, *Te Tau Ihu o te Waka a Maui, Volume III*, 1079, 1048.
85 Ibid., 1049.
86 Stevens, 'Muttonbirds and Modernity', 298.
87 Ibid.
88 Hunter, *Hunting*, 77.
89 Ibid.
90 Cost of Living Commission Report, 1912, quoted in Bailey and Earle, *Home Cooking to Takeaways*, 212.
91 Simpson, *A Distant Feast*, 253.
92 Veart, *First Catch Your Weka*, 85.
93 Bailey and Earle, *Home Cooking to Takeaways*, 212.
94 Trotter and Trotter, *Margaret's Story*, 52.
95 Welch, Diary, 4 February 1900, MSY-6129, ATL.
96 Peden and Holland, 'Settlers Transforming the Open Country', 102.
97 Ibid., 103.
98 Drake Interview, 11 December 1992, Central Stories Museum and Art Gallery.
99 Duff Interview, 8 June 2011, H0067, Box 2, Invercargill Public Library.
100 Arnold, *Farthest Promised Land*, 245.
101 Simpson, *A Distant Feast*, 83.
102 Furey, *Maori Gardening: An Archaeological Perspective*, 10–11.
103 Ibid., 9–11.
104 Petrie, *Chiefs of Industry*, 20.
105 Henare, 'Te Mahi Kai – Food Production Economics', Te Ara, https://teara.govt.nz/en/te-mahi-kai-food-production-economics
106 Adds, 'Kūmara', Te Ara, https://teara.govt.nz/en/kumara
107 Veart, *First Catch Your Weka*, 65.
108 Best, *Maori Storehouses and Kindred Structures*, 78–82.
109 Smiler, 'Eldest Son', 67–68.
110 See, for example, Johnstone-Smith, *Battles, Buggies and Babies*, 14.
111 Leach, *1,000 Years*, 98.
112 Leach, 'Cookery in the Colonial Era', 34; Hargreaves, 'Changing Maori Agriculture', 106.
113 Hargreaves, 'Changing Maori Agriculture', 106.
114 Leach, *1,000 Years*, 106–07.
115 Hargreaves, 'Changing Maori Agriculture', 105.
116 Leach, *1,000 Years*, 108.
117 Grey, *Aotearoa and New Zealand*, 138; Hargreaves, 'The Maori Agriculture of the Auckland Province', 65.
118 Leach, 'Cookery in the Colonial Era', 39.
119 Governor Grey to Earl Grey, March 25, 1847, published in the *New Zealander*, May 6, 1848, quoted in Hargreaves, 'The Maori Agriculture of the Auckland Province', 62.
120 Grey, *Aotearoa and New Zealand*, 203; Smith, *Pākehā Settlements in a Māori World*, 255.
121 Veart, *First Catch Your Weka*, 33.
122 Ibid., 46.
123 'No te Maramataka', *Anglo-Maori Warder*, 30 May 1848, 4. PP, https://paperspast.natlib.govt.nz/newspapers/AMW18480530.2.10
124 'Ko te Ritenga mo te Hanga Rewena', *Maori Messenger: Te Karere Maori*, 22 November 1849, 3. PP, https://paperspast.natlib.govt.nz/newspapers/MMTKM18491122.2.10
125 Hannah Godsiff, quoted in Mitchell and Mitchell, *Te Tau Ihu o te Waka, Volume II*, 175.
126 Mitchell and Mitchell, *Te Tau Ihu o te Waka, Volume II*, 175.
127 Grey, *Aotearoa and New Zealand*, 203–04.
128 Ibid., 204.
129 Waitangi Tribunal, *Ngati Awa Raupatu Report*, 99–102.
130 Easton, *Not in Narrow Seas*, 145–48; Binney, O'Malley and Ward, 'The Land and the People', 313.
131 Waitangi Tribunal, *The Mohaka ki Ahuriri Report*, 650.
132 Paul Morgan, Brief of Evidence, quoted in Waitangi Tribunal, *Te Tau Ihu o te Waka a Maui, Volume III*, 1076.
133 Te Maata Hineone Mokena-Gilbert, Brief of Evidence, quoted in Waitangi Tribunal, *Te Tau Ihu o te Waka a Maui, Volume III*, 1074.
134 Raine, 'The First European Gardens', 54; Leach, *1,000 Years*, 110–11.
135 Leach, *1,000 Years*, 111.
136 Raine, 'The First European Gardens', 63.
137 Leach, *1,000 Years*, 112.
138 Ibid., 113.
139 Ibid., 114; Leach, 'The European House and Garden', 77.
140 Raine and Adam, 'The Settlers' Gardens', 71–75.
141 Ibid., 73.
142 Beattie, '"Hungry Dragons"', 134–35.
143 Lee and Lam, *Sons of the Soil*, 13–14.
144 Raine and Adam, 'Victorian Gardens', 94.
145 Bailey and Earle, *Home Cooking to Takeaways*, 120–21.
146 Ibid.
147 Helen Leach provides a detailed summary of fruit and vegetable preserving techniques in the 2013 edition of *The Aristologist*, 9–36.
148 Osterud, *Bonds of Community*, 214–15.
149 Ibid., 214, 150.
150 Stewart, *My Simple Life*, 26, 34.
151 Ibid., 62.
152 Rita Ranginui, quoted in Rogers and Simpson (eds), *Te Tīmatanga Tātau Tātau*, 173.
153 Simpson, *A Distant Feast*, 60.
154 Ibid., 92.
155 Ibid., 135–36.
156 Bailey and Earle, *Home Cooking to Takeaways*, 191–92.
157 Ibid., 192.
158 Barker, *Station Life in New Zealand*, 108.
159 Barker, *Houses and Housekeeping*, 56.
160 Eldred-Grigg, *A Southern Gentry*, 52.
161 Scotter, *Run, Estate and Farm*, 18.
162 Welch, Diary, 1900–02, MSY-6129, ATL.

Notes

163 Brewis, 'The House That Jack Bought', 88.
164 Sharpe, *Country Occasions*, 67.
165 'Kitchen Recipes', *New Zealand Farmer, Bee and Poultry Journal* 13, no. 7, July 1893, 271.
166 McCloy, *Dairy Nation*, 81.
167 Mitchell, 'Reminiscences', MS-Papers-10712, ATL.
168 Ibid.
169 Easy, *Looking Backward*, 54.
170 Beaton, 'A Contemporary Māori Culinary Tradition', 58.
171 Ibid., 58–59.
172 Royal and Kaka-Scott, 'Māori Foods – Kai Māori', Te Ara, https://teara.govt.nz/en/maori-foods-kai-maori
173 Lady Mary Ann Martin, *He pukapuka whakaatu tikanga mo nga Rongoa mo nga kai*, St Stephen's College, Auckland, 1869, quoted in Beaton, 'A Contemporary Māori Culinary Tradition', 139.
174 Johnstone-Smith, *Battles, Buggies and Babies*, 26.
175 Carson, *I Was Young*, 40.
176 Sharpe, *Country Occasions*, 62.
177 Veart, *First Catch Your Weka*, 72.
178 Advertisements, *Sun* (Canterbury), 16 September 1914, 2. PP, https://paperspast.natlib.govt.nz/newspapers/sun/1914/9/16
179 Te Ūaka Lyttelton Museum, 'An Eggscellent Lyttelton Innovation – "Norton's Premier Egg Preservative"', https://www.teuaka.org.nz/news/an-eggscellent-lyttelton-innovation-nortons-premier-egg-preservative
180 Jill Brewis, 'The House That Jack Bought', 89.
181 'Home and Farm Hints', *Dairy Exporter* 9, no. 7, February 1934, 68.
182 Ibid.
183 Brewis, *Colonial Fare*, 101.
184 Carson, *I Was Young*, 41.
185 Patterson et al., *Unpacking the Kists*, 220–22.
186 White, *Springfield in the Foothills*, 34–35.
187 Wolff, Diary, MS-Papers-8078, ATL.
188 McLeod, *Punjabis in New Zealand*, 81, 118–19.
189 Beattie, 'Making Home, Making Identity', 142.
190 Ibid, 141–42; Kristiansen, 'Wilson, John Cracroft', Te Ara, https://teara.govt.nz/en/biographies/1w31ilsonn-john-cracroft
191 Duncan, 'Lands for the People', 173; Stringleman and Scrimgeour, 'Dairying and Dairy Products', Te Ara, https://teara.govt.nz/en/dairying-and-dairy-products
192 Steel, '"New Zealand *is* Butterland"', 82.
193 McCloy, *Dairy Nation*, 100.
194 *Brett's Colonists Guide and Cyclopaedia of Useful Knowledge*, 1883, quoted in McCloy, *Dairy Nation*, 73, 82.
195 Jones, *The Beginning of the Rainbow*, 15.
196 Squires, Diary, M-072, Toitū: see, for example, 24 July 1886, 6 August 1886.
197 Wharemaru and Duffié, *Through the Eye of the Needle*, 50.
198 Johnstone-Smith, *Battles, Buggies and Babies*, 12.
199 Ibid.
200 Scott, *Days That Have Been*, 103.
201 Yorke, *The Animals Came First*, 46.
202 Ibid., 50.
203 Whitaker, 'Pioneer Tales', ARC2001-134, Puke Ariki.
204 Hosken, *Life on a Five Pound Note*, 32.
205 Anderson, *A River Rules My Life*, 31.
206 Ibid.
207 Winter, *Memories*, P Box 920.72 MEM 2000, ATL, 23.
208 Easy, *Looking Backward*, 16–17.
209 Ibid., 40.
210 Duff, *Sheep May Safely Graze*, 104.
211 McWhannell, Reminiscences, Misc-MS-0784, HC, 22–23.
212 Allen, *A Childhood at Cairnsmore*, 38.
213 Waitangi Tribunal, *Muriwhenua Land Report*, 356.
214 A. G. Allan, quote from J. Henderson, *Te Kao: 75*, Kaitaia, 1957, reproduced in Waitangi Tribunal, *Muriwhenua Land Report*, 365.
215 *AJHR*, 1989, H-12, 41, quoted in Waitangi Tribunal, *Muriwhenua Land Report*, 364–65.
216 Koning and Oliver, 'Economic Decline', 6.
217 Waitangi Tribunal, *The Hauraki Report, Volume III*, 1204.
218 See for example, Waitangi Tribunal, *Te Wairarapa Ki Tararua Report, Volume II*, 589; Waitangi Tribunal, *The Mohaka ki Ahuriri Report*, 676.
219 Waitangi Tribunal, *The Mohaka Ki Ahuriri Report*, 676.
220 Waitangi Tribunal, *Te Wairarapa Ki Tararua Report, Volume II*, 593.
221 Waitangi Tribunal, *Te Wairarapa Ki Tararua Report, Volume III*, 1055.
222 Waitangi Tribunal, *Te Tau Ihu o te Waka a Maui, Volume III*, 1055.
223 S. Kaan, and R. Bull, 'Kaihaukai: The Exchanging of Foods', *Scope Contemporary Research Topics: Kaupapa Kai Tahu* 2, 72, quoted in Phillips, Jackson and Hakopa, 'Creation Narratives of Mahinga Kai', 72.

4 Women's work?

1 'A Woman's Sphere' *Home and Country* 3, no. 12, December 1930, 11.
2 Symons, *A History of Cooks and Cooking*, xi.
3 Ibid., x.
4 Makereti, *Old-Time Maori*, 160; Petrie, *Outcasts of the Gods?*, 21, 47.
5 Keane,'Tūranga i te Hapori – Status in Māori Society', Te Ara, https://teara.govt.nz/en/turanga-i-te-hapori-status-in-maori-society
6 Makereti, *Old-Time Maori*, 160.
7 Petrie, *Outcasts of the Gods*, 47.
8 Mitchell and Olsen-Reader, 'Tapu and Noa as Negotiators of Māori Gender Roles', 88.
9 Olive Wright (ed., trs), *The Voyage of the* Astrolabe, *1840: An English Rendering of the Journals of Dumont d'Urville and His Officers of Their Visit to New Zealand in 1840* (Wellington: A. H. & A. W. Reed, 1955), quoted in Fletcher, 'Religion, Gender and Rank in Maori Society', 232–33.
10 Pere, *Ako*, 22.

11 Rangimarie Rose Pere, quoted in Brief of Evidence of Leonie Pihama, 20 January 2021, Wai 2700, #A19, 38.
12 Smith, 'Māori Women: Discourses, Projects and Mana Wahine', 46.
13 Higgins and Meredith, 'Te Mana o te Wāhine – Māori Women – Tapu and Peacemaking', Te Ara, https://teara.govt.nz/en/te-mana-o-te-wahine-maori-women/page-2
14 Elsdon Best, quoted in Brief of Evidence of Leonie Pihama, 20 January 2021, Wai 2700, #A19, 37.
15 Simmonds, 'Mana Wahine: Decolonising Politics', 109.
16 Ibid.
17 Mikaere, 'Māori Women', 138.
18 Makereti, *Old-Time Maori*, 160; Hiroa, *The Coming of the Maori*, 376.
19 Taylor, *Te Ika a Maui*, 389.
20 Baucke, *Where the White Man Treads*, 103.
21 Stone and Langer, 'Te Ahi i te Ao Māori', 22.
22 Brief of Evidence of Patricia Tauroa, 30 June 2021, Wai 2700, #A60, 11.
23 Salmond, *Hui*, 106; see also Richardson, '3 Feet Under', 11.
24 Petrie, *Chiefs of Industry*, 12; Taonui, 'Tribal Organisation – The Significance of Iwi and Hapū', Te Ara, https://teara.govt.nz/en/tribal-organisation/page-1
25 Ballara, *Iwi*, 194–96.
26 Ibid.; Petrie, *Chiefs of Industry*, 12.
27 Hiroa, *The Coming of the Maori*, 375.
28 Binney and O'Malley, 'The Quest for Survival', 340; Keane, 'Te Rāngai Mahi – Māori in the Workforce –- European Contact', Te Ara, https://teara.govt.nz/en/te-rangai-mahi-maori-in-the-workforce/page-2
29 Rei, McDonald and Te Awekōtuku, 'Ngā Rōpū Wāhine Māori', NZHistory, https://nzhistory.govt.nz/women-together/theme/maori
30 K. Jenkins, 'Reflections on the Status of Maori Women', unpublished paper, 1986, 12, quoted in Mikaere, 'Maori Women', 139.
31 Mikaere, 'Māori Women', 140.
32 'Wai 2700 – Mana Wāhine Kaupapa Inquiry', Manatū Wāhine Ministry for Women, https://women.govt.nz/wahine-maori/wai-2700-mana-wahine-kaupapa-inquiry
33 'Mana Wāhine Kaupapa Inquiry', Waitangi Tribunal Inquiries, https://waitangitribunal.govt.nz/inquiries/kaupapa-inquiries/mana-wahine-kaupapa-inquiry/
34 Brief of Evidence of Donna Awatere-Huata, 21 January 2021, Wai 2700, #A20, 12.
35 Binney, 'Some Observations on the Status of Maori Women', 234–40; see also, Gemmell, 'A History of Marginalisation: Maori Women'.
36 K. Jenkins, 'Working Paper on Maori Women and Social Policy', written for the Royal Commission of Social Policy, quoted in Mikaere, 'Maori Women', 142.
37 Brief of Evidence of Leonie Pihama, 20 January 2021, Wai 2100, A#19, 27; L. T. Smith quoted in Johnston and Pihama, 'The Marginalisation of Māori Women', 119.
38 L. T. Smith quoted in Johnston and Pihama, 'The Marginalisation of Māori Women', 119.
39 Mikaere, *The Balance Destroyed*, 118.
40 Ibid., 118–19.
41 Hippolite, 'Wetekia Ruruku Elkington', in Macdonald, Penfold and Williams (eds), *The Book of New Zealand Women*, 206.
42 Johnston and Pihama, 'The Marginalisation of Māori Women', 122–23.
43 Mikaere, *The Balance Destroyed*, 104; Johnson and Pihama, 'The Marginalisation of Māori Women', 121.
44 Simmonds, 'Mana Wahine: Decolonising Politics', 111.
45 Blank, *For Someone I Love*, 124.
46 Phillis, *Maumahara*, 117.
47 Ibid., 13.
48 Te Kui, 'The Rhythm of Life', 82.
49 Maree Millar, quoted in Rogers and Simpson (eds), *Te Tīmatanga Tātau Tātau*, 96.
50 Kreklau, 'Neither Gendered Nor a Room', 6.
51 Bryder, *A Voice for Mothers*, 4.
52 Cooper, 'Feeding the Family', 144–53.
53 Kreklau, 'Neither Gendered nor a Room', 5.
54 Pennell, *The Birth of the English Kitchen*, 7.
55 Ibid., 130.
56 Callister and Didham, '"Man Alone" to "Woman Alone"?', n.p.
57 Macdonald, 'Too Many Men and Too Few Women', 18.
58 Butler, *A First Year in Canterbury Settlement*, 147–48.
59 William to his mother, 27 April 1884, The Mills letters, MS-Papers-10737-1, ATL.
60 Mitchell, 'Reminiscences', MS-Papers-10712, ATL.
61 Macdonald, 'Strangers at the Hearth', 52.
62 Tolerton, 'Household Services', Te Ara, https://teara.govt.nz/en/household-services; Macdonald, 'Strangers at the Hearth', 45.
63 Macdonald, 'Strangers at the Hearth', 45.
64 Ibid., 44.
65 A Lady, *Facts*, 38.
66 Ibid., 70.
67 Courage, *Lights and Shadows*, 56.
68 Ibid.
69 Barker, *Station Life*, 42.
70 Ibid., 68–69.
71 Garner and Foster (eds), *Letters to Grace*, 55, 68.
72 Ibid., 68.
73 Ibid., 139.
74 Macdonald, 'Strangers at the Hearth', 44.
75 Ibid.
76 Scott, *Days That Have Been*, 98.
77 Millar, *Joan's Journey*, 34.
78 See Phillips, *A Man's Country*?
79 Findlay, *Tooth and Nail*, 150, 154–55.
80 For a detailed analysis of rural childhoods see Goodyear, '"Sunshine and Fresh Air"'.
81 Winter, *Memories*, P Box 920.72 MEM 2000, ATL, 23.

Notes

82   Ibid., 31–32.
83   Fitz-William, *Life at the Oaks*, 24–25.
84   Ibid.
85   Kendall, *Making the Most of My Life*, 26.
86   Pauline Perry to her parents, 5 March 1928, 'Chronicle of Leonard and Pauline Perry', MS-Papers-5504, ATL. 'Mrs Beeton' is a reference to *Mrs Beeton's Book of Household Management*, first published in 1861 – a well known and comprehensive guide to running a Victorian household.
87   'Between Ourselves', *The Exporter and Farm Home Journal* 3, no. 12, June 1928, 64. See also 'Between Ourselves', *The Exporter and Farm Home Journal* 4, no. 1, July 1928, 64–67.
88   Law Commission, 'Justice: The Experiences of Māori Women', 15.
89   Rei, *Māori Women and the Vote*, 12.
90   Law Commission, 'Justice: The Experiences of Māori Women', 21–22.
91   Coney, *Standing in the Sunshine*, 282.
92   Walker, *Ka Whawhai Tonu Matou*, 136.
93   Brooking, '"Busting Up"', 78.
94   Brookes, *A History of New Zealand Women*, 135.
95   Hei Ariki Algie, quoted in Binney and Chaplin (eds), *Ngā Mōrehu*, 110.
96   Ibid.
97   Maraea Tippins, quoted in Rogers and Simpson (eds), *Te Tīmatanga Tātau Tātau*, 282.
98   Wharemaru and Duffié, *Through the Eye of the Needle*, 27.
99   Keenan, *Ahuwhenua*, 2–3, 72.
100 King, 'Cooper, Whina', Te Ara, https://teara.govt.nz/en/biographies/5c32/cooper-whina
101 Brief of Evidence of Waina Hoete Ahipene and Grace Hoet on Behalf of Themselves and the New Zealand Māori Council, 10 February 2021, Wai 2700, #A37, 1–2.
102 'Should Women Milk Cows?' *The Countrywoman* 1, no. 12, April 1934, 4.
103 'Report on the health conditions and environments of rural school-children in certain districts of New Zealand', Annual Report of Director-General of Health, *AJHR*, 1928, I, I I 01, 75.
104 Work in this context was defined as 'work other than purely domestic duties and kitchen-gardening – for example, feeding stock, assisting with haymaking and milking'. Doig, *A Survey of Standards of Life*, 55.
105 Diok, Reminiscences, 95–160, HC, 7.
106 Easy, *Looking Backward*, 43–44.
107 Hunter and Riney-Kehrberg, 'Rural Daughters', 66.
108 Toynbee, *Her Work and His*, 92.
109 Ibid., 95.
110 Richards Interview, 9–16 January 1987, OHInt-0053/25, ATL.
111 'Should Women Milk Cows?' *Countrywoman* 1, no. 12, April 1934, 4.
112 'When Mrs B Takes a Holiday', *Dairy Exporter* 11, no. 10, May 1936, 89.
113 Hunter and Riney-Kehrberg, 'Rural Daughters', 58.
114 Porter and Macdonald, '*My Hand Will Write*', 3.
115 Ibid., 146–53.
116 Paterson and Wanhalla, *He Reo Wāhine*, 9.
117 Ibid.
118 Connor, 'Writing Ourselves "Home"', 14.
119 Ibid., 93.
120 Flashoff, *Reremoana Hakiwai*, 17.
121 Ibid., 31, 36–37.
122 Reremoana Koopu, quoted in Binney and Chaplin (eds), *Ngā Mōrehu*, 63.
123 Colin Waitere and Maree Waitere, quoted in Rogers and Simpson (eds), *Te Tīmatanga Tātau Tātau*, 299.
124 Heni Brown, quoted in Binney and Chaplin (eds), *Ngā Mōrehu*, 51.
125 Ibid., 52.
126 Szaszy, 'Maori Women', 20.
127 Elsdon Craig, quoted in Szaszy, 'Maori Women', 20.
128 Vera Morgan, quoted in Grace et al (eds), *The Silent Migration*, 7–10.
129 Ibid., 10.
130 Phillis, *Maumahara*, 128.
131 Pere, *Ako*, 42.
132 Jahnke, 'Towards a Secure Identity', 510.
133 Heni Sunderland, quoted in Binney and Chaplin (eds), *Ngā Mōrehu*, 120.
134 Jahnke, 'Towards a Secure Identity', 509.
135 Witarina Harris, quoted in Grace et al. (eds), *The Silent Migration*, 17–20.
136 Jahnke, 'Towards a Secure Identity', 508–09; Pere, *Ako*, 22.
137 Edwards, *Mihipeka*, 30.
138 Ibid., 65.
139 Hunter and Squire, 'Bread and Butter', 38.
140 Osterud, 'The Meanings of Independence', 432.
141 Matthews, *Looking Back*, 123, 133.
142 'Between Ourselves', *New Zealand Dairy Produce Exporter* 2, no. 7, January 1927, 35.
143 'Between Ourselves', *Dairy Exporter* 14, no. 10, June 1939, 69.
144 Verdon, 'The Modern Countrywoman', 88.
145 'Between Ourselves', *New Zealand Dairy Produce Exporter* 2, no. 4, October 1926, 41.
146 'Between Ourselves', *New Zealand Dairy Produce Exporter* 2, no. 5, November 1926, 48.
147 'Between Ourselves', *Exporter and Farm Home Journal* 4, no. 11, May 1929, 62.
148 Hall, *On the Farm*, 221.
149 'Reward', *Exporter and Farm Home Journal* 7, no. 3, September 1931, 48.
150 Kotchemidova, 'From Good Cheer to "Drive-By Smiling"', 9.
151 'The Business of Homemaking', *New Zealand Dairy Produce Exporter* 1, no. 7, January 1926, 31.
152 'Our Christmas Present to the Women on the Farm', *New Zealand Dairy Produce Exporter* 1, no. 6, December 1925, 26.
153 Sing, 'That's How It Was', 42.
154 'Between Ourselves', *New Zealand Dairy Produce Exporter* 2, no. 8, February 1927, 38.

155 'Between Ourselves', *New Zealand Dairy Produce Exporter* 2, no. 6, December 1926, 40.
156 Maybury, 'Mapping Lived Realities', 114.
157 Daley, *Girls & Women, Men & Boys*, 71.
158 Ibid.
159 Millar, *Joan's Journey*, 7–8, 11.
160 Ibid., 18.
161 Scott, *Barbara and the New Zealand Back-Blocks*, 185.
162 Ibid., 186.
163 Hunter, *Father's Right-Hand Man*, xi.
164 Holt, *Linoleum, Better Babies*, 37.
165 Ibid., 38.
166 'Between Ourselves', *Dairy Exporter* 7, no. 10, April 1932, 74.
167 'Between Ourselves', *Dairy Exporter* 14, no. 12, August 1939, 80.
168 'Between Ourselves', *Dairy Exporter* 15, no. 1, September 1939, 77.
169 'Reducing Fatigue in the Kitchen', *New Zealand Journal of Agriculture* 58, no. 5, May 1939, 460–63.
170 Holt, *Linoleum, Better Babies*, 47.
171 Pere, *Ako*, 66–67.
172 This analysis derives from Reckwitz, 'Affective Spaces'.
173 Pere, *Ako*, 66.
174 Gee, *Creeks and Kitchens*, 1–2.
175 Helene Connor, pers. comm., 5 September 2023. See also, Connor, 'Whakapapa Back', 10.
176 Gee, *Creeks and Kitchens*, 2–3.
177 Meah, 'Reconceptualizing Power', 671.
178 'A Cure for the Blues', *New Zealand Journal of Agriculture* 69, no. 3, September 1944, 279–81.

5 Hākari, feasts and picnics

1 Boswell, *Dim Horizons*, 108–09.
2 Ibid., 28, 54.
3 Somerset, *Littledene*, 91.
4 Fairburn, *Ideal Society*, 158–77.
5 Arnold, 'Community in Rural Victorian New Zealand'; Daley, 'Taradale Meets the Ideal Society'.
6 Mead, *Tikanga Māori*, 29.
7 Petrie, *Chiefs of Industry*, 20.
8 Pere, *Ako*, 72.
9 Chapple-Sokol, 'Culinary Diplomacy', 163.
10 Phyllis Herda talks about the use of food to make 'socially significant statements' in her article 'Ladies a Plate', 165.
11 Brown, 'Raukura Erana Gillies', 63.
12 See, for example, Martin, 'Te Manaakitanga i Roto i Ngā Ahumahi Tāpoi', 19–21.
13 Duncan and Rewi, 'Tikanga', 35.
14 Mead, *Tikanga Māori*, 29.
15 Beaton, 'A Contemporary Māori Culinary Tradition', 127–28.
16 Moon, *A Tohunga's Natural World*, 84.
17 Rita Ranginui, quoted in Rogers and Simpson (eds), *Te Tīmatanga Tātau Tātau*, 176.
18 Hārata Solomon, quoted in Rogers and Simpson (eds), *Te Tīmatanga Tātau Tātau*, 206.
19 Stirling and Salmond, *Amiria*, 67.
20 Phillis, *Maumahara*, 128–29.
21 Savage Interview, 31 January 1983, OHInt-0015-06, ATL.
22 Stack and Stack, ed. Reed, *Further Maoriland Adventures*, 64.
23 Ibid., 45.
24 Thomson, *Rambles with a Philosopher*, 91.
25 Ballantyne, 'Strategic Intimacies', 5, 11.
26 Society for Promoting Christian Knowledge, *Domestic Scenes*, 89.
27 'The Spirit of Hospitality: Are Modern Conditions Changing It?', *Exporter and Farm Home Journal* 4, no. 7, January 1929, 66–67.
28 Harrington, 'You Too Might Make a Farmer's Wife', OHInt-0002/079, ATL.
29 Drummond and Drummond, *At Home in New Zealand*, 6.
30 Soper, *The Otago of Our Mothers*, 78.
31 Murphy, '"Hospitality was their byword"', 94.
32 Ibid., 87.
33 Mieville, Reminiscences, Misc-MS-1670, 68.
34 Ibid., 67–68.
35 Simpson, *The Women of New Zealand*, 136.
36 Ibid.
37 'Between Ourselves', *Dairy Exporter* 14, no. 5, January 1939, 70.
38 'Between Ourselves', *Dairy Exporter* 14, no. 7, March 1939, 67.
39 Hatch, *Respectable Lives*, 57.
40 Belshaw, 'Agricultural Labour', 26.
41 Martin, *The Forgotten Worker*, 2–4.
42 Hatch, *Respectable Lives*, 135.
43 Ibid., 140.
44 Martin, *The Forgotten Worker*, 14.
45 Eldred-Grigg, *A Southern Gentry*, 19, 56, 89.
46 Courage, *Lights and Shadows*, 12. Although Courage was a member of the landowning elite there were aspects of her lifestyle which did not fit Eldred-Grigg's characterisation. For example, his contention that 'although ladies might pat at bits of pastry . . . [these] gentlefolk could drop their self-appointed tasks whenever they chose' is not borne out in this case (Eldred-Grigg, *A Southern Gentry*, 92).
47 Courage, *Lights and Shadows*, 118.
48 Wevers, *Reading on the Farm*, 79.
49 Ibid., 106–117.
50 Ibid., 79.
51 Phillips, 'Class', Te Ara, https://teara.govt.nz/en/class; Hatch, *Respectable Lives*, 152.
52 Brooking, 'Agrarian Businessmen Organise', 45.
53 Ibid., 47, 48.
54 See Hatch, *Respectable Lives*, 158.
55 Ibid.
56 Mackay, 'Memoirs of Longlands', Misc-MS-1044, HC, 2, 13.

Notes

57 Phillips, *A Man's Country?* 26–38.
58 Ibid., 26–32.
59 Stronach, *Musterer on Molesworth*, 29.
60 Mackay, 'Memoirs of Longlands', Misc-MS-1044, HC, 5.
61 Hatch, *Respectable Lives*, 152.
62 Jim Boswell, quoted in Cowan, *Goodness Gracious Me*, 91–92.
63 'Between Ourselves', *Dairy Exporter* 11, no. 3, October 1935, 61.
64 Ibid.
65 Watson, 'The Significance of Mr. Richard Buckley's Exploding Trousers', 357–58.
66 Brooking, 'Larkrise to Littledene', 3.
67 Smyth, *Five on a Farm*, S478.5.O8 S69 1979, HC, 19.
68 Allen, *A Childhood at Cairnsmore*, 54–55.
69 Ibid., 55.
70 Beck, *These Days Were Mine*, 29; Pauline Perry to her parents, 21 February 1928, 'Chronicle of Leonard and Pauline Perry', MS-Papers-5504, ATL.
71 Ross, 'Through the Eyes of a Child', Cromwell Museum; Cranstoun, Diaries, 92-062, HC. See, for example, 19 May 1905: 'Mary then went to Flemings to help as the mill was there'; 12 February 1925: 'Ivy went to Parkers in afternoon to help with the lunch as men are harvesting there'; 8 May 1926: Georgina 'went over to Pearce's to help Mrs Pearce to prepare for the mill and went over after tea to help with the tea over there, the mill just having arrived after dark'.
72 Chitty, 'Autobiographical Sketch', qMS-0446, ATL.
73 Felix Keesing, *The Changing Maori*, Avery, 1928, quoted in Binney and O'Malley, 'The Quest for Survival', 349.
74 Fyfe (ed.), *Matriarchs*, 91.
75 Solomon, 'Solomon, Hārata Ria Te Uira', Te Ara, https://teara.govt.nz/en/biographies/5s33/solomon-harata-ria-te-uira
76 Brookes and Tennant, 'Maori and Pakeha Women', 31.
77 Harris, 'Persistence and Resilience', 364.
78 Morrison, *Te Rōpu o te Ora*, 103.
79 J. C. Sturm, 'The Maori Women's Welfare League', *Te Ao Hou* 3, no. 1, Spring 1954, 8.
80 Ibid., 9.
81 Binney and O'Malley, 'The Quest for Survival', 341.
82 Metge, 'Continuity in Change', P 572.9931 MET 1958, ATL, 26.
83 Ibid., 27.
84 Firth, *Economics of the New Zealand Maori*, 310.
85 Hiroa, *The Coming of the Maori*, 375.
86 Paterson, 'Ngā Reo o Ngā Niupepa', 169; Paterson, *Colonial Discourses*, 103–04.
87 Mead, *Tikanga Māori*, 104; Rangiwai, 'Kai Māori', 16–17.
88 Firth, *Economics of the New Zealand Maori*, 309; Keane, 'Māori Feasts and Ceremonial Eating – Hākari – Traditional Feasts', Te Ara, https://teara.govt.nz/en/maori-feasts-and-ceremonial-eating-hakari/page-2
89 Best, *The Maori, Volume 1*, 379.
90 Petrie, *Chiefs of Industry*, 23.
91 Makereti, *Old-Time Maori*, 157.
92 Ibid., 158.
93 Ibid., 160, 164.
94 Petrie, *Chiefs of Industry*, 53–56.
95 Keane, 'Māori Feasts and Ceremonial Eating – Hākari', Te Ara, http://www.TeAra.govt.nz/en/maori-feasts-and-ceremonial-eating-hakari; Firth, *Economics of the New Zealand Maori*, 319.
96 'Auckland', *New Zealand Spectator and Cook's Strait Guardian*, 6 October 1849, 2. PP, https://paperspast.natlib.govt.nz/newspapers/NZSCSG18491006.2.4
97 Maning, Papers and Reflections, Misc-MS-0082, HC.
98 Ibid.
99 Firth, *Economics of the New Zealand Maori*, 321–25.
100 Taylor, *Te Ika a Maui*, 169.
101 Hiroa, *The Coming of the Maori*, 377–78.
102 Ballara, *Iwi*, 224–25; Salmond, *Hui*, 18.
103 Te Whaiti, Diary, 14 March 1907, MS-Papers-7033, ATL.
104 Binney and Chaplin (eds), *Ngā Mōrehu*, 87.
105 Ballara, *Iwi*, 225.
106 Vera Morgan, quoted in Grace et al. (eds), *The Silent Migration*, 10.
107 Savage Interview, 31 January 1983, OHInt-0015-06, ATL.
108 Stirling and Salmond, *Amiria*, 67.
109 Hei Ariki Algie, quoted in Binney and Chaplin (eds), *Ngā Mōrehu*, 104.
110 Grace, 'Two Worlds', 54.
111 Stirling and Salmond, *Amiria*, 54.
112 Mead, *Tikanga Māori*, 16; Salmond, *Hui*, 105.
113 Brown, *Māori Architecture*, 84.
114 Ibid., 85–90.
115 Bennett, 'Marae: A Whakapapa', 222; Mead, *Tikanga Māori*, 104.
116 Bennett, 'Marae: A Whakapapa', 222; Brown, *Māori Architecture*, 92.
117 Brown, *Māori Architecture*, 92.
118 Ellis, *Whakapapa of Tradition*, 242.
119 Graham, 'The Pioneers 1840–1870', 64.
120 Mitchell, 'Picnics in New Zealand', 45.
121 'Picnic at Otaria', *Mataura Ensign*, 4 January 1884, 2–3. PP, https://paperspast.natlib.govt.nz/newspapers/mataura-ensign/1884/1/4
122 'Kelso Annual Picnic', *Mataura Ensign*, 19 February 1892, 3. PP, https://paperspast.natlib.govt.nz/newspapers/mataura-ensign/1892/2/19
123 Carson, *I Was Young*, 30.
124 Begg, *Low Country Liz*, q511022, ATL, 14–15.
125 Courage, *Lights and Shadows*, 204.
126 Sharpe, *Country Occasions*, 152.
127 Hollard, 'Reminiscences', qMS-0989, ATL.
128 A Lady, *Facts*, 66.
129 Ibid. A charming example of this type of fundraising is given by Nellie Johnson in her oral history for the Lakes District Museum. She describes a 'basket concert', organised by the community of Macetown each year, where each woman would bring a basket of food to be auctioned off: the man who placed the winning bid

would be treated to supper with the lady who supplied it. (Interview 8 June 1976, LD0035).
130 Newman, 'The Late Great Country Hall', 4.
131 Ibid., 8.
132 Sharpe, *Country Occasions*, 152.
133 Schepens, *Ring Back the Curtain*, P q920 SCH 1963, ATL, 19.
134 'Matarawa Picnic and Sports', *Wairarapa Standard*, 3 January 1883, 3. PP, https://paperspast.natlib.govt.nz/newspapers/wairarapa-standard/1883/1/3
135 'Canterbury Settlers in Hokianga: A Picnic with the Ngapuhi', *Star* (Canterbury), 11 January 1889, 4. PP, https://paperspast.natlib.govt.nz/newspapers/star/1889/1/11
136 Millar, *Joan's Journey*, 11–12.
137 Bell, 'Rural Way of Life', 16–17.
138 Ibid., 14, 220.

Conclusion

1 Stevens, 'Muttonbirds and Modernity'.
2 Mintz, *Tasting Food, Tasting Freedom*, 7.

Bibliography

Archival Sources and Oral Histories

Alexander Turnbull Library, Wellington (ATL)

Begg, Elvira M., *Low Country Liz: An Autobiography* [John Begg, Mosgiel, 1991], q511022.
Bryant, Agnes, 'Reminiscences and Reflections about Reikorangi', MS-Papers-3899.
Buckland, Kate, 'Reminiscences – Homes of Ours', MS-Papers-3892-3.
Chitty, Alicia, 'Autobiographical Sketch', qMS-0446.
Harrington, Pamela, 'You Too Might Make a Farmer's Wife', Open Country Sound Recordings, Radio New Zealand, OHInt-0002/079.
Hollard, Elizabeth, 'Reminiscences', qMS-0989.
Metge, Joan, 'Continuity in Change: Urbanisation and Modern Maori Society: The Structure and Organisation of Maori Society in an Urban Area and a Rural Community in Northern New Zealand', unpublished typescript, 1958, P 572.9931 MET 1958.
Mills Family, Letters, Anderson family: Papers, MS-Papers-10737-1.
Mitchell, Lydia, 'Reminiscences', MS-Papers-10712.
Perry, Robin, 'Chronicle of Leonard and Pauline Perry', MS-Papers-5504.
Richards, Myrtle, Interview by Rosie Little, 9–16 January 1987, Nelson and Golden Bay Oral History Project, Nelson Provincial Museum, OHInt-0053/25. Quoted with permission of David Richards.

Savage, Naki, Interview by Judith Fyfe, 31 January 1983, Masterton South Rotary Club Oral History Project, OHInt-0015-06. Quoted with permission of Georgina Scouller and whānau.

Schepens, Daisy K., *'Ring Back the Curtain': A True New Zealand Story* [D. K. Schepens, Kaikohe, 1963], P q920 SCH 1963.

Te Whaiti Family Papers, Translations of Diaries of Iraia Te Whaiti by Rangi Pouwhare, 1907 [2000], MS-Papers-7033. Quoted with permission of the Te Whāiti whānau.

Turbott, Harold, Maori Health File, Papers, Series 4 Papers on Maori Health, 88-059-2/09.

Warner, Pamera Te Ruihi, Interview by Gabrielle Hildreth, 26 July 1995, Memories of the Kaipara Oral History Project: Part Two, OHInt-0633/5.

Welch, George, Diary, 1900-02, MSY-6129.

Winter, Lily, *Memories* [L. Winter, Nelson, 2000], P Box 920.72 MEM 2000

Wolff, Johanna, Diary (photocopied translation and transcript) with supplement, 1888–1889, MS-Papers-8078.

Archives New Zealand, Wellington (ANZ)

Anaura Housing Survey, Department of Maori Affairs, Memoranda and Registered Files, ACIH 16036 MA1 607/ 30/3/35, R19528233.

Makarita[sic] Housing Survey, Department of Maori Affairs, Memoranda and Registered Files, ACIH 16036 MA1 607/ 30/3/16, R19528225.

Rural Housing Designs and Specifications, State Advances Corporation, Registered Files, AELE 19203 SAC1 233/ 35/113/1, R20054195.

Tintown Housing Survey, Department of Maori Affairs, Memoranda and Registered Files, ACIH 16036 MA1 607/ 30/3/37, R19528234.

Waimiha Housing Survey, Department of Maori Affairs, Memoranda and Registered Files, ACIH 16036 MA1 608/ 30/3/65, R19528259.

Central Stories Museum and Art Gallery, Alexandra

Drake, Christina Elizabeth, Interview by L. R. Phillips, 11 December 1992.

Duncan, Anne, Interview by Jan Morgan, 28 July 1996.

Bibliography

Cromwell Museum

Ross, Emily, '"Through the Eyes of a Child", As Told by Mrs. Emily Ross (née Elliott) Formerly of Queensberry in July, 1978'.

Hocken Collections, Dunedin (HC)

Cranstoun, Mary, Diaries, January 1905–1908, 1925–1926, 92-062.
Dick, Eliza, Reminiscences, transcribed by Mrs de Hamell, 95-160.
Hooker, Ray, Hemi Te Rakau, Kelly R. Wilson, Gordon McLaren, Albert Naihi-McLaren, Iris Climo, James M. Russell and Allan L. Russell, H8 – Evidence on Mahinga Kai, Arahura Area (1988). AG-653/177.
Mackay, J. S., 'Memoirs of Longlands, 1919–1923', Misc-MS-1044.
Mackenzie, Alice, Diary, 1890-1, MS-0137.
Maning, Maria Amina, Papers and Reflections on Māori Life, Misc-MS-0082.
McWhannell, Rhoda, Reminiscences, Misc-MS-0784.
Mieville, Frederick Louis, Reminiscences 1851–1858, transcribed by Marsha Donaldson, Misc-MS-1670.
Smyth, Rosemary, *Five on a Farm* [R. Smyth, Oamaru, 1979], S478.5.08 S69 1979. Quoted with permission of Rosemary Smyth.
Tau, Rawiri Te Maire and Henare Raikiihia Tau, H6 – Evidence on Mahinga Kai, Tuahuiri Area (1988). AG-653/176.

Invercargill Public Library, Invercargill

Duff, Albert Gordon (Bert), Interview by Avis McDonald, 8 June 2011, H0067, Box: 2, Southland Oral History Project, http://archives.ilibrary.co.nz/repositories/4/resources/702.

Lakes District Museum Archives, Arrowtown

Johnson, Nellie, interviewed 8 June 1976, LD0035.

Owaka Museum

Guthrie, Frances, 'Happy Days at Spring Hill, Tahatika', 2010.182.9.

Puke Ariki, New Plymouth

Whitaker, Mabel, 'Pioneer Tales from Taranaki's Rough North East Backblocks', ARC2001-134.

Toitū Otago Settlers Museum, Dunedin

Squires, Catharine, Diary, 1843–1912, M-072.

Periodicals

Home and Country, 1929–1939.
New Zealand Dairy Produce Exporter, 1925–1928.
New Zealand Farm and Home, 1932–1933.
New Zealand Farmer: Bee and Poultry Journal, 1885–1900.
Te Ao Hou, 1952–1959.
The Countrywoman, 1933–1934.
The Dairy Exporter, 1932–1939.
The Exporter and Farm Home Journal, 1928–1929.
The Exporter and Home Journal, 1929–1932.
Other periodicals were consulted online via Papers Past, and specific items are cited in the footnotes. These newspapers were not surveyed, but relevant articles were found using keyword search terms. National Library of New Zealand, Papers Past, https://paperspast.natlib.govt.nz/

Official Publications

Ahipene, Waina Hoete and Grace Hoet, Brief of Evidence on Behalf of Themselves and the New Zealand Māori Council: Wai 2700 – the Mana Wāhine Kaupapa Inquiry, #A37, 10 February 2021, https:// forms.justice.govt.nz/search/Documents/WT/wt_DOC_168784595/ Wai%202700%2C%20A037.pdf

Appendix to the Journals of the House of Representatives of New Zealand(AJHR), 1871–1940, National Library of New Zealand, Parliamentary Papers, https://paperspast.natlib.govt.nz/parliamentary

Huata, Donna Awatere, Brief of Evidence: Wai 2700 – the Mana Wāhine Kaupapa Inquiry, #A20, 21 January 2021, forms.justice.govt.nz/search/Documents/WT/wt_DOC_168113441/Wai 2700%2C A020.pdf

New Zealand Official Yearbook, Statistics New Zealand, Digital Yearbook Collection, https://stats.govt.nz/indicators-and-snapshots/digitisedcollections/yearbook-collection-18932012/

New Zealand Parliamentary Debates (Hansard), Vol. CCLVI, 1939.

New Zealand Population Census, 1878–1956.

Pihama, Leonie, Brief of Evidence: Wai 2700 – the Mana Wāhine Kaupapa Inquiry, #A19, 20 January 2021, https://forms.justice.govt.nz/search/Documents/WT/wt_DOC_198605587/Wai%202700%2C%20A019.pdf

Tauroa, Patricia, Brief of Evidence: Wai 2700 – the Mana Wāhine Kaupapa Inquiry, #A60, 30 June 2021, https://forms.justice.govt.nz/search/Documents/WT/wt_DOC_173797520/Wai%202700%2C%20A060.pdf

Waitangi Tribunal, *The Hauraki Report, Volume III*, Waitangi Tribunal Report, 2006. https://forms.justice.govt.nz/search/Documents/WT/wt_DOC_68331905/Hauraki%20Vol%203.pdf

——, *The Mohaka Ki Ahuriri Report*, Waitangi Tribunal Report, 2004. https://forms.justice.govt.nz/search/Documents/WT/wt_DOC_68598011/Wai201.pdf

——, *Muriwhenua Land Report*, Waitangi Tribunal Report, 1997. https://forms.justice.govt.nz/search/Documents/WT/wt_DOC_68635760/Muriwhenua%20Land.pdf

——, *The Ngai Tahu Report. Volume III*, Waitangi Tribunal Report, 1991. https://forms.justice.govt.nz/search/Documents/WT/wt_DOC_160762113/Ngai%20Tahu%20Report%201991%20V3W.pdf

——, *The Ngāti Awa Raupatu Report*, Waitangi Tribunal Report, 1999. https://forms.justice.govt.nz/search/Documents/WT/wt_DOC_68458811/Wai46.pdf
——, *Te Roroa Claim*, Waitangi Tribunal Report, 1992. https://forms.justice.govt.nz/search/Documents/WT/wt_DOC_68462675/Wai38.pdf
——, *Te Tau Ihu o te Waka a Maui, Report on Northern South Island Claims, Volume III*, Waitangi Tribunal Report, 2008. https://forms.justice.govt.nz/search/Documents/WT/wt_DOC_68199520/Te%20Tau%20Ihu%20Vol%203.pdf
——, *The Wairarapa Ki Tararua Report, Volume II: The Struggle for Control*, Waitangi Tribunal Report, 2010. https://forms.justice.govt.nz/search/Documents/WT/wt_DOC_68640217/Wairarapa%20ki%20Tararua%20Vol%20II.pdf
——, *The Wairarapa Ki Tararua Report, Volume III: Powerlessness and Displacement*, Waitangi Tribunal Report, 2010. https://forms.justice.govt.nz/search/Documents/WT/wt_DOC_68640655/Wairarapa%20ki%20Tararua%20Vol%20III.pdf
——, *The Wananga Capital Establishment Report*, Waitangi Tribunal Report, 1999. https://forms.justice.govt.nz/search/Documents/WT/wt_DOC_68595986/Wai718.pdf
——, *The Whanganui River Report*, Waitangi Tribunal Report, 1999. https://forms.justice.govt.nz/search/Documents/WT/wt_DOC_68450539/Wai167.pdf

Other Material

Adams, Jane, *The Transformation of Rural Life, Southern Illinois, 1890–1990*, University of North Carolina Press, Chapel Hill and London, 1994.
Adds, Peter, 'Kūmara – Introducing Kūmara to New Zealand', Te Ara – the Encyclopedia of New Zealand, https://teara.govt.nz/en/kumara/page-1 (accessed 23 August 2023).
Allen, John S., *Home: How Habitat Made Us Human*, Basic Books, New York, 2015.

Bibliography

Allen, June, *A Childhood at Cairnsmore: Growing Up on a New Zealand Sheep Farm*, 2nd edn, Kwizzel Publishing, Auckland, 2014. Quoted with permission of the children of Gwen Mackenzie.

Anderson, Atholl, 'Emerging Societies: AD 1500–1800', in Atholl Anderson, Judith Binney and Aroha Harris (eds), *Tangata Whenua: An Illustrated History*, Bridget Williams Books, Wellington, 2014, pp. 102–29.

——, 'In the Foreign Gaze: AD 1642–1820', in Atholl Anderson, Judith Binney and Aroha Harris (eds), *Tangata Whenua: An Illustrated History*, Bridget Williams Books, Wellington, 2014, pp. 132–59.

——, 'Old Ways and New Means: AD 1810–1830', in Atholl Anderson, Judith Binney and Aroha Harris (eds), *Tangata Whenua: An Illustrated History*, Bridget Williams Books, Wellington, 2014, pp. 162–87.

——, 'A Fragile Plenty: Pre-European Māori and the New Zealand Environment', in Eric Pawson and Tom Brooking (eds), *Making a New Land: Environmental Histories of New Zealand*, new edn, Otago University Press, Dunedin, 2013, pp. 35–51.

Anderson, Atholl, Judith Binney and Aroha Harris (eds), *Tangata Whenua: An Illustrated History*, Bridget Williams Books, Wellington, 2014.

Anderson, Mona, *A River Rules My Life*, new edn, Beckett Publishing, Auckland, 1988.

Angus, John H., *The Ironmasters: The First One Hundred Years of H. E. Shacklock Limited*, H. E. Shacklock Ltd, Dunedin, 1973.

Arbury, Ella and Fiona Cram, 'Housing on Māori Land, c. 1870–2021', Report commissioned by the Waitangi Tribunal for the Housing Policy and Services Inquiry (Wai 2750), 2023, https://forms.justice.govt.nz/search/Documents/WT/wt_DOC_197360498/Wai%20 2750%2C%20A012.pdf

Arnold, Rollo, *New Zealand's Burning: The Settler's World in the mid-1880s*, Victoria University Press, Wellington, 1994.

——, 'Community in Rural Victorian New Zealand', *NZJH* 24, no. 1, 1990, pp. 3–21.

——, *The Farthest Promised Land: English Villagers, New Zealand Immigrants of the 1870s*, Victoria University Press/Price Milburn, Wellington, 1981.

Ashworth, Jeremy, *The Bungalow in New Zealand*, Viking, Auckland, 1994.
Austin, Michael, 'Polynesian Architecture in New Zealand', PhD thesis, University of Auckland, 1976.
Awatere, Shaun, Craig Pauling, Shad Rolleston, Rau Hoskins and Karl Wixon, 'Tū Whare Ora: Building Capacity for Māori Driven Design in Sustainable Settlement Development', Landcare Research Contract Report LC0809/039, prepared for University of Otago, 2008, https://www.maramatanga.ac.nz/project/t-whare-ora-building-capacity-m-ori-driven-design-sustainable-settlement-development
Bailey, Ray and Mary Earle, *Home Cooking to Takeaways: A History of New Zealand Food Eating*, Massey University, Palmerston North, 1993.
Ballantyne, Tony, *Entanglements of Empire: Missionaries, Māori, and the Question of the Body*, Auckland University Press, Auckland, 2015.
——, 'Strategic Intimacies: Knowledge and Colonization in Southern New Zealand', *Journal of New Zealand Studies* NS14, Special Issue: Intimacy, Race and Colonial Histories, 2013, pp. 4–18.
——, *Webs of Empire: Locating New Zealand's Colonial Past*, Bridget Williams Books, Wellington, 2012.
——, 'On Place, Space and Mobility in Nineteenth-Century New Zealand', NZJH 45, no. 1, 2011, pp. 50–70.
Ballara, Angela, *Iwi: The Dynamics of Māori Tribal Organisation from c. 1769 to c. 1945*, Victoria University Press, Wellington, 1998.
Barker, Lady, *Station Life in New Zealand* [1883], Golden Press reprint, Auckland, 1973.
——, *Houses and Housekeeping: A Fireside Gossip Upon Home and Its Comforts*, William Hunt, London, 1878.
Barker, Lady Mary Ann, *Station Amusements*, William Hunt, London, 1873. NZETC, https://nzetc.victoria.ac.nz/tm/scholarly/tei-BarAmus.html
Baucke, William, *Where the White Man Treads*, Wilson & Horton, Auckland, 1905. Wellcome Collection, https://wellcomecollection.org/works/berrbepy
Beaglehole, Ernest and Pearl Beaglehole. *Some Modern Maoris*, New Zealand Council for Educational Research [Wellington], 1946.
Beaton, Sophia, 'A Contemporary Māori Culinary Tradition: Does It Exist? An Analysis of Māori Cuisine', Masters thesis, University of Otago, 2007.

Beattie, James, '"Hungry Dragons": Expanding the Horizons of Chinese Environmental History – Cantonese Gold-Miners in Colonial New Zealand, 1860s–1920s', *International Review of Environmental History* 1, 2015, pp. 103–45.
——, 'Making Home, Making Identity: Asian Garden Making in New Zealand, 1850s–1930s', *Studies in the History of Gardens & Designed Landscapes* 31, no. 2, 2011, pp. 139–59.
Beck, Florence E. M., *These Days Were Mine*, C. Beck, Edendale, 1982.
Belich, James, *Making Peoples: A History of the New Zealanders from Polynesian Settlement to the End of the Nineteenth Century*, Penguin, Auckland, 2007.
Bell, Claudia, 'Rural Way of Life in New Zealand – Myths to Live By', PhD thesis, University of Auckland, 1993.
Belshaw, H., 'Agricultural Labour in New Zealand', *International Labour Review* 28, no. 1, July 1933, pp. 26–45.
Bennett, Adrian John Te Piki Kotuku, 'Marae: A Whakapapa of the Maori Marae', PhD thesis, University of Canterbury, 2007.
Best, Elsdon, *Maori Storehouses and Kindred Structures: Houses, Platforms, Racks, and Pits Used for Storing Food, etc.* [1916], A. R. Shearer, Government Printer, Wellington, 1974.
——, *The Maori, Volume II*, Polynesian Society, Wellington, 1941. NZETC, https://nzetc.victoria.ac.nz/tm/scholarly/tei-Bes02Maor.html
——, *The Maori, Volume I*, Wellington, 1924. NZETC, http://nzetc.victoria.ac.nz/tm/scholarly/name-204181.html
Binney, Judith, 'Some Observations on the Status of Maori Women', *NZJH* 38, no. 2, 2004, pp. 233–41.
Binney, Judith and Gillian Chaplin (eds), *Ngā Mōrehu: The Survivors*, Bridget Williams Books, Wellington, 2011.
Binney, Judith with Vincent O'Malley, 'The Quest for Survival: 1890–1920', in Atholl Anderson, Judith Binney and Aroha Harris (eds), *Tangata Whenua: An Illustrated History*, Bridget Williams Books, Wellington, 2014, pp. 318–49.
Binney, Judith with Vincent O'Malley and Alan Ward, 'Rangatiratanga and Kāwanatanga: 1840–1860', in Atholl Anderson, Judith Binney and Aroha Harris (eds), *Tangata Whenua: An Illustrated History*, Bridget Williams Books, Wellington, 2014, pp. 220–53.

——, 'The Land and the People: 1860–1890', in Atholl Anderson, Judith Binney and Aroha Harris (eds), *Tangata Whenua: An Illustrated History*, Bridget Williams Books, Wellington, 2014, pp. 286–315.

Blank, Arapera, *For Someone I Love: A Collection of Writing*, Anton Blank, Auckland, 2015.

Blunt, Alison and Robyn Dowling, *Home*, Routledge, London and New York, 2006.

Boast, Richard, 'Te Tango Whenua – Māori Land Alienation', Te Ara – the Encyclopedia of New Zealand, https://teara.govt.nz/en/te-tango-whenua-maori-land-alienation (accessed 23 August 2023).

——, *Buying the Land, Selling the Land: Governments and Maori Land in the North Island 1865–1921*, Victoria University Press, Wellington, 2008.

Boswell, Jean, *Dim Horizons*, Whitcombe & Tombs, Christchurch, 1956.

Boulton, Amohia, Jana Nee and Tanya Allport, 'Haukāinga – A Review of Māori concepts of "home"', Te Pūtake – Whakauae Raro Occasional Paper Series number 1, Whakauae Research Services, Whanganui, 2020, https://www.whakauae.co.nz/uploads/publications/publication322.pdf?1691976233.

Boyd, Joan, *Daughters of the Land: Nga Uri Wahine a Hineahuone: A Glimpse into the Lives of Rural Women in the Rotorua Area 1893–1993*, The Bathhouse Art & History Museum, Te Whare Taonga o Te Arawa, Rotorua, 1993.

Brewis, Jill, 'The House That Jack Bought: A Wanganui Childhood', *The Aristologist: An Antipodean Journal of Food History* 3, 2013, pp. 85–94.

——, *Colonial Fare*, Methuen, Auckland, 1982.

Brookes, Barbara, *A History of New Zealand Women*, Bridget Williams Books, Wellington, 2016.

——, 'Nostalgia for "Innocent Homely Pleasures": The 1964 New Zealand Controversy over *Washday at the Pa*', in Barbara Brookes (ed.), *At Home in New Zealand: History, Houses, People*, Bridget Williams Books, Wellington, 2000, pp. 210–25.

Brookes, Barbara (ed.), *At Home in New Zealand: History, Houses, People*, Bridget Williams Books, Wellington, 2000.

Brookes, Barbara and Margaret Tennant, 'Maori and Pakeha Women: Many Histories, Divergent Pasts?', in Barbara Brookes, Charlotte Macdonald and Margaret Tennant (eds), *Women in History 2: Essays on Women in New Zealand*, Bridget Williams Books, Wellington, 1992, pp. 25–48.

Brooking, Tom, '"Yeotopia" Found . . . But? The Yeoman Ideal that Underpinned New Zealand Agricultural Practice into the Early Twenty-First Century, with American and Australian Comparisons', *Agricultural History* 93, no. 1, 2019, pp. 68–101.

——, 'Use It or Lose It: Unravelling the Land Debate in Late Nineteenth-Century New Zealand', *NZJH* 30, no. 2, 1996, pp. 141–62.

——, '"Busting Up" the Greatest Estate of All: Liberal Maori Land Policy, 1891–1911', *NZJH* 26, no. 1, 1992, pp. 78–98.

——, 'Economic Transformation', in Geoffrey W. Rice (ed.), *The Oxford History of New Zealand*, 2nd edn, Oxford University Press, Auckland, 1992, pp. 230–53.

——, 'Larkrise to Littledene: The Making of Rural New Zealand Society 1880s–1939', unpublished working paper, University of Edinburgh, 1985.

——, 'Agrarian Businessmen Organise: A Comparative Study of the Origins and Early Phases of Development of the National Farmers' Union of England and Wales and the New Zealand Farmers' Union, ca 1880–1929', PhD thesis, University of Otago, 1977.

Brown, Deidre, *Māori Architecture: From Fale to Wharenui and Beyond*, Raupō, Auckland, 2009.

Brown, Helen, 'Raukura Erana Gillies (1896–1989)', in Helen Brown and Takerei Norton (eds), *Tāngata Ngāi Tahu: People of Ngāi Tahu, Volume I*, Te Rūnunga o Ngāi Tahu, Christchurch; with Bridget Williams Books, Wellington, 2017, pp. 62–67.

Bryder, Linda, *A Voice for Mothers: The Plunket Society and Infant Welfare 1907–2000*, Auckland University Press, Auckland, 2003.

Buchanan, Rachel, *The Parihaka Album: Lest We Forget*, Huia, Wellington, 2009.

Burton, David, *Two Hundred Years of New Zealand Food & Cookery*, A. H. & A. W. Reed, Auckland, 1982.

Butler, Samuel, *A First Year in Canterbury Settlement*, Longman, Green, Longman, Roberts & Green, London, 1863. ENZB, http://www.enzb.auckland.ac.nz/document/?wid=2889&action=null

Callister, Paul and Robert Didham, '"Man Alone" to "Woman Alone"?:

New Zealand Sex Ratios Since the Mid 1800s', Working Paper, Centre of Methods and Policy Application in the Social Sciences, University of Auckland, 2012, https://cdn.auckland.ac.nz/assets/arts/research-centres/compass/documents/New%20Zealand%20sex%20ratios%20since%20the%20mid%201800s%20(2).pdf

——, 'Workforce Composition', Te Ara – the Encyclopedia of New Zealand, https://teara.govt.nz/en/workforce-composition (accessed 23 August 2023).

Campbell, Hugh, *Farming Inside Invisible Worlds: Modernist Agriculture and Its Consequences*, Bloomsbury Academic Open Access Ebook, London, 2020, https://www.bloomsbury.com/uk/farming-inside-invisible-worlds-9781350327740/

Campbell, Judith A., *Between the Kitchen and the Creek*, 2nd edn, Chappell Printing, Warkworth, 2004.

Cant, Garth, and Russell Kirkpatrick (eds), *Rural Canterbury: Celebrating Its History*, Daphne Brassell Associates and Lincoln University Press, Wellington, 2001.

Carruthers, A. M., *'There Goes the Bell!!'*, A. M. Carruthers, Christchurch, 1968.

Carson, Winifred E., *I Was Young and the Grass Was Green: Impressions of Life during the Development of Back Country Communities in the Nelson Province*, Winifred E. Carson, Korere, 1996. Quoted with permission of Tom Carson.

Carter, Ian, 'Most Important Industry: How the New Zealand State Got Interested in Rural Women, 1930–1944', *NZJH* 20, no. 1, 1986, pp. 27–43.

Chapple-Sokol, Sam, 'Culinary Diplomacy: Breaking Bread to Win Hearts and Minds', *Hague Journal of Diplomacy* 8, 2013, pp. 161–83.

Coleman, John Noble, *A Memoir of the Rev. Richard Davis, For Thirty-Nine Years a Missionary in New Zealand*, John Nisbet, London, 1865. ENZB, http://www.enzb.auckland.ac.nz/document/?wid=1149&page=0&action=null

Coney, Sandra, *Standing in the Sunshine: A History of New Zealand Women Since They Won the Vote*, Viking, Auckland, 1993.

Connor, Helene, 'Whakapapa Back: Mixed Indigenous Māori and Pākehā Genealogy and Heritage in Aotearoa/New Zealand', *Genealogy* 3, no. 4, 2019, https://doi.org/10.3390/genealogy3040073. Quoted with permission of Helene Connor.

——, 'Writing Ourselves "Home", Biographical Texts, A Method for Contextualizing the Lives of Wahine Maori, Locating the Story of Betty Wark', PhD thesis, University of Auckland, 2006.

——, 'Land, Notions of "Home", and Cultural Space', in Katarina Ferro and Margit Wolfsberger (eds), *Gender and Power in the Pacific: Women's Strategies in a World of Change*, LIT Verlag, London, 2003, pp. 159–84.

Cooper, Katie, 'Feeding the Family: Pākehā and Māori Women in Rural Districts, c. 1900–1940', in Barbara Brookes, Jane McCabe and Angela Wanhalla (eds), *Past Caring? Women, Work and Emotion*, Otago University Press, Dunedin, 2019, pp. 135–61.

Counihan, Carole and Penny Van Esterik, 'Introduction', in Carole Counihan and Penny Van Esterik (eds), *Food and Culture: A Reader*, Routledge, New York and London, 1997, pp. 1–7.

Courage, Sarah Amelia, *Lights and Shadows of Colonial Life: Twenty-Six Years in Canterbury New Zealand* [1896], Whitcoulls, Christchurch, 1976.

Cowan, Ruth Schwartz, *More Work for Mother: The Ironies of Household Technology from the Open Hearth to the Microwave*, Basic Books Inc., New York, 1983.

Cowan, Valerie, *Goodness Gracious Me*, Cape Catley, Queen Charlotte Sound, 1998.

Cromley, Elizabeth Collins, *The Food Axis: Cooking, Eating, and the Architecture of American Houses*, University of Virginia Press, Charlottesville and London, 2010.

Cyclopedia Company Limited, *Cyclopedia of New Zealand, Volume 4: Otago and Southland Provincial Districts*, Christchurch, 1905. NZETC, http://nzetc.victoria.ac.nz/tm/scholarly/tei-Cyc04Cycl.html

——, *Cyclopedia of New Zealand, Volume 3: Canterbury Provincial District*, Christchurch, 1903. NZETC, http://nzetc.victoria.ac.nz/tm/scholarly/tei-Cyc03Cycl.html

Dacker, Bill, *Te Mamae me te Aroha: The Pain and the Love. A History of Kai Tahu Whānui in Otago, 1844–1994*, University of Otago Press in association with the Dunedin City Council, Dunedin, 1994.

——, *The People of the Place: Mahika Kai*, New Zealand 1990 Commission, Wellington, 1990.

Daley, Caroline, *Girls & Women, Men & Boys: Gender in Taradale 1886–1930*, Auckland University Press, Auckland, 1999.

——, 'Taradale Meets the Ideal Society and Its Enemies', *NZJH* 25, no. 2, October 1991, pp. 129–46.

Davidoff, Leonore and Catherine Hall, *Family Fortunes: Men & Women of the English Middle Class 1780–1850*, Hutchinson, London, 1987.

Davidson, Alexander, *A Home of One's Own: Housing Policy in Sweden and New Zealand from the 1840s to the 1990s*, Almqvist & Wiksell International, Stockholm, 1994.

Davidson, Janet, 'Explorers and Pioneers: The First Pacific People in New Zealand', in Sean Mallon, Kolokesa Māhina-Tuai and Damon Salesa (eds), *Tangata o le Moana: New Zealand and the People of the Pacific*, Te Papa Press, Wellington, 2012, pp. 37–55.

——, *The Prehistory of New Zealand*, Longman Paul, Auckland, 1987.

Denison, Edward and Guang Yu Ren, *The Life of the British Home: An Architectural History*, John Wriley & Sons, Chichester, 2012.

Derby, Mark, 'Māori–Pākehā Relations – Māori Urban Migration', Te Ara – the Encyclopedia of New Zealand, https://teara.govt.nz/en/maori-pakeha-relations/page-5 (accessed 23 August 2023).

Dieffenbach, Ernest, *Travels in New Zealand; With Contributions to the Geography, Geology, Botany, and Natural History of that Country, Volume II* [John Murray, London, 1843], Capper Press, Christchurch, 1974. ENZB, http://www.enzb.auckland.ac.nz/document/?wid=243&action=null

Doig, W. T., *A Survey of Standards of Life of New Zealand Dairy-Farmers*, E. V. Paul, Government Printer, Wellington, 1940.

Dow, Derek A., *Maori Health & Government Policy 1840–1940*, Victoria University Press, Wellington, 1999.

Drummond, Alison and L. R. Drummond, *At Home in New Zealand: An Illustrated History of Everyday Things before 1865*, Blackwood and Janet Paul, Auckland, 1967.

Duff, G. J., 'The Development of House Styles in New Zealand 1840–1990', *New Zealand Real Estate* 41, no. 8, Special Issue: 150 Years of Housing in New Zealand, September 1990, pp. 11–20.

Duff, Geoffrey P., *Sheep May Safely Graze: The Story of Morven Hills Station and the Tarras District, Central Otago* [1978], Cadsonbury Publications, Christchurch, 1998.

Duncan, J. S., 'The Land for the People?: Land Settlement and Rural Population Movements, 1886–1906', in Murray McCaskill (ed.), *Land and Livelihood: Geographical Essays in Honour of George Jobberns*, New Zealand Geographical Society, Christchurch, 1962, pp. 170–90.

Duncan, Suzanne and Poia Rewi, 'Tikanga: How Not to Get Told Off!', in Michael Reilly, Suzanne Duncan, Gianna Leoni, Lachy Paterson, Lyn Carter, Matiu Rātima and Poia Rewi (eds), *Te Kōparapara: An Introduction to the Māori World*, Auckland University Press, Auckland, 2018, pp. 30–47.

Durie, E. T., 'Ancestral Laws of Māori: Continuities of Land, People and History', in Danny Keenan (ed.), *Huia Histories of Māori: Ngā Tāhuhu Kōrero*, Huia, Wellington, 2012, pp. 2–11.

——, 'Will the Settlers Settle? Cultural Conciliation and Law', *Otago Law Review* 8, no. 4, 1996, pp. 449–65.

Durie, Mason, *Whaiora: Maori Health Development*, 2nd edn, Oxford University Press, Auckland, 1998.

Easton, Brian, *Not in Narrow Seas: The Economic History of Aotearoa New Zealand*, Victoria University of Wellington Press, Wellington, 2020.

Easy, Ann M., *Looking Backward* [I. Easy], Wellington, 1991.

Edwards, Mihi, *Mihipeka: Early Years*, Penguin Books, Auckland, 1990.

Eldred-Grigg, Stevan, *A Southern Gentry: New Zealanders Who Inherited the Earth*, A. H. and A. W. Reed, Wellington, 1980.

Ellis, Ngarino, *A Whakapapa of Tradition: 100 Years of Ngāti Porou Carving, 1830–1930*, Auckland, Auckland University Press, 2016.

Endt-Ferwerda, Annemarie, *Aunt Dorothy's Memories of Sunnydale*, Landsendt Publications, Auckland, 2006.

Fairburn, Miles, *The Ideal Society and Its Enemies: The Foundations of Modern New Zealand Society, 1850–1900*, Auckland University Press, Auckland, 1989.

——, 'The Rural Myth and the New Urban Frontier: An Approach to New Zealand Social History, 1870–1940', *NZJH* 9, no. 1, 1975, pp. 3–21.

Fearnley, Charles, *Colonial Style: Pioneer Buildings of New Zealand*, Gordon Ell, Bush Press, Auckland, 1986.

Ferguson, Gael, *Building the New Zealand Dream*, The Dunmore Press Limited with the assistance of the Historical Branch, Department of Internal Affairs, Palmerston North, 1994.

Findlay, Mary, *Tooth and Nail: The Story of a Daughter of the Depression*, A. H. & A. W. Reed, Wellington, 1974.

Fink, Deborah, *Open Country, Iowa: Rural Women, Tradition and Change*, State University of New York Press, Albany, 1986.

Firth, Raymond, *Economics of the New Zealand Maori*, R. E. Owen, Government Printer, Wellington, 1959.

Fitzgerald, Tanya, 'Archives of Memory and Memories of Archive: CMS Women's Letters and Diaries 1823–1835', *History of Education* 34, no. 6, 2005, pp. 657–74.

Fitz-William, Elsie, *Life at the Oaks: Memories of Raglan and Hamilton 1890–1912*, Pegasus, Christchurch, 1975.

Flanders, Judith, *The Making of Home: The 500-Year Story of How Our Houses Became Our Homes*, Thomas Dunne Books, St Martin's Press, New York, 2014.

Flashoff, Ruth, *Reremoana Hakiwai*, Reremoana Hakiwai Educational Trust, Napier, 1981.

Fletcher, Adele Lesley, 'Religion, Gender and Rank in Maori Society: A Study of Ritual and Social Practice in Eighteenth and Nineteenth-Century Documentary Sources', PhD thesis, University of Canterbury, 2000.

Furey, Louise, *Maori Gardening: An Archaeological Perspective*, Science and Technical Publishing, Department of Conservation, 2006, https://www.doc.govt.nz/our-work/heritage/heritage-publications/maori-gardening-an-archaeological-perspective/

Fyfe, Judith (ed.), *Matriarchs: A Generation of New Zealand Women Talk to Judith Fyfe*, Penguin Books, Auckland, 1990.

Gaffney, Brendan, *The New Zealand Coal Range Handbook* [Brendan Gaffney], Wellsford, 2021.

Galbreath, Ross, 'Agricultural and Horticultural Research – Early days', Te Ara – the Encyclopedia of New Zealand, https://teara.govt.nz/en/diagram/19623/kumara-pits (accessed 13 September 2023).

Gardner, W. J., 'A Colonial Economy', in Geoffrey W. Rice (ed.), *The Oxford History of New Zealand*, 2nd edn, Auckland University Press, Auckland, 1992, pp. 57–86.

——, *The Amuri: A County History*, Amuri County Council, Culverden, 1956.

Garner, Jean and Kate Foster (eds), *Letters to Grace: Writing Home from Colonial New Zealand*, Canterbury University Press, Christchurch, 2011.

Gee, Maurice, *Creeks and Kitchens: A Childhood Memoir*, Bridget Williams Books, Wellington, 2013.

Gemmell, Monique, 'A History of Marginalisation: Maori Women', Masters thesis, Victoria University of Wellington, 2013.

Gilabert, Violeta, 'Labours of Love: Marriage and Emotion in Aotearoa New Zealand 1918–1970s', PhD thesis, University of Otago, 2020.

Goodyear, Rosemary K., '"Sunshine and Fresh Air": An Oral History of Childhood and Family Life in Interwar New Zealand, with Some Comparisons to Interwar Britain', PhD thesis, University of Otago, 1998.

Grace, Patricia, 'Two Worlds', in Witi Ihimaera (ed.), *Growing Up Māori*, Tandem Press, Auckland, 1998, pp. 47–57.

Grace, Patricia, Irihapeti Ramsden and Jonathan Dennis (eds), *The Silent Migration: Ngāti Pōneke Young Māori Club 1937–1948*, Huia, Wellington, 2001.

Graham, Jeanine, 'The Pioneers (1840–1870)', in Keith Sinclair (ed.), *The Oxford Illustrated History of New Zealand*, Oxford University Press, Auckland, 1993, pp. 49–74.

Grey, Alan, *Aotearoa and New Zealand: A Historical Geography*, Canterbury University Press, Christchurch, 1994.

Halfacree, K. H., 'Locality and Social Representation: Space, Discourse and Alternative Definitions of the Rural', *Journal of Rural Studies* 9, no. 1, 1993, pp. 23–37.

Hall, David, *On the Farm: New Zealand's Invisible Women*, Atuanui Press, Pōkeno, 2022.

Hareven, Tamara K., 'The Home and the Family in Historical Perspective', *Social Research* 58, no. 1, Spring 1991, pp. 253–85.
Hargreaves, R. P., 'Changing Maori Agriculture in Pre-Waitangi New Zealand', *Journal of the Polynesian Society* 72, no. 2, 1963, pp. 101–17.
——, 'The Maori Agriculture of the Auckland Province in the Mid-Nineteenth Century', *Journal of the Polynesian Society* 68, no. 2, 1959, pp. 61–79.
Harman, Kristyn, '"Some Dozen *Raupo Whares*, and a Few Tents": Remembering Raupo Houses in Colonial New Zealand', *Journal of New Zealand Studies* NS17, 2014, pp. 39–57.
Harris, Aroha, 'Persistence and Resilience: 1920–1945', in Atholl Anderson, Judith Binney and Aroha Harris (eds), *Tangata Whenua: An Illustrated History*, Bridget Williams Books, Wellington, 2014, pp. 352–79.
——, 'Maori Land Development Schemes, 1945–1974, with Two Case Studies from the Hokianga', Masters thesis, Massey University, 1996.
Harris, Olive (compiler), ed. Chris Lancaster, *Remember the Hokianga*, O. Harris, Waikanae, 2006.
Hatch, Elvin, *Respectable Lives: Social Standing in Rural New Zealand*, University of California Press, Berkeley, 1992.
Hedley, Max J., 'Mutual Aid between Farm Households: New Zealand and Canada', *Sociologia Ruralis* 25, no. 1, 1985, pp. 26–39.
Henare, Manuka, 'Te Maki Kai – Food Production Economies', Te Ara – the Encyclopedia of New Zealand, https://teara.govt.nz/en/te-mahi-kai-food-production-economics (accessed 23 August 2023).
Herda, Phyllis, 'Ladies a Plate: Women and Food', in Julie Park (ed.), *Ladies a Plate: Change and Continuity in the Lives of New Zealand Women*, Auckland University Press, Auckland, 1991, pp. 144–72.
Higgins, Rawinia and Paul Meredith, 'Te Mana o te Wāhine – Māori Women – Tapu and Peacemaking', Te Ara – the Encyclopedia of New Zealand, https://teara.govt.nz/en/te-mana-o-te-wahine-maori-women/page-2 (accessed 23 August 2023).
Hippolite, Joy, 'Wetekia Ruruku Elkington', in Charlotte Macdonald, Merimeri Penfold and Bridget Williams (eds), *The Book of New Zealand Women: Ko Kui Ma Te Kaupapa*, Bridget Williams Books, Wellington, 1991, pp. 205–07. Quoted with permission of Joy Hippolite.

Bibliography

Hiroa, Te Rangi, *The Coming of the Maori*, Maori Purposes Fund Board, Wellington, 1949. NZETC, https://nzetc.victoria.ac.nz/tm/scholarly/tei-BucTheC.html

Hodgson, Terence E., *The Big House: Grand and Opulent Houses in Colonial New Zealand*, Random Century, Auckland, 1991.

Hoggart, Keith, 'Let's Do Away with Rural', *Journal of Rural Studies* 6, no. 3, 1990, pp. 245–57.

Holland, Peter, *Home in the Howling Wilderness: Settlers and the Environment in Southern New Zealand*, Auckland University Press, Auckland, 2013.

Holt, Marilyn Irvin, *Linoleum, Better Babies & the Modern Farm*, University of New Mexico Press, Albuquerque, 1995.

Hosken, Evelyn, *Life on a Five Pound Note*, E. Hoskens, Timaru, 1964.

Hoskins, Rau, Rihi Te Nana, Peter Rhodes, Philip Guy and Chris Sage, 'Ki te Hau Kainga: New Perspectives on Māori Housing Solutions', Design Guide Prepared for Housing New Zealand Corporation, 2002, https://kaingaora.govt.nz/assets/Publications/Design-Guidelines/ki-te-hau-kainga-new-perspectives-on-maori-housing-solutions.pdf

Hunter, Kate, *Hunting: A New Zealand History*, Random House NZ, Auckland, 2009.

Hunter, Kate and Lynette Squire, 'Bread and Butter: Rural Women at the Stove and Churn in Nineteenth-Century New Zealand and Australia', in Kate Hunter and Michael Symons (eds), *Eating In, Dining Out: Proceedings of the New Zealand Culinary History Conference*, History Programme and Stout Research Centre, Victoria University, Wellington, 2005, pp. 38–50.

Hunter, Kathryn M., *Father's Right-Hand Man: Women on Australia's Family Farms in the Age of Federation*, Australian Scholarly Publishing, Melbourne, 2004.

Hunter, Kathryn and Pamela Riney-Kehrberg, 'Rural Daughters in Australia, New Zealand, and the United States: An Historical Perspective', in Ruth Panelli, Samantha Punch and Elsbeth Robson (eds), *Global Perspectives on Rural Childhood and Youth: Young Rural Lives*, Routledge, New York and London, 2007, pp. 57–68.

Husband, Dale, 'Mike Stevens: Bluffies and Kāi Tahu', *E-Tangata*, 2 December 2018, https://e-tangata.co.nz/korero/mike-stevens-bluffies-and-kai-tahu/

Ihimaera, Witi (ed.), *Growing Up Māori*, Tandem Press, Auckland, 1998.

Isaacs, Nigel, 'Foundations of Control – New Zealand Building Legislation in the 1840s', in Christine McCarthy (ed.), *'A Massive Colonial Experiment': New Zealand Architecture in the 1840s: A One Day Symposium*, Centre for Building Performance Research, Wellington, 2014.

——, 'Early Building Legislation', *Build* 122, February/March 2011, pp. 90–91.

——, 'Hot Water the Old-Fashioned Way', *Build* 99, April/May 2007, pp. 94–95.

Isaacs, Nigel, Michael Camilleri and Lisa French, 'Hot Water Over Time: The New Zealand Experience', conference paper delivered at the XXXVth International Association of Housing Science (IAHS) World Congress on Housing Science, RMIT University, 2007.

Jackson, Moana, 'Where to Next? Decolonisation and the Stories in the Land', in Bianca Elkington, Moana Jackson, Rebecca Kiddle, Ocean Ripeka Mercier, Mike Ross, Jennie Smeaton and Amanda Thomas (eds), *Imagining Decolonisation*, Bridget Williams Books, Wellington, 2020, pp. 133–55.

Jahnke, Huia Tomlins, 'Towards a Secure Identity: Maori Women and the Home-Place', *Women's Studies International Forum* 25, no. 5, Sept–Oct 2022, pp. 503–13.

Johnston, Patricia and Leonie Pihama, 'The Marginalisation of Māori Women' [originally printed in *Hecate*, 1994], in Leonie Pihama, Linda Tuhiwai Smith, Naomi Simmonds, Joeliee Seed-Pihama and Kirsten Gabel (eds), *Mana Wahine Reader: A Collection of Writings 1987–1998, Volume 1*, Te Kotahi Research Institute, Hamilton, 2019, pp. 114–25.

Johnstone-Smith, Sophie May, *Battles, Buggies and Babies*, Rice Printers, Hamilton, 1975.

Jones, Verna, *Crock of Gold*, V. Jones, Ohaeawai, c. 1988.

——, *The Beginning of the Rainbow*, V. Jones, Ohaeawai, 1981. Quoted with permission of Margaret Ludbrook.

Kake, Bonnie Jade, 'Pehiāweri Marae Papakāinga: A Model for Community Regeneration in Te Tai Tokerau', Masters thesis, Unitec Institute of Technology, 2015.

Keane, Basil, 'Māori Feasts and Ceremonial Eating – Hākari – Traditional Feasts', Te Ara – the Encyclopedia of New Zealand, https://teara.govt.nz/en/maori-feasts-and-ceremonial-eating-hakari/page-2 (accessed 23 August 2023).

——, 'Tūranga i te Hapori – Status in Māori Society', Te Ara – the Encyclopedia of New Zealand, https://teara.govt.nz/en/turanga-i-te-hapori-status-in-maori-society (accessed 23 August 2023).

——, 'Te Māori i te Ohanga – Māori in the Economy', Te Ara – the Encyclopedia of New Zealand, https://teara.govt.nz/en/te-maori-i-te-ohanga-maori-in-the-economy (accessed 23 August 2023).

——, 'Te Rāngai Mahi – Māori in the Workforce – European Contact', Te Ara – the Encyclopedia of New Zealand, https://teara.govt.nz/en/te-rangai-mahi-maori-in-the-workforce/page-2 (accessed 23 August 2023).

——, 'Te Tāhere Manu: Bird Catching', in Te Ara – the Encyclopedia of New Zealand, *Te Taiao: Māori and the Natural World*, David Bateman, Auckland, 2010, pp. 152–60.

Keenan, Danny, *Ahuwhenua: Celebrating 80 Years of Māori Farming*, BNZ & Huia Publishers, Wellington, 2013.

Kendall, Florence Ada, *Making the Most of My Life: Recollections from 1906–1960*, Judy Graham and Family, Auckland, 1996.

King, Michael, 'Cooper, Whina', *Dictionary of New Zealand Biography*, Te Ara – the Encyclopedia of New Zealand, https://teara.govt.nz/en/biographies/5c32/cooper-whina (accessed 23 August 2023).

King, Pita, Darrin Hodgetts, Mohi Robert Rua and Mandy Morgan, 'When the Marae Moves into the City: Being Māori in Urban Palmerston North', *City & Community* 17, no. 4, December 2018, pp. 1189–208.

Kohere, Reweti T., *The Autobiography of a Maori*, Reed Publishing, Wellington, 1951. NZETC, https://nzetc.victoria.ac.nz/tm/scholarly/tei-KohAuto.html

Koning, J. P. and W. H. Oliver, 'Economic Decline and Social Deprivation in Muriwhenua 1880–1940', Report Commissioned by Council for Claimants to Present Submission to Waitangi Tribunal, 1993.

Kotchemidova, Christina, 'From Good Cheer to "Drive-By Smiling": A Social History of Cheerfulness', *Journal of Social History* 39, no. 1, Fall 2005, pp. 5–37.

Kreklau, Claudia, 'Neither Gendered Nor a Room: The Kitchen in Central Europe and the Masculinization of Modernity, 1800–1900', *Global Food History* 7, no. 1, 2021, pp. 5–35.

Kristiansen, Tessa, 'Wilson, John Cracroft', *Dictionary of New Zealand Biography*, Te Ara – the Encyclopedia of New Zealand, https://teara.govt.nz/en/biographies/1w31/wilson-john-cracroft (accessed 23 August 2023).

Krivan, Mark, 'The Department of Maori Affairs Housing Programme, 1935 to 1967', Masters thesis, Massey University, 1990.

Lady, A [Mrs William], *Facts, Or, The Experiences of a Recent Colonist in New Zealand*, Mrs William, Yalding, 1883.

Lange, Raeburn, 'The Social Impact of Colonisation and Land Loss on the Iwi of the Rangitikei, Manawatu and Horowhenua Region, 1840–1960', Research Report Commissioned by the Crown Forestry Rental Trust, Porirua ki Manawatu Inquiry, 2000.

——, *May the People Live: A History of Maori Health Development 1900–1920*, Auckland University Press, Auckland, 1999.

Law Commission, 'R53 Justice: The Experiences of Māori Women', Commission's Report, 1999, https://www.lawcom.govt.nz/our-projects/justice-experiences-m%C4%81ori-women

Leach, Helen, *Kitchens: The New Zealand Kitchen in the 20th Century*, Otago University Press, Dunedin, 2014.

——, 'Fruit and Vegetable Preservation in 20th Century New Zealand Homes', *The Aristologist: An Antipodean Journal of Food History* 3, 2013, pp. 9–36.

——, 'Cookery in the Colonial Era (1769–1899)', in Helen Leach (ed.), *From Kai to Kiwi Kitchen: New Zealand Culinary Traditions and Cookbooks*, Otago University Press, Dunedin, 2010, pp. 31–48.

——, 'Maori Cookery before Cook', in Helen Leach (ed.), *From Kai to Kiwi Kitchen: New Zealand Culinary Traditions and Cookbooks*, Otago University Press, Dunedin, 2010, pp. 13–30.

——, 'Cooking with Pots – Again', in Atholl Anderson, Kaye Green and Foss Leach (eds), *Vastly Ingenious: The Archaeology of Pacific Material*

Culture in Honour of Janet M. Davidson*, Otago University Press, Dunedin, 2007, pp. 53–68.

——, 'The European House and Garden in New Zealand: A Case for Parallel Development', in Barbara Brookes (ed.), *At Home in New Zealand: History, Houses, People*, Bridget Williams Books, Wellington, 2000, pp. 73–88.

Leach, Helen, with illustrations by Nancy Tichborne, *1,000 Years of Gardening in New Zealand*, A. H. & A. W. Reed, Wellington, 1984.

Lee, Lily and Ruth Lam, *Sons of the Soil: Chinese Market Gardeners in New Zealand*, Dominion Federation of New Zealand Chinese Commercial Growers, Pukekohe, 2012.

Lévi-Strauss, Claude, 'The Culinary Triangle', in Carole Counihan and Penny Van Esterik (eds), *Food and Culture: A Reader*, Routledge, New York and London, 1997, pp. 28–35.

Macdonald, Charlotte, 'Strangers at the Hearth: The Eclipse of Domestic Service in New Zealand Homes c. 1830s–1940s', in Barbara Brookes (ed.), *At Home in New Zealand: Houses, History, People*, Bridget Williams Books, Wellington, 2000, pp. 41–56.

——, 'Too Many Men and Too Few Women: Gender's "Fatal Impact" in Nineteenth-Century Colonies', in Caroline Daley and Deborah Montgomerie (eds), *The Gendered Kiwi*, Auckland University Press, Auckland, 1999, pp. 17–35.

Mackenzie, Alice, *Pioneers of Martins Bay*, Otago Daily Times and Witness Newspapers, Dunedin, 1947.

Makereti [Maggie Papakura], *The Old-Time Maori*, Victor Gollancz, London, 1938. NZETC, http://nzetc.victoria.ac.nz/tm/scholarly/tei-MakOldT.html. Quoted with permission of June Grant.

Manaaki Whenua Landcare Research, 'Ngā Raupori Whakaoranga', https://rauropiwhakaoranga.landcareresearch.co.nz/

Manatū Wāhine Ministry for Women, Wai 2700 – Mana Wāhine Kaupapa Inquiry, https://women.govt.nz/wahine-maori/wai-2700-mana-wahine-kaupapa-inquiry (accessed 6 January 2024).

Martin, David Robert, 'The Maori Whare After Contact', Masters thesis, University of Otago, 1996.

Martin, Frances Kahui, 'Te Manaakitanga i roto i ngā Ahumahi Tāpoi: The Interpretation of Manaakitanga from a Māori Tourism

Supplier Perspective', Masters thesis, Auckland University of Technology, 2008.

Martin, John, *The Forgotten Worker: The Rural Wage Earner in Nineteenth-Century New Zealand*, Allen and Unwin and Trade Union History Project, Wellington, 1990.

Massey, Doreen, *Space, Place, and Gender*, University of Minnesota Press, Minneapolis, 1994.

Matthews, S. Leigh, *Looking Back: Canadian Women's Prairie Memoirs and Intersections of Culture, History, and Identity*, University of Calgary Press Ebook, Calgary, Alberta, 2010, https://library.oapen.org/bitstream/handle/20.500.12657/57453/9781552385951.pdf?sequence=1&isAllowed=y

Maudlin, Daniel and Bernard L. Herman, 'Introduction', in Daniel Maudlin and Bernard L. Herman (eds), *Building the British Atlantic World: Spaces, Places, and Material Culture, 1600–1850*, University of North Carolina Press, Chapel Hill, 2016, pp. 1–27.

Maybury, Jan, 'Mapping Lived Realities onto Social Representations of Rurality and Gender', Masters thesis, University of Auckland, 1998.

McAloon, Jim, 'Land Ownership', Te Ara – the Encyclopedia of New Zealand, https://teara.govt.nz/en/land-ownership (accessed 23 August 2023).

——, *No Idle Rich: The Wealthy in Canterbury and Otago 1840–1914*, University of Otago Press, Dunedin, 2002.

——, 'The Colonial Wealthy in Canterbury and Otago: No Idle Rich', *NZJH* 13, no. 1, 1996, pp. 43–60.

McCloy, Nicola, *Dairy Nation: The Story of Dairy Farming in New Zealand*, Random House New Zealand, Auckland, 2014.

McDowall, R. W., *Ikawai: Freshwater Fishes in Māori Culture and Economy*, Canterbury University Press, Christchurch, 2011.

McLeod, W. H., *Punjabis in New Zealand: A History of Punjabi Migration*, Guru Nanak Dev University, Amritsar, 1986.

McNeill, Joanne, 'Northland's Buried Treasure', *New Zealand Geographic* 10, April–June 1991, https://www.nzgeo.com/stories/northlands-buried-treasure/

Mead, Hirini Moko, *Tikanga Māori: Living by Māori Values*, Huia Publishers, Wellington, 2003.

Meah, Angela, 'Reconceptualizing Power and Gendered Subjectivities in Domestic Cooking Spaces', *Progress in Human History* 38, no. 5, 2014, pp. 671–90.

Mercier, Ocean Ripeka, 'What is Decolonisation?', in Bianca Elkington, Moana Jackson, Rebecca Kiddle, Ocean Ripeka Mercier, Mike Ross, Jennie Smeaton and Amanda Thomas (eds), *Imagining Decolonisation*, Bridget Williams Books, Wellington, 2020, pp. 40–82.

Meredith, Paul, 'Te Hī Ika: Māori Fishing', in Te Ara – the Encyclopedia of New Zealand, *Te Taiao: Māori and the Natural World*, David Bateman, Auckland, 2010, pp. 138–43.

Metson, Norma, 'The Farm Home', *New Zealand Journal of Agriculture* 71, no. 4, 1945, pp. 357–70.

Middleton, Angela, *Pēwhairangi: Bay of Islands Missions and Māori 1814 to 1845*, Otago University Press, Dunedin, 2014.

Mikaere, Ani, 'Māori Women: Caught in the Contradictions of a Colonised Reality' [originally printed in *Waikato Law Review*, no. 2, 1994], in Leonie Pihama, Linda Tuhiwai Smith, Naomi Simmonds, Joeliee Seed-Pihama and Kirsten Gabel (eds), *Mana Wahine Reader: A Collection of Writings 1987–1998, Volume 1*, Te Kotahi Research Institute, Hamilton, 2019, pp. 137–54.

——, *The Balance Destroyed: The Consequences for Māori Women of the Colonisation of Tikanga Māori*, Auckland International Research Institute for Māori and Indigenous Education and Ani Mikaere, Auckland, 2003.

Millar, Joan, *Joan's Journey: The Autobiography of Joan Millar*, Sycamore Print, Invercargill, 1992. Quoted with permission of Rodger Millar.

Miller, C. Holmes, *Sturdy Sons: A Flashback into the Cheerful Yesterday of a New Zealand Family*, Otago Daily Times & Witness Newspapers, Dunedin, 1958.

Ministry for Culture and Heritage, 'Māori Land Loss: 1860–2000', NZHistory website, https://nzhistory.govt.nz/media/interactive/maori-land-1860-2000 (accessed 23 August 2023).

——, 'Summary – British and Irish Immigration, 1840–1914', NZHistory website, https://nzhistory.govt.nz/culture/immigration/home-away-from-home/summary (accessed 23 August 2023).

Mintz, Sidney W., *Tasting Food, Tasting Freedom: Excursions into Eating, Culture, and the Past*, Beacon Press, Boston, 1996.

Mitchell, Hilary and John Mitchell, *Te Tau Ihu o te Waka: A History of Māori of Nelson and Marlborough, Volume II: Te Ara Hou – The New Society*, Huia Publishers in association with the Wakatū Incorporation, Wellington, 2007.

Mitchell, Isabella, 'Picnics in New Zealand During the Late Nineteenth and Early Twentieth Centuries: An Interpretive Study', Masters thesis, Massey University, 1995.

Mitchell, Kelly and Vini Olsen-Reeder, 'Tapu and Noa as Negotiators of Māori Gender Roles in Precolonial Aotearoa and Today', *MAI Journal* 10, no. 2, 2021, pp. 84–92.

Moeke-Pickering, Taima, 'Maori Identity Within Whanau: A Review of Literature', working paper, University of Waikato, 1996.

Moffats Limited, *Cooking By Moffat*, Moffats, Weston, Ontario; Blackburn, England [193–?].

Moon, Paul, *A Tohunga's Natural World: Plants, Gardening and Food*, David Ling Publishing, Auckland, 2005.

Moore, Evelyn E., 'The Farmhouse Kitchen in New Zealand', *New Zealand Journal of Agriculture* 83, no. 5, 1951, pp. 405–08.

——, 'The Farmhouse Kitchen in New Zealand', *New Zealand Journal of Agriculture* 83, no. 3, 1951, pp. 232–36.

Moorfield, John C., *Te Aka: Māori–English, English–Māori Dictionary*, 3rd edn, Pearson, Auckland, 2011.

Morrison, Laurie, *Te Rōpu o te Ora: The Founding of the Te Arawa Women's Health League 1937*, Women's Health League, Rotorua, 2018.

Murphy, Mary, '"Hospitality was their byword": Food, Tradition, and Creativity in Borderlands Kitchens', in Cynthia C. Prescott and Maureen S. Thompson (eds), *Backstories: The Kitchen Table Talk Cookbook*, Digital Press at the University of North Dakota, Grand Forks, ND, 2021, pp. 87–95, https://commons.und.edu/press-books/18/

Narotzky, Susana, 'Provisioning', in James G. Carrier (ed.), *A Handbook of Economic Anthropology*, 2nd edn, Elgar Online, 2012, https://www.elgaronline.com/display/edcoll/9781849809283/9781849809283.00012.xml

Nevill, Jane Kathryn, 'The "Electric Servant" in Rural New Zealand: A Study of the Impact of Electrification on Rural Domestic Life', BA (Hons) thesis, University of Otago, 1985.

Newby, Howard, 'Locality and Rurality: The Restructuring of Rural Social Relations', *Regional Studies* 20, no. 3, 1986, pp. 209–15.

Newman, Mary, 'Contact Period Houses from the Lake Rotoaira Area, Taupo', *Archaeology in New Zealand* 32, no. 1, March 1989, pp. 7–25.

Newman, Sara, 'The Late Great Country Hall', in New Zealand Memories, *Her Story: Women Shaping New Zealand History*, New Zealand Memories, Auckland, 2007, pp. 4–8. Quoted with permission of Sara Newman.

Newport, Jeff, 'Country Living in the 1920s', *Journal of the Nelson and Marlborough Historical Societies* 2, no. 4, 1990, pp. 29–33. NZETC, https://nzetc.victoria.ac.nz/tm/scholarly/tei-NHSJ05_04-t1-body1-d8.html

Northcote-Bade, S., 'Early Housing in New Zealand, With Particular Reference to Nelson and Cook Straight Area', *Nelson Historical Society Journal* 1, no. 3, November 1958, pp. 2–7. NZETC, https://nzetc.victoria.ac.nz/tm/scholarly/tei-NHSJ01_03-t1-body1-d1.html

O'Donnell, Jean Marie, '"Electric Servants" and the Science of Housework: Changing Patterns of Domestic Work, 1935–1956', in Barbara Brookes, Charlotte Macdonald and Margaret Tennant (eds), *Women in History 2: Essays on Women in New Zealand*, Bridget Williams Books, Wellington, 1992, pp. 168–83.

Olssen, Erik, 'Families and the Gendering of European New Zealand in the Colonial Period, 1840–80', in Caroline Daley and Deborah Montgomerie (eds), *The Gendered Kiwi*, Auckland University Press, Auckland, 1999, pp. 37–62.

Osterud, Nancy Grey, 'The Meanings of Independence in the Oral Autobiographies of Rural Women in Twentieth-Century New York', *Agricultural History* 89, no. 3, 2015, pp. 426–43.

——, *Bonds of Community: The Lives of Farm Women in Nineteenth-Century New York*, Cornell University Press, Ithaca and London, 1991.

Paama-Pengelly, Julie, *Māori Art and Design: Weaving, Painting, Carving and Architecture*, New Holland, Auckland, 2010.

Paris, Susan, *Two Per Mile: A History of the Rural Electrical Reticulation Council*, Morris Communications Group, Wellington, c. 1996.

Park, Geoff, '"Swamps which might doubtless Easily be drained": Swamp Drainage and Its Impact on the Indigenous', in Eric Pawson and Tom Brooking (eds), *Making a New Land: Environmental Histories of New Zealand*, new edn, Otago University Press, Dunedin, 2013, pp. 174–89.

Parker, Sally K., 'Farm Women in the 1950s', in Barbara Brookes, Charlotte Macdonald and Margaret Tennant (eds), *Women in History 2: Essays on Women in New Zealand*, Bridget Williams Books, Wellington, 1992, pp. 205–24.

Paterson, Lachy, 'Rēweti Kōhere's Model Village', *NZJH* 41, no. 1, 2007, pp. 27–44.

——, *Colonial Discourses: Niupepa Māori 1855–1863*, Otago University Press, Dunedin, 2006.

——, 'Ngā Reo o Ngā Niupepa: Māori-Language Newspapers 1855–1863', PhD thesis, University of Otago, 2004.

Paterson, Lachy and Angela Wanhalla, *He Reo Wāhine: Māori Women's Voices from the Nineteenth Century*, Auckland University Press, Auckland, 2017.

Patterson, Brad, Tom Brooking and Jim McAloon with Rebecca Lenihan and Tanja Bueltmann, *Unpacking the Kists: The Scots in New Zealand*, McGill-Queens University Press, Montreal & Kingston, London, and Ithaca; Otago University Press, Dunedin, 2013.

Paulin, Chris D., 'Perspectives of Māori Fishing History and Techniques. Ngā Āhua me ngā Pūrākau me ngā Hangarau Ika o te Māori', *Tuhinga* 18, 2007, pp. 11–47.

Peden, Robert, *Making Sheep Country: Mt. Peel Station and the Transformation of the Tussock Lands*, Auckland University Press, Auckland, 2011.

Peden, Robert and Peter Holland, 'Settlers Transforming the Open Country', in Eric Pawson and Tom Brooking (eds), *Making a New Land: Environmental Histories of New Zealand*, new edn, Otago University Press, Dunedin, 2013, pp. 89–105.

Pehi, Phillipa and Marion Johnson, 'Whenua Whānau: Walking the Land with Indigeneity and Science to Find Our Home', in Mere Kēpa, Marilyn McPherson and Linitā Manuʻatu (eds), *Home: Here to Stay*, Huia Ebook, Wellington, 2015, pp. 138–63.

Pennell, Sara, *The Birth of the English Kitchen, 1600–1850 (Cultures of Early Modern Europe)*, Bloomsbury Academic, Kindle Ebook, 2016.

Pere, Rangimarie Rose, *Ako: Concepts and Learning in the Maori Tradition*, Te Kohanga Reo National Trust Board, Wellington, 1994.

Petersen, Anna K. C., *New Zealanders at Home: A Cultural History of Domestic Interiors 1814–1914*, University of Otago Press, Dunedin, 2001.

Petrie, Hazel, *Outcasts of the Gods? The Struggle Over Slavery in Māori New Zealand*, Auckland University Press, Auckland, 2015.

——, 'Decoding the Colours of Rank in Māori Society: What Might They Tell Us About Perceptions of War Captives?' *Journal of the Polynesian Society* 120, 2011, pp. 211–40.

——, *Chiefs of Industry: Māori Tribal Enterprise in Early Colonial New Zealand*, Auckland University Press, Auckland, 2006.

Phillipps, W. J. and John Huria, *Māori Life & Custom*, Raupō, North Shore, 2008.

Phillips, Chanel, Anne-Marie Jackson and Hauiti Hakopa, 'Creation Narratives of Mahinga Kai: Māori Customary Food-Gathering Sites and Practices', *MAI Journal* 5, no. 1, 2016, pp. 63–75.

Phillips, Jock, 'Class', Te Ara – the Encyclopedia of New Zealand, https://teara.govt.nz/en/class (accessed 23 August 2023).

——, 'Rural Mythologies', Te Ara – the Encyclopedia of New Zealand, https://teara.govt.nz/en/rural-mythologies (accessed 23 August 2023).

——, 'Rural Recreation', Te Ara – the Encyclopedia of New Zealand, https://teara.govt.nz/en/rural-recreation (accessed 23 August 2023).

——, *A Man's Country? The Image of the Pakeha Male*, Penguin Books, Auckland, 1987.

Phillis, Onehou, *Maumahara: The Memories of Te Onehou Phillis*, Kapohia, Ōtaki, 2012. Quoted with permission of Katrina Te Hana Phillis and Teri Phillis.

Porter, Frances and Charlotte Macdonald, 'Introduction', in Frances Porter and Charlotte Macdonald (eds), *'My Hand Will Write What My Heart Dictates': The Unsettled Lives of Women in Nineteenth-Century*

New Zealand as Revealed to Sisters, Family, and Friends, Auckland University Press with Bridget Williams Books, Auckland, 1996, pp. 1–22.

Prickett, Nigel J., 'Houses and House Life in Prehistoric New Zealand', Masters thesis, University of Otago, 1974.

Raine, Katherine, '1815–1840s: The First European Gardens', in Matthew Bradbury (ed.), *A History of the Garden in New Zealand*, Viking, Auckland, 1995, pp. 52–63.

Raine, Katherine and John P. Adam, '1840–1860s: The Settlers' Gardens', in Matthew Bradbury (ed.), *A History of the Garden in New Zealand*, Viking, Auckland, 1995, pp. 64–85.

——, '1860s–1900: Victorian Gardens', in Matthew Bradbury (ed.), *A History of the Garden in New Zealand*, Viking, Auckland, 1995, pp. 86–111.

Rangiwai, Byron, 'Some Brief Notes on Kai Māori', *Te Kaharoa* 14, no. 1, 2021. https://www.tekaharoa.com/index.php/tekaharoa/article/view/359

Reckwitz, Andreas, 'Affective Spaces: A Praxeological Outlook', *Rethinking History: The Journal of Theory and Practice* 16, no. 2, 2012, pp. 241–58.

Reed, A. H., *The Kauri Gumdiggers*, 3rd edn, Bush Press, Auckland, 2006.

Rei, Tania, *Maori Women and the Vote*, Huia Publishers, Wellington, 1993.

Rei, Tania, Geraldine McDonald and Ngāhuia Te Awekōtuku, 'Ngā Rōpū Wāhine Māori', NZHistory website, https://nzhistory.govt.nz/women-together/theme/maori (accessed 23 August 2023).

Reilly, Helen, *Connecting the Country, New Zealand's National Grid 1886–2007*, Steele Roberts Publishers, Wellington, 2008.

Rennie, Neil, *Power to the People: 100 Years of Public Electricity Supply in New Zealand*, Electricity Supply Association of New Zealand, Wellington, 1989.

Richardson, Robert, '3 Feet Under: Is the Traditional Hāngī in Danger of Cultural Disappearance?' Masters thesis, Auckland University of Technology, 2017.

Riney-Kehrberg, Pamela, 'New Directions in Rural History', *Agricultural History* 81, no. 2, Spring 2007, pp. 155–58.

Rogers, Anna and Mīria Simpson (eds), *Te Tīmatanga Tātau Tātau: Early Stories from Founding Members of the Māori Women's Welfare League*, Māori Women's Welfare League and Bridget Williams Books, Wellington, 1993.

Rolshoven, Johanna, 'The Kitchen: Terra Incognita', in Klaus Spechtenhauser (ed.), Bill Martin and Laura Bruce (trans.), *The Kitchen: Life World, Usage, Perspectives*, Burkhäuser – Publisher for Architecture, Basel, 2006, pp. 9–15.

Rosenberg, Gerhard, 'House Plans for Maori Families', *Te Maori* 1, no. 3, Summer 1970, pp. 15–17, 45–47.

Ross, Mike, 'The Throat of Parata', in Bianca Elkington, Moana Jackson, Rebecca Kiddle, Ocean Ripeka Mercier, Mike Ross, Jennie Smeaton and Amanda Thomas (eds), *Imagining Decolonisation*, Bridget Williams Books, Wellington, 2020, pp. 21–39.

Royal, Charles and Jenny Kaka-Scott, 'Māori Foods – Kai Māori', Te Ara – the Encyclopedia of New Zealand, https://teara.govt.nz/en/maori-foods-kai-maori (accessed 23 August 2023).

Sales, R., 'Early New Zealand Cottages, 1850–70', Subthesis/Building report for B. Arch, University of Auckland, 1970.

Salmond, Anne, *Hui: A Study of Maori Ceremonial Gatherings*, 2nd edn., Reed Books, Auckland, 1994.

Salmond, Jeremy, *Old New Zealand Houses, 1800–1940*, Reed Publishing, Auckland, 1986.

Savage, John, *Some Account of New Zealand, Particularly the Bay of Islands and Surrounding Country with a Description of the Religion, Arts, Manufactures, Manners and Customs of the Natives & c. & c.* [J. Murray, London, 1807], Hocken Library facsimile, 1966. ENZB, http://www.enzb.auckland.ac.nz/document?wid=56&action=null

Schmidt, Tyson, '". . . The Menace Posed to Public Health by 'Insanitary Pahs": Sir Maui Pomare's Clean Up of Maori Architecture', in Christine McCarthy (ed.), *The Proceedings of Elegance and Excesses: 'Good Architecture Should Not Be a Plaything': A One Day Symposium*, Centre for Building Performance Research, Wellington, 2011.

Schrader, Ben, *The Big Smoke: New Zealand Cities 1840–1920*, Bridget Williams Books, Wellington, 2016.

——, 'A Bi-cultural Townscape: Wellington in the 1940s [sic]', *Architectural History Aotearoa* 11, 2014, pp. 11–18.
——, 'Māori Housing: Te Noho Whare', Te Ara –the Encyclopedia of New Zealand, https://teara.govt.nz/en/maori-housing-te-noho-whare (accessed 23 August 2023).
——, 'Housing and Government', Te Ara – the Encyclopedia of New Zealand, https://teara.govt.nz/en/housing-and-government (accessed 23 August 2023).
——, 'Housing – Interior Planning and Living', Te Ara – the Encyclopedia of New Zealand, https://teara.govt.nz/en/interactive/38650/housing-floor-plans (accessed 8 January 2024).
——, *We Call It Home: A History of State Housing in New Zealand*, Reed Publishing, Auckland, 2005.
Scott, Mary, *Days That Have Been: An Autobiography*, Longman Paul, Auckland, 1966.
——, *Barbara and the New Zealand Back-Blocks*, Thomas Avery & Sons, New Plymouth, 1936.
Scotter, W. H., *Run, Estate and Farm: A History of the Kakanui and Waiareka Valleys, North Otago*, Capper Press, Christchurch, 1978.
Sharp, Andrew (ed.), *Duperrey's Visit to New Zealand in 1824*, Alexander Turnbull Library, Wellington, 1971. ENZB, http://www.enzb.auckland.ac.nz/document/?wid=4889&page=1&action=null
Sharpe, R. D., *Country Occasions*, A. H. & A. W. Reed, Wellington, 1962.
Shaw, Louise and Barbara Brookes, 'Constructing Homes: Gender and Advertising in *Home and Building*, 1936–1970', *NZJH* 33, no. 2, 1999, pp. 200–20.
Shaw, Peter, *New Zealand Architecture: From Polynesian Beginnings to 1990*, Hodder & Stoughton, Auckland, 1991.
Shoebridge, Tim and Gavin McLean, 'Feeding Britain', NZHistory website, https://nzhistory.govt.nz/war/public-service-at-war/feeding-britain (accessed 23 August 2023).
Simmonds, Naomi, 'Mana Wahine: Decolonising Politics' [originally printed *Women's Studies Journal* 25, no. 2, 2011], in Leonie Pihama, Linda Tuhiwai Smith, Naomi Simmonds, Joeliee Seed-Pihama and Kirsten Gabel (eds), *Mana Wahine Reader: A Collection of Writings 1999–2019, Volume 2*, Te Kotahi Research Institute, Hamilton, 2019, pp. 105–22.

Simmons, Alexy, 'Te Wairoa, The Buried Village: A Summary of Recent Research and Excavations', *Australian Journal of Historical Archaeology* 9, 1991, pp. 56–62.

Simpson, Helen, *The Women of New Zealand*, Paul's Book Arcade, Auckland and Hamilton; George Allen and Unwin, London, 1962.

Simpson, Tony, *A Distant Feast: The Origins of New Zealand's Cuisine*, 2nd edn, Godwit, Auckland, 2008.

Sing, Margaret, 'That's How It Was: Rural Women of Tatuanui District 1919–1992', Masters thesis, University of Waikato, 1992.

Smiler, Tom Junior, 'Eldest Son', in Witi Ihimaera (ed.), *Growing Up Māori*, Tandem Press, Auckland, 1998, pp. 64–71. Quoted with permission of Witi Ihimaera.

Smith, Ian, *Pākehā Settlements in a Māori World New Zealand Archaeology, 1769–1860*, Bridget Williams Books, Wellington, 2020.

Smith, Linda Tuhiwai, 'Māori Women: Discourses, Projects and Mana Wahine' [originally printed in *Women and Education in Aotearoa, Volume 2*, 1992], in Leonie Pihama, Linda Tuhiwai Smith, Naomi Simmonds, Joeliee Seed-Pihama and Kirsten Gabel (eds), *Mana Wahine Reader: A Collection of Writings 1987–1998, Volume 1*, Te Kotahi Research Institute, Hamilton, 2019, pp. 39–52.

Smith, Rosemarie, 'Rural Organisations', NZHistory website, https://nzhistory.govt.nz/women-together/theme/rural-women (accessed 23 August 2023).

Society for Promoting Christian Knowledge, *Domestic Scenes in New Zealand*, Committee of General Literature and Education, London 1845.

Solomon, Eleanor Ria, 'Solomon, Hārata Ria Te Uira', *Dictionary of New Zealand Biography*, Te Ara – the Encyclopedia of New Zealand, https://teara.govt.nz/en/biographies/5s33/solomon-harata-ria-te-uira (accessed 23 August 2023).

Somerset, H. C. D., *Littledene*, New Zealand Council for Educational Research, Wellington, 1938.

Soper, Eileen L., *The Otago of Our Mothers*, Whitcombe & Tombs, Dunedin, 1948. Quoted with permission of Gavin Service.

Stack, James West and Eliza Stack, edited by A. H. Reed, *Further Maoriland Adventures of J. W. and E. Stack*, A. H. & A. W. Reed,

Dunedin and Wellington, 1938. ENZB, http://www.enzb.auckland.ac.nz/document/?wid=3792&action=null
——, edited by A. H. Reed, *Early Maoriland Adventures of J. W. Stack*, A. H. & A. W. Reed, Dunedin and Wellington, 1935. ENZB, http://www.enzb.auckland.ac.nz/document/?wid=3832&action=null
Stacpoole, John, *Colonial Architecture in New Zealand*, A. H. and A. W. Reed, Wellington, 1976.
Staples, Irene, *Cooks and Shepherds Come Away*, A. H. & A. W. Reed, Wellington, Auckland and Sydney, 1964.
Star, Paul, *Thomas Potts of Canterbury: Colonist and Conservationist*, Otago University Press, Dunedin, 2020.
——, 'On the Edge of Canterbury Settlement: Thomas Potts up the Rakaia, 1854–58', paper read at Making Rural New Zealand: Environment, Economics and Politics conference, Dunedin, 2018.
Steel, Frances, '"New Zealand *Is* Butterland": Interpreting the Historical Significance of a Daily Spread', *NZJH* 39, no. 2, 2005, pp. 179–94.
Stevens, Michael, 'Muttonbirds and Modernity in Murihiku: Continuity and Change in Kāi Tahu Knowledge', PhD thesis, University of Otago, 2009.
Stewart, Adela B., *My Simple Life in New Zealand*, R. Banks, London, 1908.
Stewart, Di, *The New Zealand Villa: Past and Present*, Viking Pacific, Auckland, 1992.
Stirling, Amiria Manutahi, as told to Anne Salmond, *Amiria: The Life Story of a Maori Woman*, Penguin, Auckland, 2005.
Stone, Grace Aroha and E. R. (Lisa) Langer, 'Te Ahi i te Ao Māori: Māori Use of Fire: Traditional Use of Fire to Inform Current and Future Fire Management in New Zealand', *MAI Journal* 4, no. 1, 2015, pp. 15–28.
Strasser, Susan, *Never Done: A History of American Housework*, Pantheon Books, New York, 1982.
Stringleman, Hugh and Frank Scrimgeour, 'Dairying and Dairy Products', Te Ara – the Encyclopedia of New Zealand, https://teara.govt.nz/en/dairying-and-dairy-products (accessed 23 August 2023).
Stronach, Bruce, *Musterer on Molesworth*, Whitcombe and Tombs, Christchurch, 1953.
Swarbrick, Nancy, *Creature Comforts: New Zealanders and Their Pets: An Illustrated History*, Otago University Press, Dunedin, 2013.

Bibliography

——, 'Rural Services', Te Ara – the Encyclopedia of New Zealand, https://teara.govt.nz/en/rural-services (accessed 23 August 2023).

Symons, Michael, *A History of Cooks and Cooking*, University of Illinois Press, Urbana, IL, 2004.

Szaszy, Mira, 'Maori Women – from Community Hostess to Family Drudge?', *New Zealand Listener*, 15 October 1973, 20–21.

Takiari, Kiritahi (ed.), *Women of the River, Part One*, ICT Whanganui Charitable Trust, Whanganui, 2002.

Taonui, Rāwiri, 'Tribal Organisation', Te Ara – the Encyclopedia of New Zealand, https://teara.govt.nz/en/tribal-organisation (accessed 23 August 2023).

Taylor, Richard, *The Ika a Maui, or, New Zealand and Its Inhabitants*, Wertheim and Mackintosh, London, 1855. ENZB, http://www.enzb.auckland.ac.nz/document/?wid=460&action=null

Te Ara – the Encyclopedia of New Zealand, *Te Taiao: Māori and the Natural World*, David Bateman, Auckland, 2010.

Te Kui, 'The Rhythm of Life', in Witi Ihimaera (ed.), *Growing Up Māori*, Tandem Press, Auckland, 1998, pp. 81–87. Quoted with permission of Margaret Taurere and whānau.

Te Rūnanga o Ngāi Tahu, 'Claim History', The Settlement, https://ngaitahu.iwi.nz/ngai-tahu/the-settlement/claim-history/ (accessed 1 October 2023)

Te Ūaka Lyttelton Museum, 'An Eggscellent Lyttelton Innovation – "Norton's Premier Egg Preservative"', News Article, 2023, https://www.teuaka.org.nz/news/an-eggscellent-lyttelton-innovation-nortons-premier-egg-preservative (accessed 1 October 2023).

Teal, F. Jane, 'Changing Kitchen Technology', in Helen Leach (ed.), *From Kai to Kiwi Kitchen: New Zealand Culinary Traditions and Cookbooks*, Otago University Press, Dunedin, 2010, pp. 71–96.

Thomson, Arthur S., *The Story of New Zealand: Past and Present, Savage and Civilised, Volume I*, John Murray, London, 1859. ENZB, http://www.enzb.auckland.ac.nz/document/?wid=787&action=null

Thomson, John Turnbull, *Rambles with a Philosopher or, Views at the Antipodes*, Mills, Dick & Co., Dunedin, 1867. ENZB, http://www.enzb.auckland.ac.nz/document?wid=1862&p=1

Tolerton, Jane, 'Household services', *Te Ara – the Encyclopedia of New Zealand*, https://teara.govt.nz/en/household-services (accessed 23 August 2023).

Toomath, William, *Built in New Zealand: The Houses We Live In*, Harper Collins, Auckland, 1996.

Toynbee, Claire, *Her Work and His: Family, Kin and Community in New Zealand 1900–1930*, Victoria University Press, Wellington, 1995.

Trapeznik, Alexander, *Dunedin's Warehouse Precinct*, Genre Books Ebook, Dunedin, 2014, http://www.genrebooks.co.nz/ebooks/DunedinsWarehousePrecinct.pdf

Trotter, Margaret, with June Trotter, *Margaret's Story: A Southland Childhood in the 1920s*, Sycamore Print, Invercargill, 2011. Quoted with permission of June Trotter and Ann Irving.

Turbott, H. B., 'Health and Social Welfare', in I. L. G. Sutherland (ed.), *The Maori People Today*, Whitcombe and Tombs, Christchurch, 1940, pp. 229–68.

Veart, David, *First Catch Your Weka: A Story of New Zealand Cooking*, Auckland University Press, Auckland, 2008.

Verdon, Nicola, '"The Modern Countrywoman": Farm Women, Domesticity and Social Change in Interwar Britain', *History Workshop Journal* 70, Autumn 2010, pp. 86–107.

Waitangi Tribunal, Mana Wāhine Kaupapa Inquiry, https://waitangitribunal.govt.nz/inquiries/kaupapa-inquiries/mana-wahine-kaupapa-inquiry/ (accessed 6 January 2024).

Wakefield, Edward Jerningham, *Adventure in New Zealand, From 1839 to 1844; With Some Account of the Beginnings of the British Colonization of the Islands. Volume I*, John Murray, London, 1845. ENZB, http://www.enzb.auckland.ac.nz/document/?wid=553&action=null

Walker, Ranginui, *Ka Whawhai Tonu Matou: Struggle Without End*, Penguin Books, Auckland, 1990.

Wanhalla, Angela, 'Living on the River's Edge at the Taieri Native Reserve', in Zoë Laidlaw and Alan Lester (eds), *Indigenous Communities and Settler Colonialism: Land Holding, Loss and Survival in an Interconnected World*, Palgrave Macmillan, New York, 2015, pp. 138–57.

——, 'Housing Un/healthy Bodies: Native Housing Surveys and Maori Health in New Zealand 1930–45', *Health and History* 8, no. 1, Special Issue: History, Health and Hybridity, 2006, pp. 100–20.

Ward, Peter, *A History of Domestic Space: Privacy and the Canadian Home*, UBC Press, Vancouver and Toronto, 1999.

Waterhouse, Richard, *The Vision Splendid: A Social and Cultural History of Rural Australia*, Curtin University Press, Fremantle, 2005.

Watson, James, 'The Significance of Mr. Richard Buckley's Exploding Trousers: Reflections on an Aspect of Technological Change in New Zealand Dairy Farming between the World Wars', *Agricultural History* 78, no. 3, Summer 2004, pp. 346–60.

Weaver, John C., *The Great Land Rush and the Making of the Modern World 1650–1900*, McGill-Queens University Press, Montreal and Kingston, 2003.

Weaver, John C. and Doug Munro, 'Country Living, Country Dying: Rural Suicides in New Zealand, 1900–1950', *Journal of Social History* 42, no. 4, 2009, pp. 933–61.

West, Jonathan, *The Face of Nature: An Environmental History of the Otago Peninsula*, Otago University Press, Dunedin, 2017.

Wevers, Lydia, *Reading on the Farm: Victorian Fiction and the Colonial World*, Victoria University Press, Wellington, 2010.

Whaanga, Mere, 'Mātaitai: Shellfish Gathering', in Te Ara – the Encyclopedia of New Zealand, *Te Taiao: Māori and the Natural World*, David Bateman, Auckland, 2010, pp. 144–51.

Wharemaru, Heeni and Mary Katharine Duffié, *Through the Eye of the Needle: A Māori Elder Remembers*, Harcourt College Publishers, Fort Worth, Texas, 2001.

Whatmore, S., 'On Doing Rural Research (Or Breaking the Boundaries)', *Environment and Planning A: Economy and Space* 25, no. 2, Feb. 1993, pp. 605–07.

White, Yuilleen, *Springfield in the Foothills*, Yuilleen White, Marlborough, 1996.

Wilkes, Chris and Brennon Wood, 'The Social Relations of Housing in Early New Zealand', in Chris Wilkes and Ian Shirley (eds), *In the Public Interest: Health, Work and Housing in New Zealand*, Benton Ross, Auckland, 1984, pp. 183–212.

Williams, Erin, 'Māori Fire Use and Landscape Changes in Southern New Zealand', *Journal of the Polynesian Society* 118, no. 2, 2009, pp. 175–89.

Williams, Jim, 'Mahika Kai: The Husbanding of Consumables by Māori in Precontact Te Wāipounamu', *Journal of the Polynesian Society* 119, no. 2, June 2010, pp. 149–80.

———, 'E Pākihi Hakinga a Kai: An Examination of Pre-Contact Resource Management Practice in Southern New Zealand', PhD thesis, University of Otago, 2004.

Williams, Melissa Matutina, *Panguru and the City: Kāinga Tahi, Kāinga Rua: An Urban Migration History*, Bridget Williams Books, Wellington, 2015.

Wilmhurst, Janet, 'Human Effects on the Environment', Te Ara – the Encyclopedia of New Zealand, https://teara.govt.nz/en/human-effects-on-the-environment (accessed 23 August 2023).

Wilson, Helen, *My First Eighty Years*, Paul's Book Arcade, Hamilton, 1950.

Women's Division, Federated Farmers of New Zealand, *My Rural Home*, Women's Division, Federated Farmers of New Zealand, Wellington, 1953.

Woods, Michael, *Rural Geography: Processes, Responses and Experiences in Rural Restructuring*, SAGE Publications, London, 2005.

Worsley, Lucy, *If Walls Could Talk: An Intimate History of the Home*, Walker, New York, 2011.

Wynn, Graeme, 'Scoping Yeotopia: Tom Brooking and the Making of Rural New Zealand', *International Review of Environmental History* 6, no. 2, 2020, pp. 5–23.

———, 'Destruction Under the Guise of Improvement? The forest, 1840–1920', in Eric Pawson and Tom Brooking (eds), *Making a New Land: Environmental Histories of New Zealand*, new edn, Otago University Press, Dunedin, 2013, pp. 122–38.

Yorke, Amy Tremenheere, *The Animals Came First: Farming in New Zealand during the Depression of the Thirties*, Heinemann, Auckland, Melbourne, London, 1980.

Glossary of Māori words

Some of the words listed have multiple meanings. The definitions given relate to this book.

aho fishing line
ao world
ao Māori Māori world
ao mārama Earth, physical world
ariki paramount chief, first-born in a high-ranking family
aroha affection, sympathy, love
aruhe fern root
aute paper mulberry, *Broussonetia papyrifera*
hahunga ceremony for uplifting bones
hākari feast, banquet, celebration
hāngī earth oven
hapū subtribe
harakeke New Zealand flax, *Phormium tenax*
hereumu cooking shed, kitchen
hīnaki eel trap
hīnau a tall forest tree with edible berries, *Elaeocarpus dentatus*
hinu fat, grease
hue calabash, gourd, *Lagenaria siceraria*
hui gathering, meeting
hunga slave
īnanga whitebait, *Galaxias maculatus*
iwi tribe

kai food
kaihaukai present of food, feast
kaimoana seafood, shellfish
kāinga home, village, settlement
kaitiaki trustee, custodian, guardian
kākā forest parrot, *Nestor meridionalis*
kākaho toetoe stem
kamokamo squash, marrow, *Cucurbita* spp
kāmuri cooking shed
kānga corn, maize
kaponga ponga, silver treefern, *Cyathea dealbata*
karaka fruit of the *Corynocarpus laevigatus*
karanga ceremonial call, call of welcome
kareao supplejack, *Ripogonum scandens*
karengo edible seaweed, *Porphyra columbina*
kaumātua adult, elder
kaupapa topic for discussion, subject, issue
kāuta cooking shed, cookhouse, kitchen
kawenga load, pack
kererū New Zealand pigeon, *Hemiphaga novaeseelandiae*
kete basket, kit
kiekie thick native vine, *Freycinetia banksia*

Glossary of Māori words

kina sea urchin, *Evechinus chloroticus*
kō digging stick
kōaro whitebait, *Galaxias brevipinnis*
kōhua pot for boiling food
kōkopu whitebait, *Galaxias fasciatus*
kōrero speech, narrative, discussion
kōura various species of crayfish and lobster
kui/kuia elderly woman, grandmother, female elder
kuki cook, chef
kuku green-lipped mussel, *Perna canaliculus*
kūmara sweet potato, *Ipomoea batatas*
kupenga fishing net
mahi apū communal work
mahinga kai food and resource gathering place, food source
mana prestige, authority, power, status
manaaki to support, take care of
manaakitanga hospitality
manuhiri visitor, guest
Māori indigenous New Zealanders
Māoritanga Māori culture, way of life
marae ceremonial courtyard in front of the wharenui, complex of buildings around marae
marae ātea courtyard, open area in front of meeting house
marahea commoner
maramataka Māori lunar calendar
matau fish hook
mātauranga Māori Māori knowledge
mate death, misfortune
mīti meat
mōkai servant, slave
motu island, country
ngāwhā boiling spring, boiling mudpool

nīkau native palm, *Rhopalostylis sapida*
noa ordinary, unrestricted
pā fortified village
pā tuna eel weir
Pākehā New Zealander of European descent
papakāinga home base, village
Papatūānuku Earth mother
parakaraka a potato cultivar
pātaka raised storehouse, pantry, larder
pātia spear for fishing
pāua abalone, *Haliotis* spp.
paukena, poukena pumpkin
pāwhara dried fish
pikopiko young fern roots
pipi edible bivalve, *Paphies australis*
pōhā kelp bag
ponga treefern, *Cyathea dealbata*
pononga servant, slave
pōwhiri rituals of encounter, welcome ceremony
pūhā sow thistle (various species)
pūkeko swamp hen, *Porphyrio porphyrio*
rangatira chief
rangatiratanga chiefly authority, right to exercise authority
raupatu confiscation of land
raupō bulrush, *Typha orientalis*
rēwena bread made with potato yeast
rīwai potato
rohe district, region
rongoā remedy, medicine
rua storage pit
taha Māori Māori identity
tahu to cook
taikōwhatu hāngī stones
tāne husband, male

Glossary of Māori words

tangata whenua local people, hosts, indigenous people
tangihanga funeral
taonga possession; treasure
tapu sacred, restricted, prohibited
taro vegetable, *Colocasia esculenta*
taurekareka captive taken in war, slave
tawa tree, *Beilschmiedia tawa*
tāwhara edible bracts of the kiekie, *Freycinetia banksii*
tī cabbage tree (various species)
tī pore Pacific Island cabbage tree, *Cordyline fruticosa*
tikanga correct procedure, custom
tio rock oyster, *Saccostrea cucullata*
tītī muttonbird, sooty shearwater, *Puffinus griseus*
toetoe native grass, *Cortaderia* spp
toheroa bivalve mollusc, *Paphies ventricosa*
tohunga/tohuka skilled person, expert
tuangi New Zealand cockle, *Austrovenus stutchburyi*
tuatua bivalve mollusc, *Paphies subtriangulata*
tūī parson bird, *Prosthemadera novaeseelandiae*
tuna eel (various species)
tupuna, tipuna ancestor, grandparent
tūrangawaewae place to stand, place where one has rights of residence
tūtūā person of low birth, commoner, ordinary person
umu earth oven
uwhi yam, *Dioscorea alata*
wāhi tapu sacred place
wāhine women, females
waiata song
waikaka mudfish, *Neochanna apoda*
waka canoe
ware commoner
waruwaru scrape
weka woodhen, *Gallirallus australis*
whakanoa to remove tapu
whakapapa genealogy
whānau extended family
whanaungatanga relationship, kinship
wharau temporary shelter, shed
whare house, building, residence, dwelling
whare tapere house of entertainment, theatre
whare whakairo carved house, meeting house
wharekai dining hall
wharenui meeting house, large house
wharepuni main house of village, guest house, sleeping house
whareumu cooking shed
whata elevated platform, storage place
whekī rough treefern, *Dicksonia squarrosa*
whenua land
whio blue duck, *Hymenolaimus malacorhynchos*
wīwī rushes (various species)

Drawn from Anderson, Binney and Harris *Tangata Whenua: An Illustrated History*; Moorfield, *Te Aka: Māori–English, English–Māori Dictionary*, 3rd edn; Te Ara – the Encyclopedia of New Zealand, *Te Taiao: Māori and the Natural World*; Manaaki Whenua Landcare Research, 'Ngā Raupori Whakaoranga'.

Imperial to metric conversion

1 pound (lb)   454 grams
10 pounds   4.54 kilograms

1 inch   2.54 centimetres
1 foot   30.48 centimetres
1 mile   1.61 kilometres

Acknowledgements

This book is based on my PhD, completed at the University of Otago in 2016. My first note of thanks must go to my supervisors Angela Wanhalla and Mark Seymour, who guided me through my PhD with generosity and dedication – I could not have asked for better mentors. I am very grateful for the guidance I received from other members of the Department of History and Art History, and in particular I would like to thank Tom Brooking, Tony Ballantyne, Barbara Brookes and Jane McCabe for their encouragement and advice.

I completed this manuscript while in the role of Curator New Zealand Histories and Cultures at Te Papa. It would not have been possible without the support of my colleagues in the New Zealand Histories and Cultures team and my managers Bronwyn Labrum and Safua Akeli Amaama. I would also like to thank the Knowledge and Information team, especially Mary Smart, Nicola Caldwell and Martin Lewis for sourcing books and journal articles on my behalf and alerting me to interesting research. Thank you also to Dougal Austin, Josefine Ørsted Christensen, Chrissie Locke and Isaac Te Awa for their advice.

About halfway through this project I found myself losing steam and direction, and were it not for my wonderful writing group – Angela Wanhalla, Lachy Paterson, Kate Stevens, Violeta Gilabert and Sarah Christie – I might still be in the doldrums. They provided critical feedback which made this a far better book (although of course any errors are my own).

I have been lucky enough to meet many scholars whose work I admire, and without exception I have found them to be helpful and

Acknowledgements

encouraging. Thank you to James Beattie, David Hall, Kate Hunter, Amanda Mulligan, Anna Petersen, Jonathan West and Rose Young for taking time to discuss the project with me at various stages, and to Alison Clarke, Brian Easton, Helen Leach, Robert Peden, Ann Pomeroy, Rosemary Smith and Paul Star for answering questions and sharing some of their research with me.

I would like to thank the reviewers for their encouraging and useful comments on the manuscript. Deidre Brown, Aroha Harris and Jane Teal also provided extremely valuable feedback on sections of the book, for which I am very grateful.

It has been my great joy and privilege to visit libraries, museums and archives around the country over the course of this research and I would like to sincerely thank the staff of the Alexander Turnbull Library, Archives New Zealand, Central Stories Museum and Art Gallery, Cromwell Museum, Hocken Library, Invercargill City Library and Archives, the Lakes District Museum Archives, Owaka Museum, Puke Ariki, Rural Women New Zealand and Toitū Otago Settlers Museum. I would also like to thank the staff at Mangawhai Museum, Raglan Museum and Tairāwhiti Museum for pointing me to interesting objects and archives.

I am very grateful to the publishers and copyright holders of material I have quoted in this book for their permission to reproduce it here. Thank you to: June Allen, Bridget Williams Books, Chappell Printing, Valerie Cowan, Huia Publishers, Maraea Hunia, David Ling, Penguin Random House New Zealand, Anne Salmond and Sycamore Print. For permission to reproduce images and other archival material, thank you to: Albertland Heritage Museum; Alberton; Alexander Turnbull Library; Aotea Utanganui Museum of South Taranaki; Ashburton Museum & Historical Society Collection; Auckland Libraries – Ngā Whare Mātauranga o Tāmaki Makaurau; Auckland War Memorial Museum Tāmaki Paenga Hira; Bluff Maritime Museum; Canterbury Museum; Central Stories Museum and Art Gallery; Christchurch City Libraries Ngā Kete Wānanga o Ōtautahi; Waitangi Clarke, Pou Ahurea of Ngāti Rangitihi; Cromwell Museum; Harata Gibson, chairperson of Te Poho o Rawiri marae; Helensville and District Historical Society; Hocken Collections Uare Taoka o Hākena University of Otago; Invercargill City Libraries and Archives; Kāpiti Coast District Council; Rick Kingi, Pipiriki;

Acknowledgements

Rosie Little; Mangawhai Museum; Mataura Historical Society; MTG Hawke's Bay Tai Ahuriri; Museum of New Zealand Te Papa Tongarewa; Nelson Provincial Museum Pupuri Taonga o Te Tai Ao; New Zealand Media and Entertainment; Owaka Museum; Palmerston North City Library; Tā Selwyn Parata KNZM; Puke Ariki; Radio New Zealand; South Canterbury Museum; Tairāwhiti Museum; Te Pūranga Kōrero o Wairarapa/Wairarapa Archive; Te Ūaka The Lyttelton Museum; Rewi Tolich, chairperson of Tauteihiihi marae; Richard Woodman, chairperson of Ngāwhā marae; and Wyndham and Districts Museum.

My sincere and humble thanks to the individuals or descendants of individuals mentioned in this book who have given their blessing for me to include their stories. Thank you to: Tom Carson, Helene Connor, June Grant, Joy Hippolite, Witi Ihimaera, Ann Irving, the Love whānau, Kerry and Margaret Ludbrook, the whānau of Gwen Wingate Mackenzie, Alister Matheson, Rodger Millar, Sara Newman, Katrina Te Hana Phillis and Teri Phillis, David Richards, Gavin Service, Georgina Scouller and whānau, Rosemary Smyth, Margaret Taurere and the Penfold whānau, the whānau of Irāia Te Whāiti and June Trotter.

To my mum Nicki, my brothers Mike and Tom, and my wonderful family, thank you for the pride and confidence you've always shown in me. And to Tim, thank you for your endless encouragement and support. This would not have been possible without you.

Finally, a very big thank you to the team at Auckland University Press: director Sam Elworthy, production manager Katharina Bauer, editor Gillian Tewsley, graphic designer Kalee Jackson, proofreader Kate Stone and indexer Daphne Lawless. They have been wonderful to work with and have made this a far better book.

Index

Entries in *italics* refer to picture captions. An endnote is indicated by a page number followed by 'n' and then the note number.

Abbot, Edward 81
adaptive acculturation 55
Adkin, Maud *11*
Ahuwhenua Trophy 199
Alexander, Charles and Johanne 71
Anderson, Mona 171
Angus, John 92, 96
animals, in the kitchen 35–36
Apatū, Mare Nepe 205
apples 154, 158
Arahanga, Ruku 135
Arama Karaka Pī 252
Ariki Algie, Hei 113, 198, 256
Arnold, Rollo 228
Arthur, John 185
aruhe 79, 128, 151, 249
Associated Country Women of the World 74
Association for Country Education 218
aute 148

Bailey, Ray 145
Ballantyne, Tony 232
Barker, Mary Anne 44, 159–60, 192
Barningham & Co 92
basket concert 290n129
baths, tin *17*, 40
Baucke, William 182
Bay of Islands, Māori housing in 28–32, 34
Beaglehole, Ernest and Pearl 67

Beaton, Sophia 79
Beattie, Herries 229
Beck, Florence 245
beef 46, 130, 159, 161, *163*, 165
Begg, Elvira 262
Belich, James 131
Bell, Claudia 267
Belshaw, Horace 236
berries 125, 139, 154, 249
Best, Elsdon 32, 50, 181, 248–49
Bettany, Muriel *224*
'big houses' 44–46, 236–38
billies *32*, *36*, 81–83, *113*
Birch, Edward 132
birds: Māori use of 79, 128, 131, 136, 139; settler use of 143; vulnerability of populations 140–41
blacklead brush 96–97, *96*
Blank, Arapera 186
Blunt, Alison 18
boiling 80
boil-ups 161, 186
Boswell, Jean 116, 227
Boswell, Jim 242
bread 111, 152; baking 46, 85, 165; buying 170–72
Brewis, Jill 160, 163
Brinsley & Co 92, *94*
Brookes, Barbara 246
Brooking, Tom 22, 114–15, 129, 238, 243
Broomielaw 44, 159
Brown, Heni 130, 206
Bryant, Agnes 88
Buchanan, Rachel 278n4

Buck, Peter *see* Te Rangi Hīroa
Buckland, Kate 283n158
Bull, Ron 176
bungalows 17, 27, 56–59, *61*; floor plan of 59
Burton, David 139
bush camps *191*
butchers 45–46, 163, 171, *174*, 235, 271
Butler, Samuel 188
butter 104, 115, 126–27, 129, 160, 165; churning 119, 167–68, *168*, 197

cabbages 151, 154, 165
Cameron, Stan and Mabel 194
camp ovens *32*, 81–82, *82*, 85–86, *113*; bread in 152; for labourers 111; preserving meat using 139; storage of 40
Campbell, Hugh 12, 16, 127, 131
Campbell, Judith 68
Canterbury, rural 22, 235, 238
carrots 151, 154
Carruthers, Alice 45–46
Carson, Winifred 36, 85, 92, 163–64, 262
Champion ranges *94*, 97, *99*
chapatis 165
cheerfulness 210–12
cheese hoop *168*
chimneys 39–42; in Māori housing 47, 85
Chinese goldminers 155, *156*
Chitty, Alicia 92, 245
Christianity 185; and family life 65–66; and gender 179; influence on housing 33, 47; and land use 129; and privacy 70
Christmas parties 265

337

Index

CMS (Church Missionary Society) 66, 70
coal 90–91
coal range 88–97, *90*, 118, *120*, 186; cleaning 95–96; heating water 119
colonial ovens *8*, 86, 88–89, *89*, 109, 111
colonisation 13; and conceptions of home 64, 66; and housing 25, 27, 73–74; and Māori writing 205; and wāhine Māori 184; Wakefield on 34; *see also* settlers
commoners, in te ao Māori 180
community picnics 261
community spirit 228, 232, 262
Connor, Helene 125, 205, 220–21
Cook, James 28, 132
cookhouses 30, 36, 39, 45–46, *46*, *241*; culture of 240–41; eating in 236–38; *see also* kāuta
cooking 19, 22; in te ao Māori 79–81, 180–87; for early settlers 81–83, 188–89; in rural Pākehā life 59, 72, 191–93, 195, 197; women's role in 274
cooking areas 11, 17, 51, 73–74, 273; in te ao Māori 26, 29–32, 47, 65
cooking fire 15, 39–40, 42, 182
cooking techniques 77; traditional Māori 117; variations in 109–22
cooking technologies 13, 18, 77–78; variations in 109–22
cooks, male 188–89
Cooper, Whina 199
copper 102, 119–20, *120*
corn 130, 148, 151, 207
cottages 26, 38–41, *38*, *41*, 43; box cottages 27, 43–44; plans for *39*
Counihan, Carole 11
Courage, Sarah 30, 69, 191–92, 237–38, 262, 289n46
Cowan, Ruth Schwartz 108
Cracroft Wilson, John 165
Cranstoun, Mary 245
Cromley, Elizabeth 278n9
cucumbers 151, 154
culinary diplomacy 228–29, 233, 268
cultural misunderstanding 246
curry 165, *167*
Curtis family 35

Dacker, Bill 142
dairy (room) 44–45
Dairy Exporter magazine 97, 164, 204, 210–11, 217, 235, 242

dairy farms 167; and electricity 101; Māori 114; refrigerators on 104; and women 213
dairy industry 130, 167
dairy products 129, 167–68
Dalbeth, Maisie 107
Daley, Caroline 228
dances 235, 259, 274
Darwin, Charles 155
Davidson, Dorothy 107
Davis, Dot 136
Davis, Richard 70, 155
Dawes, Charles Peet *154*, *255*, *259*, *263*
Dawes, Jessie *255*
de Surville, Jean-François 151
debt 62, 172, 175
Department of Maori Affairs 54, 60, 114
Dick, Eliza 200, 203
Dieffenbach, Ernst 30
dining rooms 40, 44–46, 59, 63; on marae 63, 208, 231, 259; outdoor 111; social hierarchy in 238, 242; *see also* wharekai
dining tables 219, 221, 242
Doig, W. T. 104
domestic labour 59, 116–18; children and 195–96, 245, 290n71; and coal ranges 92; efficiency in 218–19; and kitchen appliances 108–9; men and 197; women and 20, 179, 187, 193; women's writing on 204–18
domestic servants 44, 188–89, 191–95, 224, 237
domestic spaces 18; in te ao Māori 29; underlying understandings of 25–26
domestic standards 66, 187
domestic violence 69
domesticated foods 131, 148
Dowling, Robyn 18
Duff, Albert Gordon 148
Duff, Geoffrey 171
Duncan, Anne 118
Duncan, Suzanne 230
Durie, E. T. 128
Durie, John Mason 284n26
d'Urville, Jules Dumont 29

Earle, Mary 145
Earnscleugh Station 145
earth ovens 30, 77–86, 109, 182; *see also* hāngī; umu
Easy, Ann M. 119, 161, 171, 203
eating arrangements, and class 22

Edwards, Mihipeka 135, 209
egalitarianism 238, 261, 271
eggs 125–26, 160, 163–64, *164*, 242
Eldred-Grigg, Stevan 237
electric stoves 77, 99–102, 108–9, 118, 217
electricity 13, 101–2, 195, 273
Elkington, Alfred 141
Elkington, Wetekia Ruruku 185
embers 79, 85, 88, 182
emotional norms 179, 224
Esterik, Penny Van 11
European settlement *see* colonisation; settlers
export economy 19, 128–30

Fairburn, Miles 20, 62, 228
family: nuclear ideal of 18, 65; settler notions of 65–66; *see also* whānau
family farms 16, 56; idealisation of 62; and land use 128; and mobility 110–11
family rituals 274
Farmers' Union 199
farming: commercial 56, 110–11, 151, 153; economic alternatives to 176; golden age of 16; intensive 110–11, 114, 129, 155; *see also* family farms; Māori farming; small farming
fire risk 41–42, 73
Firth, Raymond 248
fish *148*; Māori use of 79, 113, 131–36, *134*; settler use of 143–45, *144*; *see also* kaimoana
fishhooks *132*
Fitness, Alice 246
Fitz-William, Elsie 196
Flanders, Judith 70, 72
flour 125; bulk storage of 60; buying 170–71; rations of 160; trading 127
flue brush 96, *97*
food axis 278n9
food cultures 148, 158, 165
food paths 126–27, 131
food purchases 131, 170–71
food rituals 13, 228, 236, 274–75
food safe 104, *106–7*
foodways 16
forests 15; food from 125–26, 139–40
Fraser, Peter 102
front rooms 57
fundraising 265, 290n129
Fyfe, Judith 119

Index

Gardner, W. J. 129
Gee, Maurice 220-21
gender 19; colonial ideas about 185-86; in traditional Māori society 180-85; *see also* women
German migrants 165
gift exchange 145
Gilabert, Violeta 65
Gilbert, Te Maata 153
Gillies, Raukura Erana 229-30
go-ashore pots 81, *81*
Godsiff, Hannah 152
Gold, Charles Emilius *148*
Grace, Patricia 258
Great Depression 194
Grey, Alan 153
Grey, George 151
grocers 172-75, *173*, 235, 271
gumdigging 113-14, 175, 227

Hadfield, Octavius 33
hākari 20, 248-58; preparations for *255*
hākari stages 249-52, *252*
Hakiwai, Reremoana 205
Halfyard, Bob 242-43
Hall, Agnes 192-93
Hall, Tetai 199
hāngī 30, 79, *182*; for hui 259; techniques of 117; women's role in 182-83, 203, 205
hāngī stones *see* taikōwhatu
Harrington, Pamela 232
Harris, Aroha 131
Harris, Witarina 208
harvest camps 111
harvesters 111, 243, 245
Hatch, Elvin 22, 235, 242
Health Act 1920 51
hearths *8*, *38*, 40, 43; large alcove for 81-83
Herda, Phyllis 289n10
hereumu 29
Herman, Bernard 25
hīnaki 136
hīnau meal 80
Hoani, Rupini 266
Hoet, Grace 199
Hollard, Elizabeth 118
Holt, Marilyn Irvin 216
home: Christian ideas of 68; and houses 25; Māori and Western perceptions of 63-64, 273

home ownership, individual 16, 49, 55
home science 59, 187, 219
homesteads 44-46; *see also* 'big houses'
horticulture 13, 150
Hosken, Evelyn 170
hospitality 20, 229-35; rural 229-30, 235; *see also* manaakitanga
hot water 102, 119-20
housing 16-17; Māori and Pākehā constructions of 25-26; *see also* Māori housing; rural Pākehā housing
housewives 108, 160, 188, 213, 219
hue 148, 249
hui: manaakitanga at 229-30, 234; meals at 30, 207-8, 249, 253, 256, *257*
Hunter, Kathryn (Kate) 143, 203-4, 209
Huria, John 30
Hursthouse, Charles 139
Hutchinson, Mere 284n68

individualism 70-71
industrialisation 108
influenza epidemic of 1918-19 50, 113
intimacy 22, 71, 271, 274
Irish stew 165
iron pots *see* metal pots
isolation, social 20, 228, 233

Jackson, Moana 25, 27, 63, 73
jams 158, 193, 207, 262
jellies 107, 158
Jenkins, Kuni 184
Johnson, Nellie 290n129
Johnstone, Lindsay and Bernice 71-72
Johnstone-Smith, Sophie May 95, 161, 168
Jones, Maaka 253
Jones, Verna 167

Kaa, Sophie 119
Kaan, Simon 176
kaimoana 125, 128, 132-35
kāinga 28-30, 141, 184, 220; internal order of 64-65
kākā 139
kākaho 37
Kameta, Te Toiroa Charles 118
Kameta, Te Uruhina 118
kamokamo 205, 208
kāmuri 29
karaka berries 125, 153

karanga 230
kāuta *14*, 27-30, *32*, 206, 268, 273; in kāinga 65; large 249, 256-59; Māui Pōmare on 49-50; set-up of 83-85; shape of 32
Keane, Basil 128
Keesing, Felix 246
Kelly, Gwen *224*
Kendall, Florence 197
Kereopa, Hohepa 230
kererū 139-41
Kerikeri 154-55
kerosene 102
kerosene tins 77, 119, 137, 139, 164, 258, 284n68
Kerr Taylor, Alan *167*
kettles *32*, 34-35, *35*, 40, *81*, 83, *85*-87
kitchen appliances 18-19, 117-18; electric 99-109, 121, 217
kitchenettes 59-60
kitchens: as conservative spaces 121; in cottages 39-40, 43; efficient design of 218, *219*; in the eighteenth and nineteenth centuries 28-34; historical sources on 15-16; in homesteads 44; labourers eating in 237-38; in Māori housing 49-50, 53-54, 259; in rural Pākehā housing 59-61, *61*, 68-69, 72-73; as sites of adjustment 272-73; social practices of 11-12, 219-24, 271, 273-75; use of term 15, 27; in villas 56-57; as women's sphere 19-20, 66, 179, 188
kō 151
Kōhere, Rēweti Tūhorouta 55, 67, 70
kōhua 80
Koopu, Reremoana Reweti 85, 130, 205
kōrero 26, 206, 274
Kōtukutuku, Mihi 256
Krippner, Nessie 119
kūmara 79, 130, 148-50; for hākari 249-53, *255*; storage 32; wāhine Māori and 205, 207
kupenga 132, *134*

labour: casual 131, 170; and one-table households 22; in rural economy 110-13, 117; *see also* domestic labour; Māori labour; rural workforce
labour-saving innovations 59, 92, 108-9, 117, 213
land ownership 19; collective 63
land use 12, 19, 126-31
Lange, Raeburn 50, 283n26
Leach, Helen 17-18, 100, 285n147

339

Index

Lepper, Anne 196
Lesson, René Primavère 28
Long Depression 116
Longbeach Station *45–46*
Longlands Station 239, 241
Love, Avarua *53*
Love, Chris 130

Macdonald, Charlotte 188, 204
Macdonald, Luckie 130
Mackay, J. S. 239, 241
Mackenzie, Alice 41, 85
Mackenzie, Gwen Wingate 118, 172, 245
McWhannell, Rhoda 72, 172
mahinga kai 128, 136, 141–43, 153, 183–84
maize *see* corn
mana: and feasts 228, 248, 252; and manaakitanga 51, 208
mana wāhine 181, 184–85, 199
manaakitanga 20, 117, 228–34, 273; and hosting guests 51, 53, 125; and wāhine Māori 205–8
Mangapouri 29
Maning, Maria Amina 252
Mantell, Walter *81*
Manuka Point Station *245*
Māori: building settler houses 37; dispossession of 19; extended family structures of 51–53; socialising with Pākehā 238, 246, 266–67; urbanisation of 15
Māori communities: and culinary diplomacy 268; cycle of poverty in 19; domesticated food sources in 148–51, 153; electrification of 102; feasts in *see* hākari; food production 130, 176; land use by 127–28; maintenance of culture in 117; Pākehā views of 121; structure of 272; traditional food sources 131–43, 208; urbanisation of 15
Māori councils, local 49–51, 121
Māori farming 12, 114, 131, 284n26; wāhine as farmers 199–200
Māori food paths 126
Māori housing 26–27; cooking technologies in 92, 273; European-style 33, 66–67; and home 64; impact of settlement on 47; nineteenth-century *85*; pre-colonial 28–33; privacy in 71; state involvement in 49–56, *56*, 60–62; water in 119; *see also* whare Māori
Māori identity 63, 71, 121
Māori labour 47, 113, 172–75, 180

Māori land: alienation of 129–30, 198; development 53, 130–31; and poverty 175–76
Māori Land Boards 130
Māori women *see* wāhine Māori
Māori Women's Welfare League 121, 206, 246
Māori world *see* te ao Māori
Māori-driven design 68
marae 26, 51, 63, 65, 68, 208, 248, 274
market gardening 155
marrows 151
Marsden, Māori 29
Marsh, Grace *195*
Martin, David Robert 47
Martin, John 113, 236
Martin, Mary Ann 161
Marumaru, Hoeroa 284n26
Massey, Doreen 15
Matatā *30*
mātauranga Māori 176; and gardening knowledge 153
mateship 240–41
Matthews, Leigh 210
Maudlin, Daniel 25
Maxwell, David 85
Maybury, Jan 214
Mead, Hirini Moko 230
Meah, Angela 221
meat: consumption of 158–64; preservation of 139; sharing and trading 168
meat safes 107
melons 154, 252
Merrett, Joseph 30
metal pots 34, 40, 79–81, *87*, 258
Metge, Joan 246–47
Metson, Norma 44
middle classes 65–66, 70, 179, 189, 224
Mieville, Frederick 233–34
Mikaere, Annie 184–85
milking 95, 118, 167; by women 200, 203
milking shed 45
Millar, Joan 96, 193, 214, 267
Millar, Maree 187
Milliken, Robert 165
Mills, George 245
Mills, William 189
Mintz, Sidney W. 274
missionaries 26, 252; concept of family 66; and domestic space 33; food production by 151, 154–55

Mitchell, Hilary and John 152
Mitchell, Lydia and family 40, 60, 161, 189
moa 78, 131
mobile cookshop *4*, 111
modernity: and tradition 143, 273; trappings of 19, 117, 121, 214
Moffat stoves 99–100, *100*, *102*, 118
Mokikiwa, Mereana 67
Moon, Paul 230
Morgan, Paul 153
Morgan, Vera 206–7, 253–56
Mrs Beeton's Book of Household Management 197, 288n86
Munro, Doug 113
Murphy, Mary 233
musterers 111, 113, 241
mutton 158–60, 165; keeping fresh 164; Māori use of 130, 136, 139; settler use of 145
muttonbirds 128, 139, 141–43
mutuality 229, 271
Myers, Frederick 189

Native Housing Act 1935 53–54, 92
Native Land Court 130, 185, 198
native schools 185, 284n28
The Neck, Rakiura Stewart Island *49*
NEECO (National Electric and Engineering Co. Ltd.) 99
'new woman' 214
New Zealand Farm and Home 121
New Zealand Farmer 73, 86

New Zealand Wars 129, 153, 185
Newman, Mary 47
Newman, Sara 265
Ngāi Tahu, food sources of 126, 136, 139, 142–43
Ngata, Apirana 53–55, 130, 259
Ngāti Porou 114
ngāwhā 208
nīkau 37
noa 29, 180–81; *see also* tapu; whakanoa
nostalgia 121

oatmeal 165, 170–71
Ōhinemutu 54, 208
one-table households 22, 236, 238–42
onions 151, 154–55, 165, 189, 207
open-fire cooking 27, *32*, 77–86, 109; in te ao Māori 30, 51, *85*; for labourers 110–11

Index

optimism 170, 210
Orbell family 43
orchards 46, 158, 176, 229
Orion ranges 90–92, *90*, *92*, 94–95, *94*
Ormondville 119, 171
Orongorongo Station 44
Osterud, Nancy Grey 158, 209
Otago, early settlers in 81
Ovaline 163, *164*; see also eggs
overcrowding 49, 53

pā 28
pā tuna 136, *139*
packmen 110, *113*
Pākehā communities: cohesion in 20; gender and cooking in 187–94; rural see rural Pākehā; see also settlers
Pākehā men, community and culture of 240–41
Pākehā women 187–88, 224; autobiographical writings of 204, 209–14; and food preparation 274; relationships with Māori 246; working the land 200–203
Panguru 102, 199, 277n6
papakāinga 63, 199
Papakura, Mākereti 32, 64, 71, 79, 180, 249
Papatūānuku 63, 153
parakaraka 153
Paratene, Keita Kaikiri 67
Parihaka *14*, 278n4
pastoralism 128–29, 153, 188, 238
pātaka 32
Paterson, Lachy 55
pāua 79, 132, 208
Paul, Priscilla 284n77
pears 154, 158
peas 151, 154
Penfold, Merimeri 186–87
Pennell, Sarah 188
Pere, Rangimarie Rose 181, 220, 228
Perry, Pauline 72–73, 197, 245
Petrie, Hazel 150, 228
Phillipps, W. J. 30
Phillis, Te Onehou 186, 207, 231
picnics 234–35, 261–67, *263–64*
pigeons 140, 227
pioneering 43, 77, 210, 212, 240, 272
pipi 132, 208
Pleugh, Ernie 72, 172
plough camps 110–11, 282n107
plums 158, 262

Poff, Basil 242
Pōmare, Māui 49, 54
ponga logs 30–32
pork 46, 145, 161, *163*; Māori use of 130, 139, 208–9; wild 143
Porter, Frances 204
Porter family *245*
potatoes *11*, *14*, 130, 150–51, 153–55; baskets for 65; for hākari 252; in migrant food cultures 165; and mutton 160; wāhine Māori and 205, 207–8
poultry 125, 130, 141
poverty, cycle of 19
pōwhiri 248
pragmatism 19, 122
prayers 70
prefabricated houses 37
preserving jars *159*
Preston, Joseph 239
Prickett, Nigel 30
primary sector, workforce in 62
privacy 26, 70–73
provisioning 60, 126–27; Māori systems of 128, 131–32
public and private spaces 57, 70, 72–73
public health 47–50, 187
pūhā 207
pūkeko 136, 148
pumpkins 151, 154, 207–8, 252
Punaomaru pā *81*
Punjabi migrants 165

rabbits 139, 145, *148*
Radiation NZ Ltd 97
radishes 151, 154
Rangataua Women's Institute *247*
rangatira 33, 150–51, 180, 183–84, 253
rangatiratanga 176
Ranginui, Rita 158, 230
Rangitūkehu, Maata Te Taiawatea 198
raupō *37*; see also whare raupō
reception rooms 44
refrigerated shipping 129, 238
refrigerators 15, 77, *104*, 107, 217
Rei, Matiu 176
relief work 170
Rene, Ariana 113
Rennie, Anne 212–13
rēwena 118, 152, 207, 209
Reweti-Logan, Maudie Ruaka 51

Rewi, Poia 230
Reynolds, H. C. 102
rice 151, 167, 171, 252
Richards, Myrtle 60, 203
Rikihana, Rawinia *53*
Riney-Kehrberg, Pamela 203–4
Ringatū faith 253
Rolshoven, Johanna 18
rongoa 142
Ross, Emily 245
rural, use of term 13
Rural Electrical Reticulation Council 102
rural history, and Māori 12, 16
Rural Housing Act 1939 60–62
rural life: and cooking technologies 109; diversity of 16; hospitality in see hospitality, rural; images of 12; and the kitchen 22, 275; mythology of 128–29, 267, 271–72; women's commitment to 213–14
rural Pākehā 12–13, 16; and coal ranges 92; as community 227–28; farming 114–16; hospitality of see hospitality, rural; Māori neighbours of 246–47; social status among 235–42; values of 267–68
rural Pākehā housing 16–17, 26, 56–60, 68–69, 273; see also 'big houses', bungalows; cottages; villas
rural women 167; and community events 265–66; culture of emotions 212; domestic work by 107–9, 115–17, 204; engagement with feminist movement 211; farm work by 200–203, 274; feeding workers 243–45; and hospitality 232–33, 235; institutions for 68, 187; and kitchens 20, 221, *224*; and modernisation 214–18; oral histories of 209–10; partnership with husbands 212–13
rural workforce, eating arrangements 158, 236–45

salesmen *90*
Salmond, Anne 183
Salmond, Jeremy 40
sanitary regulations 49–50
Savage, Dorothy 231, 256
Savage, John 30
Savage, Michael Joseph 54
Schepens, Daisy 265
School of Maori Arts and Crafts 259
Scott, John Halliday *85*

Index

Scott, Mary 170, 193, 216
Scott Bros 92, 99
Scottish migrants 233, 241
sealers 33-34
seasonal employment 111, 237
Second World War 13
self-sufficiency 127, 128, 204, 233
settler housing 37-39; state intervention in 56
settlers: attitudes to land 128-29; domesticated food 151-52, 154-58; gender imbalance among 188; hunting and fishing by 143-48; meat consumption 158-64; and traditional food sources 141-42
Shacklock, Henry 90-91
sharing meals 20, 22, 236, 267
Sharpe, R. D. 163, 265
shearers 111, *200*; feeding 239-40, 243-45; Māori 113, 172
shearers' huts *241*
sheep runs 114, 237
shellfish 30, 79-80, 132-35; *see also* kaimoana
shepherds 113, 160, 188, 191, 238
Simpson, Helen 234
Simpson, Tony 126, 144, 158
Sing, Margaret 213
sitting room 61, 72-73
Skelton, Lulu and Leslie 125-26
slaves, in te ao Māori 28-29, 116, 180-81
small farming 19, 176; and economic instability 117, 127; idealisation of 129; number of 62; state support for 56, 129
Smiler, Tom Jr. 51, 150
Smith, Linda Tuhiwai 181
smoko 243-45
Smyth, Rosemary 218
social connection 22, 261
social distance 22, 236, 238-39
social equality, relative 20, 238, 243, 272
social interactions 15, 22, 204, 229, 246, 266, 274-75
social organisation 20, 184, 247
Society for Promoting Christian Knowledge 232
soldiers, discharged 111
Solomon, Hārata 231, 246
Somerset, H. C. D. 19, 69
Soper, Eileen 81, 233
Squire, Lynette 209
Squires, Catharine 168

St Helens Station *113*
Stack, James West 29, 232
Staples, Irene 118
Star, Paul 16
State Advances Corporation 53, 60
state lending, for Māori housing 53-54
Stephens, Ropata 142
Stevens, Michael 143, 273
Stewart, Adela 158
Stirling, Amiria Manutahi 67, 231, 256-58
Stirling, Duncan 256
Stirling, Eruera Kawhia Whakatane 67, 258
Strasser, Susan 117
Strutt, William 42
Sturm, J. C. 246
subsistence farming 56, 111, 114, 129-30, 148, 163
subsistence needs 126, 129
sugar 125; bulk storage of 60; buying 170-71; rations of 160; trading 127
Sunderland, Heni 139, 208
Swarbrick, Nancy 35-36
Symons, Michael 180
Szaszy, Mira 206

Taiāmai *30*
taikōwhatu 79
Tairāwhiti 54, 113-14
Tāmihana Te Rauparaha 33
tangihanga 68, 248, 258
tapu 29, 273; and cooking 81, 180-81; and Māori housing 55; raising 248; and water supply 119
taro 148, 151, 249
Tau, Rakiihui 140-41
Tau, Rawiri Te Maire 130, 142
Tauroa, Patricia 182
tāwhara 153
Tāwhiao, Tūkāroto Matutaera Pōtatau Te Wherowhero 205
Taylor, Richard 30, 182, 253
te ao Māori: food in 20; gender and cooking in 180-87; and hāngī 117; houses and home in 26-27, 274; and Pākehā farming 12-13, 16, 272; tapu and noa in 29; use rights over land 128, 184, 197; *see also* Māori communities; tikanga Māori
Te Huki, Hori 238
Te Kao 114
Te Keepa Te Rangipūawhe 249, 278n45
Te Puea Hērangi 53, *55*

Te Rangi Hīroa 50-51, 55, *134*, 182, 248, 253
Te Ropu o te Ora Women's Health League 246
Te Ture, Poutama *139*
Te Wairoa 249, 278n45
Te Whāiti, Irāia 253
tea 111; purchasing 170; rations of 160; trading 127
Tennant, Margaret 246
thatched houses 37, 51
Thomson, John Turnbull 83, 232
threshing mills 111
tī 79, 128, 148
tikanga Māori 25-26, 64, 272-73; and manaakitanga 228, 230
tin houses 40
tio 132
Tipene, Raiha and Eruera 102
Te Tiriti o Waitangi 34, 185
tītī *see* muttonbirds
Tivie, Walles 102
Tiwini, Warren 142-43
toetoe 37
toheroa *137*
Tōnore, Airini 198
Totaranui House *89*
Toynbee, Claire 203
trade, informal 168, 170
transience 20, 34, 110
Trotter, Margaret 73, 145
tuangi 132
tuatua 132
Tuhoro, Stephanie 118
tūī *139*
tuna (eel) 100, 109, 133, 204n67
tūrangawaewae 63-64
turnips 151, 154, 165
two-table households 22, 236, 242

umu 79
urban areas: housing in 27, 49; raupō housing in 37
urban population 19, 62, 282n58
usefulness, culture of 203
uwhi 148

vacuum cleaners 108, 217
Veart, David 144, 152
vegetable gardens 46, 125, 155-58, *156-57*, 217
villas 17, 27, 56-57, *58*; floor plans of *57*

342

wāhine Māori: autobiographical writings 204–5; and colonisation 185–87, 209; cooking and preparing food 180–84, 205–8, 274; and food production 130, 132; and kitchens 224; land rights 197–98; Pākehā views of 184–85; and wāhine Pākehā 246; work on the land 198–99, *200*
waiata 26, 150, 184
Wairau Bar 79
Waitangi Tribunal 16, 19; and mana wāhine 182, 184; on Māori food sources 130, 132, 136, 140–42, 153
Waitere, Daisy 206
Wakefield, Edward Jerningham 33–34
Walker, Jimmy 243
Walker, Laurie *245*
Wardel, Freddy 168
Wark, Betty 205
Warner, Pamea Te Ruihi 53
Washday at the Pa 121
washing machines 102, 121, 217
water supply 41, 119, 155, 213
Waterhouse, Richard 13
Watson, James 242
WDFU (Women's Division of the Farmers Union) 68, 115, 200, 217
weatherboard housing 26, 33, 50–51, *53*, 67, *107*, 278n45
Weaver, John C. 113
weka 128, 136, 139
Welch, George 145, 160
wetback 102, 120
wetlands 136, 139, 208
whakanoa 181, 248
whakapapa 63–64; and access to natural resources 143; and social dynamics 181
Whakarewarewa 32, 54, 64, 182
Whakatau 29
whalers 33–34, 233
whānau 64–69, 272; connections to 51; and hapū 183–84; and mahinga kai 128; and Māori identity 71
wharau 32, 65, 249
whare Māori 33, 37, 63, *154*
whare raupō 26–27, *49*, 51
wharekai 26, *53*, 63, 207, 259–60, *260*, 268, 274–75
Wharemaru, Heeni 114, 168, 199
wharenui 63, 274; modernising 259
wharepuni 29, 47, 54

whareumu 29, 51, 259
whata 30, 81, 249
wheat 151, 153, 165
whenua 63; connection with 117
Whitaker, Mabel 43, 170
whitebait 113, 136
WI (Women's Institute) 68, 187, 217, 246
wild foods 131, 148
Williams, Marianne and Henry 66
Wilson, Helen 111, 115
Wilson, Kelly Russell 135
Winter, Lily 119, 171, 195
Witheford, Isabel *214*
wīwī 37
Wolff, Johanna 41, 165
woman's sphere 179, 203, 206, 224, 274
women: butter-churning 167; and farming 115–17, 203–4, *203*; in the home 20, 66; and urbanisation 15; *see also* domestic labour; Pākehā women; rural women; wāhine Māori
women's pages 210–11
Worsley, Lucy 121
Wynen, James *148*

Yorke, Amy Tremenheere 95

Katie Cooper grew up on a small sheep farm just out of Gore and is the daughter of an agriculture teacher and a history teacher. She completed her PhD in history at the University of Otago, and since 2016 has been a curator at the Museum of New Zealand Te Papa Tongarewa. Katie's research focus is the social and material history of nineteenth-century New Zealand, and she has been working to highlight women's histories in Te Papa's collections.